I0057208

INSPIRING WORK ANNIVERSARIES

How to Improve Employee Experience and
Strengthen Workplace Culture through the
Untapped Power of Work Anniversaries

RICK JOI

Quintriple Publishing

New York

quintriple
publishing

books that make things at least fifteen times better!

Published in the United States of America by Quintriple Publishing
767 Broadway #1204, New York, NY 10003
www.quintriple.com

Design by the Bookery | bookery.design

All trademarks are the property of their respective companies
The warranty disclaimer covering the entire book is on page 348

First edition
LCCN: 2023939569
ISBN: 979-8-9883454-4-2

Proudly printed on demand

SPECIAL SALES

Quintriple books are available at a special discount for bulk purchases, for sales promotions and premiums, and for use in corporate training programs. Special editions—including personalized covers, a custom foreword, corporate imprints, and bonus content—are also available.

WWW.QUINTRIPLE.COM/SPECIAL-SALES

CONTENTS

INTRODUCTION

E VERYTHING, EVERYTHING, *EVERYTHING* in our lives
is dependent on the work of others.

The food we eat, the clothes we wear, the many objects and machines that make our lives easier, the experiences that bring us joy, the homes we live in, the neighborhoods and roads, all the things we have and do—they're all made possible by the work of countless others.

Consider something as simple as the last time you appreciated a moment in nature. You probably weren't naked, and you probably didn't make your own clothes. And if you did, you probably didn't make the fabric or the thread or the buttons or the zippers, much less the sewing machine or the electricity to run the sewing machine, or even the *seemingly* simple needle.

And what's more, many of us would be dead were it not for the work of others.

Were it not for an appendectomy, I would have died at age eleven.

Thank you Dr. Abo. And thank you to all the doctors and nurses and assistants who aided with the surgery and my recovery, and to all those in nonmedical roles who kept the hospital running, plus the countless more who made the instruments, built the hospital, built the roads for me to get there, built the 1979 Chevy LUV truck that my dad drove me there in, built the traffic lights and the road signs that kept us safe on the way, made the paint and nuts and bolts that were used to make the traffic lights and the road signs, and a great big thanks to everyone who worked at the Palmer Township Pizza Hut that my mom took me to after each of my many post-surgery checkups.

I could go on, but you get the idea.

What does any of this have to do with work anniversaries?

Put simply, work anniversaries celebrate the work each of us does. In grander terms:

> **Work anniversaries celebrate the many unique and varied ways that we contribute to each other's lives in an indescribably beautiful web of interconnectedness**

And yet, inconsistent with the grandeur of that statement, work anniversaries just don't get the attention they deserve. As holidays go, they're rather poorly celebrated. Perhaps your organization is a rare exception, but they're generally mediocre—or ignored altogether.

Will patriotism, religion, and family always drive holidays that are better celebrated?

Probably.

But the following three statements are also true:

- Almost all of us will spend more time at work than in patriotic activities
- Almost all of us will spend more time at work than in religious activities
- Almost all of us will spend more time at work than with our kids

To be clear, I'm not saying that work is more important than those things, but I *am* saying work anniversaries deserve to be much better celebrated than they currently are.

How bad is it?

Fewer than one out of three first-year work anniversaries are celebrated.[1] Even worse, after that it falls to fewer than one out of eight annually, until year five.[2]

Encouragingly, most fifth work anniversaries are celebrated.[3] Unfortunately, the average tenure of an employee in the United States is four years.[4] That means most people rarely, if ever, receive acknowledgment of their work anniversary.

And even when work anniversaries *are* celebrated, it's often a deflating experience. It's common for work anniversaries to be acknowledged late. It's also common for the organization to have the wrong date, to misspell the person's name, or to mispronounce the person's name. And it's common for work anniversary gifts to completely miss the scale of the moment—like a twenty-fifth work anniversary "celebrated" by casually leaving a paper certificate on an employee's desk while the employee isn't there.

Spending more money isn't the solution. Say a company gives every employee a super-expensive Tiffany bowl with the company's name and logo emblazoned on it for their fifth work anniversary. Few employees actually want a fancy glass bowl, those who do want it don't want the company's name on it, and for everyone else the engraving has made it woefully unregiftable, so the expense accomplishes nothing.

Another common failure is the automated email inviting employees to pick a generic gift from a vendor's catalog. The web page for choosing a gift is hard to use, the gifts aren't great, and they aren't in any way related to the organization. Any organization could give those same gifts. Many employees give up and don't pick anything. Or maybe the employee chooses the vacuum to give to their spouse (true story!). This is not helping the connection between the employee and the organization, nor is it helping that employee's marriage.

But it doesn't have to be this way!

This book is your guide on the epic journey from the desolate land of missing and mediocre work anniversaries to the promised land of memorable and meaningful work anniversaries.

missed or mediocre	memorable and meaningful
before you read this book	**after you read this book**

At the beginning of your quest, you'll learn the magical power of the three sources of work anniversary value: (1) purpose; (2) belonging; and (3) perceived organizational support.

Armed with this power, you'll be equipped for your heroic journey to transform your organization's work anniversaries—huzzah!

But every hero's journey has at least one villain. Unfortunately, the work anniversaries journey has three. They're the three forces of work anniversary mediocrity: (1) avoiding favoritism; (2) limiting spending; and (3) limiting effort.

Together these villains make a powerful team. They push organizations to do something generic, low cost, and low effort, which is a perfect description of something so mediocre that it triggers employee cynicism—the opposite of the intended effect. When the villains have their way, work anniversaries do more harm than good.

And there are clear signs that the villains are winning:

> **Employees are twice as likely to leave during the month of their work anniversary than during any other month**[5, 6, 7]

While that statistic might be new to you, it's not new to recruiters. When a recruiter is targeting one of your employees, they know they can't call every month, so they'll reach out around the employee's work anniversary.

But while the forces of work anniversary mediocrity are formidable, there are beacons of hope to encourage you on your journey:

- **Think your organization is too big to have meaningful work anniversaries?** T-Mobile has their inclusive, team-spirited "Magentaversaries" with magenta-colored gifts, giant balloons, and #bleedmagenta hashtags, proving that large organizations can do it

- **Think your organization is too small to afford memorable work anniversaries?** The vast majority of the ideas in this book require no additional budget

- **Think your company is too focused on financial return?** While it's hard to show a direct return on investment for most workplace culture work, if that's what your organization needs, just start with the many ideas throughout this book that don't require additional budget—then check out the **Ideas for IT support** chapter on page 139, which is rich with ROI

‣ **Think you're stuck because HR or leaders aren't on board?** Grassroots change can start with a single person, which is especially clear in the chapters for managers, executive assistants, and frontline employees

I've talked to hundreds of people from dozens of countries about their work anniversaries, and the difference between success and failure is stark.

Many of those forgotten on their bigger milestones remain deeply hurt long after. In sharp contrast, it's truly heartwarming to see the beaming pride in those who have had truly meaningful work anniversaries, which are often recounted as some of the best highlights of their careers. Work anniversaries are moments when emotion is magnified, which is great when the emotion is positive—but bad when missed work anniversaries magnify alienation or when *meh* work anniversaries magnify apathy.

Your organization has its own work anniversary challenges and strengths, so your journey will be unique. This book presents all kinds of different ideas for people in all kinds of different roles at all kinds of different organizations. You *will* find something that works for you.

Is the work anniversary journey worth the effort? In a word, yes! If you want your organization to have a better workplace culture, there's just no simpler or more cost-effective place to start.

While they won't achieve the following things on their own, well-done work anniversaries can meaningfully contribute to these objectives:

- **Reduce attrition** by providing a memorable and meaningful experience during the month when employees are otherwise twice as likely to quit [8, 9, 10]

- **Make it easier to hire top candidates** by providing concrete, easy-to-communicate evidence that your organization cares more about employees than other organizations do

- **Improve team effectiveness** by providing opportunities for teams to build trust and understanding through shared celebration of moments unique to your organization

- **Increase skip-level communication** by providing a non-threatening, easy-to-explain, and hard-to-postpone opportunity for senior leaders to have meaningful conversations with employees who are multiple levels below them

- **Reinforce your organization's culture** by providing regular opportunities to remind employees of your organization's purpose, mission, brand promise, core values, and/or inspirational slogans

- **Support marketing** by providing a regular stream of compelling material that conveys the quality of your employees to your prospects, customers, and other external stakeholders

What's more, work anniversaries can deliver all of that cost effectively. Most of the ideas in this book will optimize money you're already spending rather than requiring additional budget.

Are you ready to start your inspiring work anniversaries journey?

One organization at a time, one person at a time, one work anniversary at a time—*you* will be a big part of improving how work anniversaries are celebrated.

I know you'll succeed, because you're the kind of person who opened a book about work anniversaries and read all the way to the end of the introduction!

> **You'll be helping there be less apathy, less hurt, and more meaning in the world**

This matters because, as I said at the beginning of this introduction, the work all of us do matters.

PART 1

THE WHYS

DO YOU MAKE recommendations or decisions about your organization's work anniversary program? Are you an organizational development nerd or an organizational psychology geek? Or are you simply a curious person who likes to understand things deeply?

If so, the next two chapters are for you.

If you'd rather skip the theory and get right to the practical part, then jump to **Part 2: Ideas by role** on page 41 for the start of the tactical how-to advice for each of the many roles that can contribute to better work anniversaries.

Still reading? Cool. I'm an organizational development nerd *and* an organizational psychology geek too, which at least partly explains why I wrote this book.

These next two chapters explain (1) what there is to gain and (2) the obstacles and headwinds you'll encounter. Understanding both will help you appropriately aim for the level of ambition that your organization is *realistically* capable of. This book isn't about some imaginary ideal—it's about making a real difference in the lives of your employees.

These chapters will also help you interact with stakeholders. They'll prepare you to lead more constructive conversations about potential changes, and then they'll enable you to succinctly explain why various decisions made sense if anyone asks later.

1

WHY WORK ANNIVERSARIES ARE SO VALUABLE

IF THE LEADER of your organization asked you why work anniversaries are worth the time and money spent on them, would you have a compelling answer?

Too often, work anniversaries are celebrated just because that seems better than doing nothing—but without an intent to achieve anything specific for either the employee or the organization.

As with all things in life, lack of intentionality gets in the way of achieving something great. If you don't know where you're going, you're not going to get there.

It doesn't have to be that way. There are specific, valuable outcomes that work anniversaries can achieve.

Work anniversaries are intertwined with several powerful core needs and emotional triggers that have been wired into humans (and other primates) for tens of thousands of years:

- ▸ **Purpose** – Is my work meaningful? Am I making a difference?

- ▸ **Belonging** – Does this organization have a unique identity that's worth belonging to? Am I included as a valued member of this organization?

- ▸ **Perceived organizational support** – Does the organization support me? Will they be there for me when I need them?

Each of these drivers has been scientifically shown to have a substantial impact on organizational performance. Getting them wrong can do a lot of quiet damage to your organization's culture. Getting them right can unlock a lot of value.

The key to implementing inspiring work anniversaries is understanding these drivers and crafting your work anniversary decisions around enhancing them.

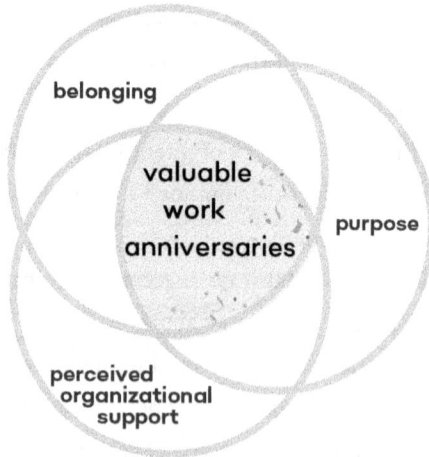

PURPOSE

A strong sense of purpose is known to improve both personal and organizational well-being. Simply put, individuals are healthier when they can feel a sense of meaningful achievement, and so are teams.

Psychology Today summarizes the impact of purpose on **personal** well-being like this:

> Cross-sectional research has shown that possessing a sense of purpose in life is a powerful predictor of numerous positive outcomes. Purposeful people have stronger immune systems (Fredrickson et al., 2013), recover more quickly from surgery (Kim et al., 2013), and even live longer (Hill & Turiano, 2014). Possessing a sense of purpose has also been shown to correlate with economic success (Hill et al., 2019). Finally, people at every stage of life are happier when they possess a sense of purpose (Bronk et al., 2009).[1]

Forbes summarizes the impact of purpose on **organizational** well-being like this:

> A study published by *Harvard Business Review* found when companies had a clearly articulated purpose which was widely understood in the organization, they had better growth as compared with companies which hadn't developed or leveraged their purpose. Specifically, 52% of purpose-driven companies experienced over 10% growth compared

with 42% of non-purpose-driven companies. Purpose-driven companies benefited from greater global expansion (66% compared with 48%), more product launches (56% compared with 33%) and success in major transformation efforts (52% compared with 16%).[2, 3]

HOW ARE PURPOSE AND WORK ANNIVERSARIES RELATED?

Although work anniversaries are obviously associated with the passage of time, there's more to consider than mere tenure.

If you want to improve how your organization celebrates work anniversaries and simultaneously improve both employee morale and performance, think bigger than time.

> A work anniversary is a celebration of the hallowed moment when a person became a part of something larger than themself

It's the moment when the individual and the organization chose to join forces to work together toward a common purpose. That's how humans have achieved every major endeavor, from Stonehenge to space travel, isn't it?

That's worth celebrating!

WHAT IF YOUR ORGANIZATION DOESN'T HAVE A PURPOSE?

If your organization has a mission or vision statement, that's quite likely close enough. Ask yourself why the mission and/or vision are important. That's the organization's purpose.

If you don't have anything close to a purpose, or the purpose is just implicitly to make money for the owners, then that's where to start:

> **Defining and communicating your organization's purpose may well be the most important thing you can do to elevate work anniversaries at your organization**

An inspiring purpose is the foundation of valuable work anniversaries.

More than that, it's the foundation of great *organizations*. It's how groups of people can make good individual decisions, make sense of each other's decisions, and work together on efficiently making progress toward shared goals. Strong purpose helps maximize the efficiency of everyone working together.

HOW TO EMBED PURPOSE IN EVERY WORK ANNIVERSARY

Once you have a clear, well-communicated purpose, it's as easy as the following three steps:

STEP 1

What is your organization's purpose or mission? How is your organization making the world a better place in a way that your organization is uniquely positioned to do?

Whatever the answer, remind employees of it *every* work anniversary. Not in a cheesy, insincere way, but authentically. Assume everyone works there because they believe in the purpose that unites them.

Train your managers to mention purpose when they wish employees a happy work anniversary. Mention purpose when you announce work anniversaries in your all-hands meeting or newsletter. If you have work anniversary certificates, make sure they have the organization's purpose on them.

However you celebrate work anniversaries, make sure the organization's purpose is a part of it.

STEP 2

Why does the purpose matter?

For many employees, their organization's purpose feels vague and abstract. Thus it's important to share concrete stories about the human impact of your organization's pursuit of its purpose.

Who has been positively impacted over the past year and how? Can you share specific stories?

If your organization has a longer-term purpose, how can you paint a picture of your vision for the future that the organization is striving toward?

STEP 3

How has the person having the work anniversary specifically contributed to the purpose?

Maybe it's really concrete and numerical. Maybe they've prevented untold illnesses by administering twelve hundred vaccines in the past year. Maybe they've been a part of assembling twelve thousand high chairs that will make it easier for tired parents to help their babies learn how to eat. Maybe it's a single major video game release that's brought joy to millions around the world.

Or maybe it's harder to quantify. Maybe it's keeping the front desk area both efficient and welcoming so people coming through are just that little bit better positioned to help with the company's purpose of finding a cure for lupus.

Whatever the answer, every work anniversary needs an individualized reminder of how that specific employee is contributing to the purpose, mission, and/or vision of the entire organization.

THE THREE STEPS TOGETHER

A meaningful work anniversary reminds everyone of the organization's purpose, why it matters, and the employee's contributions to that purpose.

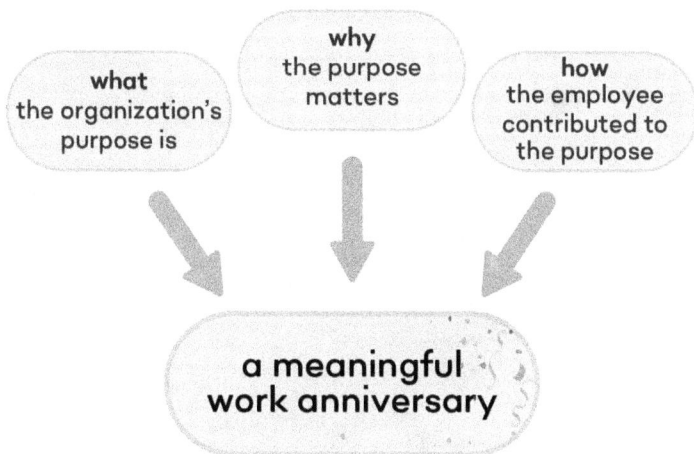

ACCOMPLISHING MORE TOGETHER THAN ALONE

Working collectively toward an inspiring shared purpose helps prevent politics and self-interest from breeding inefficiency and slowing the organization down.

The resulting higher velocity is what helps groups of people accomplish impossible things together. Or, in the words of Aristotle (and the Google People Analytics team), this causes "the whole to be greater than the sum of its parts."[4]

Looking broadly at the collective celebration of work anniversaries as a society, they're how we honor that we are all capable of accomplishing far more working together than working alone.

This is more crucial now than ever. The era when important problems could be solved by a genius or two working in isolation is over. Going forward, problems like traveling to Mars, responding to climate change, combating misinformation, and strengthening democracy are going to require increasingly larger groups of humans working together toward a common purpose.

But no matter whether your organization is solving a big problem or a small one:

> **Your organization will be more likely to succeed if you remember to talk about work anniversaries in terms of purpose and impact rather than just time passing**

18

BELONGING

Like purpose, belonging is a powerful driver of human achievement that directly impacts group performance.

The Social Issues Research Centre in Oxford, England, describes belonging like this:

> The notion of belonging, or social identity, is a central aspect of how we define who we are. We consider ourselves to be individuals, but it is our membership of particular groups that is most important in constructing a sense of identity. Social identity is a fundamental aspect of what it is to be human.[5]

Scientific research conducted at UCLA shows that lack of belonging, beyond merely making us emotionally uncomfortable, is damaging to a person's physical health and can decrease life span.[6] And not only does it affect our personal health, but it also affects the health and performance of the organizations we work for.

BELONGING AND ORGANIZATIONAL PERFORMANCE

A sense of belonging in the workplace powerfully impacts employee performance. According to the Society for Human Resource Management (SHRM):

> Creating feelings of belonging for all employees is one of the best things you can do to improve employee engagement, performance, and help support business goals.

They go on to say:

> Another important finding to note is that the cor-
> relation between belonging and engagement is
> higher for historically underrepresented groups. On
> top of that, we know that the workforce is becom-
> ing more diverse. As this trend continues, it brings
> with it more unique perspectives, ideas, and poten-
> tial for innovation.[7]

Research cited in a recent *Harvard Business Review* article shares some quantifiable, concrete business benefits of belonging:

> If workers feel like they belong, companies reap
> substantial bottom-line benefits. High belong-
> ing was linked to a whopping 56% increase in job
> performance, a 50% drop in turnover risk, and a
> 75% reduction in sick days. For a 10,000-person
> company, this would result in annual savings of more
> than $52M.[8]

As more proof that belonging has a direct impact on attrition, research from elite global management consulting firm McKinsey & Company found that the second most common reason employees cited for leaving was that they lacked a sense of belonging at work.[9] (The number one reason study participants gave for leaving was that they didn't feel their contributions were valued—another thing work anniversaries can help with.)

WHY WORK ANNIVERSARIES ARE SO VALUABLE

WHY IS BELONGING SO POWERFUL?

Our history as a social species seems to be what drives our brains to value belonging so highly, and our brains drive our behavior accordingly.

It wasn't long ago in our evolutionary history that being cast out of a tribe or a village amounted to a death sentence. While times have changed, our brains haven't. Our hardwiring remains pretty much the same as it was when we were hunter-gatherers. Neuroscientific research shows that we still see a lack of belonging or the risk of not belonging as a serious—and therefore stressful—threat. Thus, one of the advantages of boosting a sense of belonging is that it reduces stress, which in turn increases our capacity to productively handle *other* work stressors.[10]

Belonging is also powerful because it's the first of the four stages of psychological safety.[11] As an added benefit, a sense of belonging as part of overall psychological safety has been shown to have a positive impact on innovation,[12] providing a further advantage to both the individual and the organization.

HOW DO WORK ANNIVERSARIES STRENGTHEN BELONGING?

For a sense of belonging to flourish at an organization, three elements are needed:

- ▸ The organization needs an agreed-on vision of success

- ▸ The organization needs a strong, clear identity that can be belonged to

- ▸ The organization needs to clearly signal to employees that they truly belong

Work anniversaries contribute strongly to the second and third, as both an opportunity to reinforce the organization's unique identity and an opportunity to reaffirm each employee's valued status as a member of the organization.

belonging

| agree on a vision of success | strengthen the organization's identity | signal that the employee belongs |

work anniversaries

While work anniversaries don't have a direct role in helping your organization with the first element, they can be used to remind employees of their contributions to that agreed-on vision of success, keeping it in the forefront of employees' minds and fostering their feeling of connection to it.

Note that a shared vision of success is different from the sense of purpose encouraged in the previous section. A clear definition of your vision of success is more concrete. It's measurable, and people are held accountable for moving toward that vision. You need both, because purpose without a vision of success is chaos, while a vision of success without purpose is unfulfilling.

STRENGTHENING THE ORGANIZATION'S IDENTITY

Although work anniversaries won't create an organizational identity all by themselves, they can play a significant role in strengthening it.

The most obvious way is by reinforcing the organization's mission, vision, and/or purpose over and over throughout the year—both for the employee being honored and for those witnessing it. For an organization with a strong purpose, work anniversaries aren't simply acknowledgments of passing time. As we've discussed, they're recognitions of working together toward a meaningful shared purpose to accomplish more than anyone could achieve alone.

A less obvious way work anniversaries strengthen organizational identity is by embracing an organization's quirks. While less important than mission, vision, or purpose, quirks are central to an organization's identity. Sports team fans are an example of the power of quirks to drive a sense of belonging. Think Green Bay Packers fans and their Cheesehead hats, Pittsburgh Steelers fans and their Terrible Towels, and Taylor University's Silent Night basketball game.

T-Mobile's embrace of their unusual brand color is an amazing example of how organizations can create a strong identity based on a quirk. The color magenta is a rallying symbol, which stands out as unique, especially in various clothing items. T-Mobile employees so deeply identify with their organization that #BleedMagenta and #WeBleedMagenta are popular hashtags used by T-Mobile employees.

Work anniversaries can be a wonderful opportunity to get creative and come up with your own traditions, using representative imagery, concepts, or even words to generate and project a strong group identity. Most organizations can find a way to work their name into their word for work anniversary, like *Googleversary, Faceversary, Ohoversary, JLGversary,* or, in the especially inventive case of T-Mobile, *Magentaversary.*

Note that this topic is explored in more depth later in the **Work anniversaries and the power of cultural uniqueness** chapter starting on page 255.

SIGNALING TO EMPLOYEES THAT THEY BELONG

The second and perhaps more impactful element is to signal to employees that they genuinely belong with the organization—that they have a meaningful place in the system, however large or small. Work anniversaries are an annual ritual reaffirming that every employee is an important member of the organization.

Work anniversaries are a terrific opportunity to collectively look backward and appreciate all that an employee has done. By remembering, appreciating, and sharing specific contributions, the organization reminds the employee that they belong—and so do their colleagues. So in essence, while each work anniversary centers on a single employee, it also strengthens the sense of organizational belonging for everyone who witnesses it.

Overall, the investment of time and effort to commemorate a work anniversary sends a strong signal of continued commitment to all employees and their respective roles in the organization.

WORK ANNIVERSARIES MAKE BELONGING TANGIBLE

Belonging is not commonly talked about or thought about outside the social sciences, but it is the most powerful force acting on your organization's workplace culture. It probably doesn't get much attention because it can feel vague and intangible, but work anniversaries make it *tangible*.

At many organizations, work anniversaries are dismissed as unimportant. Usually this stems from an organization not having an identity worth belonging to or from the organization not being committed to its employees. Either way, this serves to undermine employees' sense of belonging.

You can solve both of these problems at the same time simply by making work anniversaries an important, regular practice in your organization.

And that simple change will boost employees' sense of belonging and unlock the many performance improvements mentioned at the beginning of this section.

PERCEIVED ORGANIZATIONAL SUPPORT

The third driver of work anniversary value is *perceived organizational support*.

It's wonkier than purpose and belonging and not something most people think about. The pioneers in the field define it as "the extent to which employees believe that their organization values their contributions and cares about their well-being."[13]

In simpler terms, it's the answer to the question *do employees feel supported by the organization?* Note that the question isn't whether employees *are* supported but whether they *feel* supported. An organization might offer all kinds of incentives, perks, and rewards for achievement, but that doesn't matter if its employees *feel* that the organization doesn't value or care about them.

THE BENEFITS OF PERCEIVED ORGANIZATIONAL SUPPORT

While not a commonly discussed topic outside the industrial and organizational psychology world, this concept is widely studied. A published literature review of seventy scientific papers concluded that perceived organizational support improved employee attitudes, employee behavior (including reduced attrition and absenteeism), and organizational performance:

> There is abundant research on outcome variables of perceived organizational support. The literature analysis showed that the outcome variables of perceived organizational support could be divided into job attitudes, job behaviors, and organizational performance. Among them, attitude-related variables include affective commitment, job satisfaction, positive emotions, and organizational trust and willingness to stay or leave; behavior-related variables include organizational citizenship behavior, and turnover behavior, and withdrawal [absenteeism and attrition] behavior; organizational performance includes relationship performance and task performance.[14]

How it works is straightforward: if employees feel supported by their organization, they behave more as though they have a social relationship with the organization rather than as though it's a purely economic relationship.

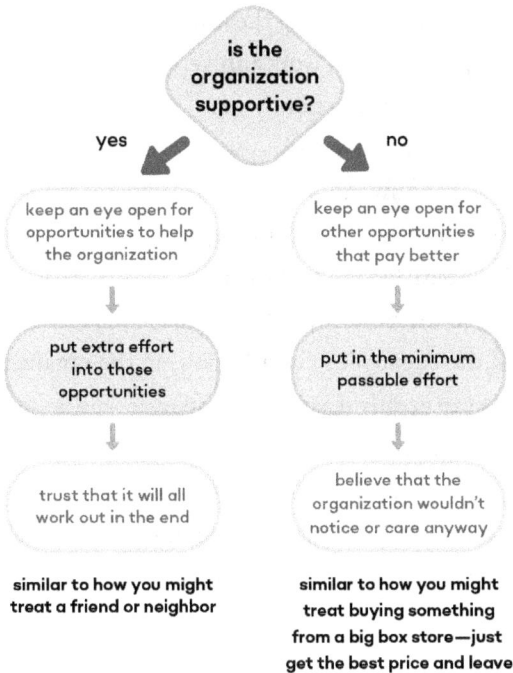

is the
organization
supportive?

yes

no

keep an eye open for
opportunities to help
the organization

keep an eye open for
other opportunities
that pay better

put extra effort
into those
opportunities

put in the minimum
passable effort

trust that it will all
work out in the end

believe that the
organization wouldn't
notice or care anyway

similar to how you might
treat a friend or neighbor

similar to how you might
treat buying something
from a big box store—just
get the best price and leave

An economic relationship is characterized by the employee—typically acting on behavior modeled by the organization—always asking *what's in it for me?*

But the social relationship encouraged by perceived organizational support is one marked by trust that the organization will reward extra effort, without the need for an explicit understanding of how or when, because the organization has demonstrated that it's worthy of that trust.

THE ROLE OF WORK ANNIVERSARIES IN FOSTERING PERCEIVED ORGANIZATIONAL SUPPORT

Clearly, daily interactions within the team and with managers play the biggest role in determining the level of organizational support an employee perceives, but work anniversaries can provide a significant push—in either direction.

A forgotten work anniversary—or one that conveys that acknowledging the work anniversary was an unwanted chore—can trigger an employee who is unsure of how supported they are to think the organization doesn't care about them.

Or it can go the other way. A genuinely appreciative acknowledgment of the employee's contributions to the organization over the past year can greatly reassure an employee who is worried about how they're perceived—and strengthen the perceived organizational support even for employees who aren't on the fence.

The impact of work anniversaries can be indirect as well. Employees, seeing a colleague they have a lot of respect for being ignored on their work anniversary, may well say to themselves, *if even that amazing employee doesn't have the organization's support, then surely I'm on shaky ground.*

> For maximal value when celebrating work anniversaries, boost perceived organizational support by actively emphasizing that the employee is a highly valued member of the team—and that the organization is fully committed to them

HOW WORK ANNIVERSARIES CAN BOOST PERCEIVED ORGANIZATIONAL SUPPORT

On each employee's work anniversary, authentically express—with details—how the employee is a uniquely valued member of the team. Say it. Write it. Smile it *genuinely*. Hug them, pat them on the back, or shake their hand (as appropriate).

Remind them of their contributions from the past year. Imagine out loud what remarkable things *wouldn't* have happened without them. Express gratitude that they're on the team and that you and the organization are lucky to start another lap around the sun with them.

Show your appreciation indirectly by putting a suitable amount of thought and/or effort into other aspects of celebrating their work anniversary.

Most important, do it all because you genuinely value them, not because of the science at the beginning of this section saying that it will boost performance. It's your intent that will be perceived. The specific details matter less than the genuine feeling behind them.

CHAPTER SUMMARY

Work anniversaries can be strong contributors to three elements of workplace culture that have repeatedly been scientifically shown to improve organizational performance:

- ▸ **Purpose** – Instead of celebrating time passing, celebrate the hallowed moment when each employee became a part of working toward something way bigger than themself

- ▸ **Belonging** – Use work anniversaries to strengthen your organization's identity as a special group to belong to, and signal to employees that they are valued members of this special group

- ▸ **Perceived organizational support** – Use work anniversaries to reinforce a reciprocal relationship of trusting support rather than a cold economic relationship where each side is trying to get by with minimal contribution

By intentionally keeping these three elements in mind as your objectives, you can unlock the full potential value of a well-run work anniversary program. This will lead to a positive return on investment from your efforts in the form of improved workplace culture, employee retention, productivity, and even innovation, rather than the usually negative net impact of the uninspired, rudderless "at least we did something" approach.

2

WHY GREAT WORK ANNIVERSARIES ARE SO HARD

WITH SO MUCH TO BE GAINED from great work anniversaries, why are they ignored—or just blah—in so many cases?

THE THREE FORCES OF WORK ANNIVERSARY MEDIOCRITY

The primary reason work anniversaries have such a bad reputation is because they are so often so very, very mediocre. They're not meaningful. They're not memorable. Instead of feeling special, employees feel like their work anniversary is just another task.

But *why*?

Typically, someone decides their organization should do something, they put a little effort into something that seems reasonable, and it ends up being mediocre. Despite the great intentions, the result is lackluster. Then, because there are so many other things to do, the organization moves on. And thus, work anniversaries remain mediocre.

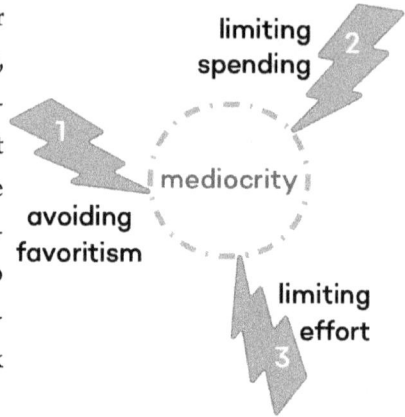

limiting spending

mediocrity

avoiding favoritism

limiting effort

On the surface, work anniversaries seem like they should be simple. No one who has been asked to be in charge of a work anniversary program has ever said, "Sorry, no, I'm not qualified to do that." Most people just wing it based on instinct in what little time they can fit into their schedules, while some look to advice from vendors who generally have priorities other than improving workplace culture.

Admittedly, work anniversaries aren't rocket surgery, but if you want to succeed, then you'll want to be aware of the three forces of work anniversary mediocrity.

FORCE OF MEDIOCRITY #1 – AVOIDING FAVORITISM

While you can do more for ten-year anniversaries than you do for five-year anniversaries, you need to do *the exact same thing* for every person hitting a specific milestone. That is, all ten-year anniversaries should be celebrated the same and all five-year anniversaries should be celebrated the same, regardless of any other factors.

People responsible for recognizing work anniversaries either understand this intuitively or learn the hard way, but either way, they will come to understand that everyone's work anniversary needs to be treated the same, or Bad Things will happen.

On the off chance you haven't experienced this yourself, I'll explain what I mean by *Bad Things*.

Imagine you have a star employee you love and for whom you want to do something amazing to celebrate their five-year work anniversary, so they get a trip to the Caribbean and a heartfelt congratulatory speech from the CEO at a company-wide meeting. That employee will certainly appreciate what you did, but they probably already knew you loved them. You'll at best only make them feel slightly better than they already did and thus not have gained much for your efforts.

However, lots of other employees will know what happened, and when *their* fifth anniversaries come around and they don't receive the same treatment, they will be hurt—far more than you made the star employee feel good. And since there are many more of them, the hurt gets multiplied.

Sure, some employees deliver more value to the organization than others. Go ahead and pay them more or give them bonuses, but *don't* celebrate their work anniversaries preferentially. If you do, you'll broadly harm belonging and perceived organizational support— rather than enhancing them.

Avoiding favoritism is also important across salaries and levels of the organization. You can't say things like "It's not favoritism because we treat all the VPs the same," or all the doctors or all the partners or whatever the case may be. One of the best ways to make a lot of people bitterly resentful is to do nicer things for the work anniversaries of higher-up or higher-paid employees.

The need to avoid favoritism is genuine, but the result is typically uninspired, generic work anniversary gifts that have nothing to do with the employee's specific interests or accomplishments. Everyone gets a coffee mug. Or a gift card to the same store. Or, on the high end, a watch that few employees would ever actually wear. It's hard to get something thoughtful *and* of the same monetary value for everyone, even in a small organization.

But there are ways to recognize and celebrate work anniversaries that avoid favoritism more skillfully, which will be covered later in the book. (And, no, it's not pick-your-own gift catalogs—why not will also be covered later in the book.)

FORCE OF MEDIOCRITY #2 – LIMITING SPENDING

At most organizations, the budget for work anniversaries is relatively limited. There are two sensible reasons for this.

SPENDING NO MORE THAN YOU'RE WILLING TO ON YOUR WORST EMPLOYEE

Once you've come to the realization that all milestones need to be celebrated the same way for every employee, you quickly arrive at the second force of mediocrity: whatever you choose to do, you need to be willing to do it for your *worst* employee.

Say you're considering two weeks off and a $5,000 travel voucher for employees celebrating their ten-year work anniversary (and you further don't mind that you'll have to gross it up because it's taxable). Look at the next five people who'll be reaching their ten-year anniversary. Are you okay with doing that for all of them? You can't get to number four on the list and say, "Oops, not them—we're about to put them on a performance improvement plan."

Some organizations don't struggle as much with this because they're disciplined about parting ways with employees who aren't great matches for the organization, but for many organizations that's not the case.

SPENDING NO MORE THAN YOU'LL BE ABLE TO DURING TOUGH TIMES

Is your business cyclical? Are there booms and busts? That should be considered when you think about how much to spend on work anniversaries.

For example, employees who hit their twenty-five-year anniversary in what happens to be a tough time for the company are going to be hurt about the work anniversary program getting cut just as they get to their big day—understandable when you consider that they'll never have another twenty-five-year work anniversary.

This can be damaging to the workplace culture, as employees will start to refer to the "old days," back when the organization cared. The organization may still care, but remember that the term from last chapter was *perceived* organizational support, and in this case the employees' perception will be that the organization has changed for the worse.

When the financial situation improves, reinstating the work anniversary program to its previous level can get awkward too, because if you don't make *retroactive* adjustments for those who weren't honored well in more austere times, they'll feel unfairly treated. But retroactively adjusting can be weird and complicated to figure out, and it just won't feel special, as was originally intended.

JUST A PAPER CERTIFICATE FOR A TWENTY-FIFTH WORK ANNIVERSARY

Pushed to the extreme, limiting spending is the force of mediocrity that leads to paper certificates as the standard workplace anniversary gift, regardless of the milestone, which puts second-year anniversaries (which tend to come with few expectations) on a par with twenty-fifth anniversaries (which come with lofty expectations). And while that might be better than nothing for some people, it's more likely to foster feelings of cynicism than belonging.

Later in the book there will be many suggestions for navigating limited budgets that avoid these pitfalls, including meaningful and memorable ideas that require very little money—or even no money at all!

FORCE OF MEDIOCRITY #3 – LIMITING EFFORT

Consider the amount of time and energy you'll have to dedicate to every workplace anniversary throughout the year, year after year. Think it's a good idea to circulate a physical card to be signed by everyone, make time to pick up helium balloons, and have a home-made cupcake get-together in the afternoon? Sounds great unless you do tax accounting, in which case, ask yourself if you'll be able to maintain that level of effort in March and April.

Or what if the person responsible for the work anniversary program gets pulled into special projects like migrating to a new payroll or HRIS system? Will they still have the time to handle the work anniversaries? Is there someone else who can fill in? Will your organization have the discipline to make sure no one gets missed?

Like the other two forces of mediocrity, the force of limiting effort can't be ignored. There will be negative consequences if you put lots of effort into some work anniversaries and not others just because of the changing schedule of the person who usually oversees them.

Work anniversary vendors will suggest that you can eliminate the effort by outsourcing work anniversaries, but that's often not worth the cost—and can do more harm than good. In the extreme, the employee will get an impersonal email from a vendor that asks them to pick their own gift and put in their own shipping address. No one they work with ever acknowledges that this happened or even mentions their work anniversary to them, and we're back to employee cynicism and dissatisfaction, but we've paid a lot to get there—running afoul of the previous force of mediocrity.

The ideas discussed throughout this book will help point you to a middle path—the path where effort is reasonably limited and deliberately focused on activities that bring you the benefits discussed in the previous chapter, and thus the effort is easier to maintain consistently over time.

THE THREE FORCES OF MEDIOCRITY TOGETHER

These three forces are pushing work anniversaries to be generic, low cost, and low effort.

> *Generic, low cost,* and *low effort—*
> that's a great description of the
> *opposite* of an amazing experience

the forces	the outcomes	the combined outcome
avoiding favoritism	generic	
limiting spending	low cost	mediocrity
limiting effort	low effort	

What makes the three forces of mediocrity so challenging is that the concerns underlying them are legitimate. Perceived favoritism *does* hurt. Money *is* limited. Time *is* limited.

And putting all three of them together makes it especially hard to have meaningful and memorable work anniversaries.

YOU CAN TRIUMPH OVER WORK ANNIVERSARY MEDIOCRITY

The main reason people continue to celebrate work anniversaries poorly is that historically, we just haven't thought deeply about them. We haven't done the research needed to figure out what works, what doesn't, and why.

But guess what? Now that the research has been done *and* collected in this book, it turns out that what works isn't hard *or* expensive. In fact, anyone who cares can make a big, positive difference in how their organization celebrates work anniversaries and have a direct impact on workplace culture, which is good for the individual, the organization, and society.

CHAPTER SUMMARY

Creating a sustainably great work anniversary program is hard because the three forces of work anniversary mediocrity are working against you:

- **Avoiding favoritism** – You can't treat some employees better than others

- **Limiting spending** – You can't spend more than you can sustain through tough times or more than you're willing to spend on your least valuable employee

- **Limiting effort** – You can't put more effort into work anniversaries than you can consistently sustain

Now that you know about these three forces, you can knowledgeably avoid unintentional missteps as you pursue the three drivers of work anniversary value from the previous chapter.

Yay, you!

THAT'S IT FOR PART 1

Now read on for concrete, tactical ideas for creating work anniversaries that promote a sense of purpose, boost belonging, and strengthen perceptions of organizational support—while also being impartial, budget-friendly, and consistently doable.

PART 2

IDEAS BY ROLE

THE NEXT NINE CHAPTERS focus on each of the roles that play a part in making work anniversaries great experiences. This is where you'll get practical ideas you can implement right away, so feel free to skip straight to the chapter(s) for your role(s):

Note: I say *role* rather than *title* because there are many titles for each role, and if you're at a smaller organization, you may well have multiple roles. For example, your title may be office manager—which means you oversee human resources *and* IT support—in which case *both* of those chapters are for you.

After you read your chapter(s), consider who else in your organization might be interested in improving work anniversaries. You can either read the chapter for them and pass along the ideas—or just pass along this book to them.

Of course, if you're an all-in work anniversary enthusiast, you're welcome to read *all* the chapters in this part whether they apply to your role or not, but know that you'll find some similar content repeated, and you may want to start skimming when that happens.

3

IDEAS FOR HUMAN RESOURCES

PEOPLE WORKING in human resources, or playing a human resources role, can have an enormous impact on making work anniversaries better.

And the great news is, you don't need to spend additional money–unless you choose to. All ten of the subsections in this chapter include ideas that don't require additional budget. Seven of the ten subsections are made up entirely of ideas that don't require additional budget.

Regardless of how much you have or don't have to spend, you can make work anniversaries better at your organization.

COMMUNICATE WORK ANNIVERSARY DATES

This is the place to start. This is the number one most important thing for the human resources team to do. If you do nothing else, do this.

Nothing great is going to happen if no
one knows *when* to make it happen

MAKE WORK ANNIVERSARY DATES EASY TO FIND

The absolute simplest thing to do is to make sure that work anniversary dates are discoverable by everyone in the organization.

This one minor step will open the door for motivated individuals throughout your organization to take matters into their own hands and celebrate the most beloved of your employees.

Some HRIS systems will have a mechanism for doing this, but if you can't figure that out, then a shared spreadsheet with everyone's name and hire date—preferably with a link to it on your intranet or wiki—will solve the problem. Then add "put new hire on work anniversary spreadsheet" to your onboarding checklist and you're all set.

There's another great option for the smallest of organizations where all employees use the same calendar system: just as things like scheduled time off, vacations, and paid holidays are put on the shared calendar, you can also include work anniversaries. This is great for encouraging colleagues to acknowledge each other, but it generally becomes unwieldy at around fifty employees.

ANNOUNCE WORK ANNIVERSARIES IN ADVANCE IN ONE OR MORE ORGANIZATION-WIDE COMMUNICATION CHANNELS

After you've made work anniversary dates findable, the next step is to find ways to "push" work anniversary dates out to employees.

This will vary by organization, but consider options like newsletters, intranets, and bulletin boards. For any of these communication channels, think about including a regularly updated section on upcoming work anniversaries. Also, the more channels the better. No single channel will reach all employees all the time, and for the employees who see them in multiple places, it will be clear that you value work anniversaries.

For each channel, decide whether you'll communicate all work anniversaries or just specific milestones. Consider the size of the organization, the age of the organization, and the frequency of the communication when you're making this decision.

Aim for there to always be at least one work anniversary announced in each communication but not more than ten. The ten rule isn't absolute, but the more you list, the less likely people are to read all the names, and thus the less effective it will be. This would mean about a hundred employees covered by a monthly communication (twelve months times ten employees rounded down), or about five hundred employees covered by a weekly communication (fifty-two weeks times ten employees rounded down).

If you can recognize every work anniversary, that's great, but if you can't, then maybe you can recognize all the "fives." Really big organizations will need to be even more selective, but there's always a way.

> The important thing is to announce
> work anniversaries *in advance*

If you put out a weekly newsletter, include the work anniversaries for the following week, not the week that's partly over already. Most people have no idea when their colleagues' work anniversaries are.

Most managers have no idea when most of their reports' work anniversaries are. If they're going to do something nice, or even just congratulate them, it's helpful for them to know ahead of time, because acknowledgment on the day is infinitely better than belated acknowledgment (especially from managers).

GET THEM RIGHT

Once you've made available a list of work anniversaries and have started announcing them regularly in a newsletter or elsewhere, you're on to the next challenge.

For some people, their work anniversary isn't simple. They will disagree with the date you have. These are the categories of cases you'll run into:

- Employees who have left and rejoined
- Employees who started out as temps or contractors
- Employees who joined as part of an acquisition
- Employees who simply remember the date wrong
- Employees whose work anniversaries were entered into the system wrong

Once you've published the work anniversaries and started announcing them, it's a sensible idea to reach out to each employee to let them know what you have as their work anniversary. Then invite them to let you know if they think you have the wrong date, so you can work through the details together. If you want to reduce the number of people who reply to you, then anytime it isn't simple, explain up front why one date was chosen over another.

In the complicated cases, which date is best? The employee will generally appreciate the more generous, earlier choice, so if you can do that, go for it; but bear in mind that means the start date will ripple through any other tenure-based benefits. Having two dates is too complicated and sets up too much opportunity for confusion. If you can't use the earlier date for the other benefits, the next best thing is to stick with a single date and be clear with the employee about which date you're using so that they aren't unpleasantly disappointed.

Here are more detailed suggestions for the complicated cases:

- **For acquired employees**, honor their original start dates with the acquired company. Acquisitions are already rife with change, risk, and angst, which you don't want to add to. You're trying to win over the acquired employees—telling them they've lost all their seniority just won't go over well.

- **For temps or contractors**, it's kindest to honor the date they started working as a temp or contractor, but this is generally handled situationally. The fewer the people you have in this situation and the more critical their role, the more likely the earlier date will be honored. The more people you have in this situation and the closer to entry level they are, the more likely the later date will be used.

- **For employees who have left and rejoined**, it can get even *more* complicated. It's nice to be generous, but that can be perceived as coming at the expense of employees who stayed with the organization all along. (To use an extreme example, you could end up with an employee celebrating a twenty-fifth work anniversary who has only actually worked for the organization for ten years, which is weird.) I recommend comparing how long the person was with the organization before the gap and how long the gap was. If they were at the organization for four years and then had a one-year gap, stick with the earlier start date. If it's reversed, with a year of working for the organization and a four-year gap, start over again with the new work anniversary. But for gaps of six years or more, always start over with the new work anniversary. Whatever cutoffs you use, publish an official policy somewhere—so you can point to it when questions arise.

And finally, don't forget to make it part of the onboarding process to be clear about employees' official start dates when any of the special cases listed above arise.

REMIND MANAGERS

After you have an agreed-on an official work anniversary date for everyone at the company, the next question to ask is, do you know who manages whom? How quickly do you find out when someone's manager changes?

Many organizations don't reliably know who manages whom. If that's your situation, just skip to the next section. But if you do know, you can move on to the next level of sophistication: reminding managers both a couple of weeks before each of their direct reports' work anniversaries *and* on the actual day of each of their direct reports' work anniversaries.

Each organization will have different technology for this. For bigger organizations, you will probably have to configure your HRIS system. For smaller organizations, you may be able to have someone manually set up scheduled emails, text messages, notifications, or whatever other schedulable communication your organization uses.

While this is harder than just publishing work anniversaries, you are now actively targeting the person who plays the most prominent role in each employee's work life, and you're setting up an expectation that they do something, which is a big step forward. Kudos!

COMMUNICATE PERFORMANCE REVIEW AND PAY RAISE TIMING

Once you're communicating work anniversary dates within an organization, the second most important thing to do is to effectively communicate performance review and pay raise timing to employees.

This one isn't glamorous, but if you don't get this right, it can undermine everything else you do.

Does your organization reliably do performance reviews? If so, when? Do all employees know when?

If your organization doesn't do performance reviews reliably, or if employees don't know how performance reviews work, many new employees will expect a performance review on their work anniversary. And when the review and/or pay raise *doesn't* happen on their work anniversary, it sets up an awkward dynamic where they don't know if they were intentionally overlooked or were inadvertently forgotten. Either way it turns out, a conversation about it will be awkward. This creates unnecessary and unproductive angst for the employee around whether or not to speak up.

IF YOU DON'T DO REVIEWS AND/OR RAISES ON OR NEAR WORK ANNIVERSARIES

This is the best-case scenario. But while *you* know that you don't do raises or reviews on work anniversaries, that doesn't mean that all your employees know this. It's vital to the success of your work anniversary program that you communicate that reviews and pay raises *do not* happen on work anniversaries.

And in that sentence, communicate doesn't mean that it was passed along once and employees *could* know, or even that you think they *should* know. It means that it was repeatedly conveyed in multiple channels so many times that it would be really, really, *really* hard for an employee *not* to know.

IF YOU DO REVIEWS AND/OR RAISES ON OR NEAR WORK ANNIVERSARIES

This scenario is not great. As you're aware, reviews and pay raises are often emotionally fraught. Employees typically want and/or expect better review ratings and bigger raises than they get, which means most of your employees will come to subconsciously associate their work anniversaries with disappointment. Obviously, that's not what you want.

(Note that this subsection is for people in a position to influence the timing of reviews and raises. If you can't change your organization's approach, jump to the next subsection, **If you can't stop doing reviews and/or raises on work anniversaries,** on page 53.)

If you want employees to have positive work anniversaries, it will greatly help to move your organization's pay raises and reviews so that they *don't* coincide with work anniversaries.

> **For pay raises, the best approach is to decide raises for everyone all at once prior to the start of each new budget year, and for them to take effect when the new budget year starts**

This approach is especially convenient for budgeting. Considering all employees at once also makes it easier to make good decisions on how to allocate limited money. It also creates an obvious annual moment to audit pay equity, and it makes it simpler to fix the pay equity disparities discovered by the audit.

However, while the all-at-once approach is great for pay raises, it's *not* great for performance reviews. Doing all the performance reviews at once is an incredible burden on managers, especially those with many direct reports. Under this circumstance, managers can't give each review sufficient attention. The managers who care the most will view the process as driving long hours that are disrupting their personal lives. Employees will pick up either overt or subconscious negative signals from their frustrated managers.

Some readers will be confused at this point because they believe that performance reviews and pay raises need to happen together and that the pay raise is based on the performance review, but that's not actually the case, and there are good reasons to keep them separate.

Doing them together can cause a fair bit of harm, because employee performance is often only a small part of what drives the size of the raise—company performance and the market rate for a particular job are typically bigger components of pay raises. A company that's losing money isn't going to give big raises. And a company can't keep giving big pay raises to a great performer who stays in a role where new hires can be brought in for a lot less.

Separating performance reviews from raises better positions employees to be aware of these exogenous financial considerations, and not to assume that raises purely reflect performance.

So if you aren't going to do reviews all at once and you're not going to do them on each employee's work anniversary, then when do you do them?

> **For most organizations, it's best to do annual reviews at a six-month offset from the work anniversary**

The six-month offset approach scatters them throughout the year so that they're just an ongoing part of the job of a manager rather than a sudden enormous burden. This schedule also has the elegant benefit of meaning that rather than having to wait a full year, new hires get a review after six months, which is a reasonable amount of time to determine if an employee is a poor fit and to address the situation sooner rather than later. For employees who are working out well, the timely attention will be appreciated.

the recommended time line

work anniversary celebration	annual performance review	annual raise

six-month gap always	different gap for each employee

the employee's work anniversary	six months after the employee's work anniversary	the start of the organization's fiscal year

While the above is best for most organizations, there are exceptions. If an employee is typically assigned to a series of single longer-term projects, then doing reviews at the conclusion of each project is a more natural schedule. There are also organizations that lean heavily into providing more frequent feedback through one-on-ones or a rigidly defined career progression path, in which case the concept of an annual review no longer makes sense.

But no matter how you separate pay raises and reviews from work anniversaries, the critical thing is to communicate how it works repeatedly, in a variety of ways, so that every employee is completely clear about not expecting a raise or a review on their work anniversary.

IF YOU CAN'T STOP DOING REVIEWS AND/OR RAISES ON WORK ANNIVERSARIES

While it's best that raises and reviews *not* happen on or near work anniversaries, you might not have the authority to make that change, or if you do have the authority, it just might not be a priority right now. That's okay. There are still some useful tweaks you can make.

Here are some tips on how to make the most of the situation.

FOR PAY RAISES:

- **Don't be late** – Decide on and share the amount of the pay raise *before* the work anniversary—put the pay raise into effect for the pay period that *includes* the work anniversary, not the pay period after the work anniversary, and if for any reason you are late, retroactively correct it

- **Prior to sharing the amount of the pay raise, be sure to communicate that two big components of pay are outside of the employee's direct control: market rates and company performance** – Employees can be enormously appreciated and do great work, but if they're at the top of the market pay scale for their role and/or the company is having any sort of financial struggles, their pay raise will be smaller than might be expected if they're just thinking about job performance in isolation

FOR ANNUAL REVIEWS:

- **Be early** – Write up and deliver the review a week or more before the work anniversary, as it gives time for any review disappointment to subside so that the work anniversary can focus on the positive. But if for any reason you can't be early and the review *is* going to happen after the work anniversary, communicate that to the employee *before* the work anniversary, because the employee will consider it late even if there's an official organizational policy that says it just has to be done in the work anniversary month, or gives you a grace period after the work anniversary, or anything like that—it's the employee that matters, not the policy

▸ **Shift annual reviews from rating to coaching** – If you can't alter the timing, this may not be an option either, but if at all possible, consider shifting your review process from a standard backward-looking "rating" methodology to a forward-looking "career coaching" methodology—rating methodologies generally come from a *scarcity* mindset where everyone is judged and compared, and shortcomings are called out, whereas career coaching methodologies have an *abundance* mentality and are about how the employee wants to grow their career—career coaching can be such a positive experience that it becomes something employees look forward to on their work anniversary!

CELEBRATE PUBLICLY

Once you've figured out everyone's work anniversary dates, have published them, and have ensured that employees know how work anniversaries relate to performance reviews and pay raises, you're ready to go a little bigger in your celebration of work anniversaries!

DO SHOUT-OUTS AT BIG MEETINGS

What are the largest groups that get together for regular "all-hands" meetings at your organization? For small and midsize organizations, it may well be the entire organization. For bigger organizations, it could be a business unit or division.

Having work anniversaries as a standing topic in your regularly scheduled meetings and calling out those who are celebrating theirs helps employees get to know each other. The size of the meeting will drive the details, but generally, everyone's work anniversary can be acknowledged on one or more presentation slides in order from shortest tenure to longest tenure. Big special work anniversaries can receive extra acknowledgment, perhaps with the person's manager saying a few words about the employee.

When possible, announce future work anniversaries rather than look back on ones that happened before the meeting. There are times when that just doesn't work well—say, when you only have a monthly meeting, and it makes more sense to show all the work anniversaries for that calendar month. But if you can do it either way, choose to announce future work anniversaries.

Ideally, have a graphic designer create the templates for the slides because this will subtly convey that work anniversaries, and thus employees, are important enough to invest in professional design. And it's just a little up-front work that can be reused month after month. You'll find more information for graphic designers in the **Ideas for graphic designers** chapter on page 183.

CELEBRATE BIG WORK ANNIVERSARIES AT AN EXISTING ANNUAL EVENT

Does your organization have an annual holiday party, or maybe a yearly summer picnic for employees and their families? These are great opportunities to acknowledge "big" work anniversaries.

First, remember that work anniversaries feel much, much more special when they're celebrated on the specific day. What I'm about to suggest is *in addition to, not a replacement for,* acknowledging work anniversaries individually throughout the year. That said:

> The wonderful thing about annual organization-wide events is that they have the biggest audience of the year

The big audiences make organization-wide events the most impactful place for a speech that reflects on the long-serving employee's time with the organization and shares collective gratitude for the employee's contributions. Done well, these speeches can be the highlight of the event, not only for the employees being honored but also for the other employees, who get to learn interesting details about their colleagues, which can enhance everyone's sense of belonging.

Here's how the work anniversary section of the event can be organized:

- The CEO *(or whatever you call the highest-ranking leader)* emcees this part and starts by sharing the organization's purpose, mission, and/or goals and how long-tenured employees are a vital part of achieving those things

- If the organization has clear core values and they can be related to long tenure, then that connection is made too. For example, if one of the organization's core values is customer focus, the CEO can explain how long-tenured employees play a special role in that core value by using their deep experience to better serve customers

- The CEO then shares that there are some big work anniversaries that occurred during the past year and that some colleagues are going to come up and share a little about each of them

- The CEO introduces the speaker by saying something like "I'd like to welcome John Smith to the stage!" *(note that it's best for the CEO not to steal the thunder of who "John Smith" is going to speak about)*

- The speaker then gives a roughly five-minute speech about the employee celebrating the milestone work anniversary and concludes by inviting them to the stage to receive a gift and/or certificate from the CEO

- The process is then repeated for each of the recipients, from shortest tenure to longest

- After everyone has been recognized, the CEO makes brief remarks about how inspiring it is to have so many great people contributing to the organization's success and asks for another round of applause for them all

Note that there's no expectation for the long-tenured employee to speak. While that might seem like a good idea, that's generally an idea pitched by someone who loves talking about themself in front of groups, which is generally uncommon. If it's known that long-tenured employees have to speak at the event, attendance will drop as the employees being recognized become unusually likely to have scheduling conflicts.

The event organizer will figure out which anniversaries are being celebrated and who will speak for each long-serving employee. Give the speakers plenty of notice, ideally letting them know before the event starts accepting RSVPs, so they can make plans to attend (or let you know they won't be able to). This also gives them time to source photos and prepare what they're going to say.

Who's best to give the speech? The employee's direct manager is the first candidate, but don't feel limited to that. Maybe the manager is new. Maybe the manager isn't a great speaker. Or maybe the manager and the employee have a tense relationship. Other candidates are leaders in the management chain above the direct manager and other long-tenured employees who have worked with the employee for many years. The employee's best friend at work can also be strongly considered, even if they aren't long-tenured, because they're likely to enjoy it and do a good (and probably entertaining) job.

Important: It's best to give all the speakers instructions/guidelines on writing and delivering the speech. As previously mentioned, not everyone is comfortable with public speaking. You will make the entire event more successful if you help ensure that each speaker is prepared and reasonably confident. In the **How to write a great celebratory work anniversary speech** appendix on page 339, you'll find a sample set of instructions, along with a link to a downloadable version you can edit for your specific situation.

Pulling off this kind of celebration well does require a little planning, so here's a timeline:

- **Six weeks before the event** – Make a list of everyone whose work anniversary will be celebrated, check it at *least* twice, and make sure you go all the way back to the cutoff for the previous event, which might not be exactly a year *(missing someone is really awkward)*

- **Five weeks before the event** – Decide who you'd like to speak on behalf of each employee and reach out to them about doing it—let them know they're on the hook for recommending someone else if they say no

- **Four weeks before the event** – Send out speech-giving guidelines, including how long the speeches should be, and aggressively work on getting answers from anyone who hasn't yet responded with a yes

- **Three weeks before the event** – Offer to let the speakers practice their speeches with you, or better yet, assumptively schedule brief meetings with each of them to practice

- **Two weeks before the event** – Remind everyone

- **One week before the event** – Remind everyone

- **One day before the event** – Remind everyone

If it's done well, many employees will view this as the most meaningful—even their favorite—part of the party. They'll get to know their colleagues better, and they'll think about what will be said about them when it's their turn. They'll have been reminded of the organization's purpose, mission, values, and/or goals, and their own roles in making those things a reality. They'll also have seen top leadership expressing that they care about employees.

While this is only thirty minutes a year, it's a tremendously powerful opportunity to reinforce the best parts of your organization's culture.

SET UP A BREAKFAST SERVED BY THE EXECUTIVE TEAM

To encourage the spirit of servant-leadership, you can use work anniversaries as a reason to have executives serve employees breakfast.

(In theory, it could also be lunch or dinner or tea, but breakfast is easier to cook, has lower culinary expectations, and is early enough in the day that "emergencies" are less likely to pull the executives away.)

If you do this annually, choose the more significant milestone anniversaries, like maybe all the fives (five, ten, fifteen, twenty, etc.). The larger the organization and the lower your turnover, the more exclusive you'll need to get. If you're a smaller organization and do this quarterly, you can include more people, perhaps even everyone celebrating a work anniversary, though you may need to spread them out over the course of a couple of hours, so you don't overburden the "staff."

This event is generally a lot of fun for everyone, as the employees get to see the executives dressed in aprons and getting messy as they take orders, cook, and serve—and the executives get to experience a different kind of relationship with the people who report to them. There will be much laughter and great photos for social media. It's the sort of thing employees will talk about when they get home after work.

And beyond being fun, it can have a noticeable impact on employees' perceptions of senior leaders. Frontline employees don't get to see executives very often. If a substantial amount of their time with the executives is spent witnessing them humbly and appreciatively serving breakfast, they're more likely to view the executives in a positive light in the future.

SET UP AN AFTER-WORK EVENT JUST FOR WORK ANNIVERSARIES

Having a work-anniversary-only event is not especially common, but it can be a viable choice if your organization is large and prestigious to work for—and has the budget to pull off an after-work event that employees won't consider a chore to attend.

Generally, these events are for employees who are celebrating a work anniversary divisible by five and their guests. They typically involve fancy dinner, drinks, speeches, and gifts.

However, there are some reasons it might not be a good fit for your organization's culture:

- **Bringing a guest can be awkward** – Consider the experience for your divorced employees, widowed employees, single employees, same-sex relationship employees who aren't out at work, and employees with strained marriages

- **Alcohol can be awkward** – Some of your employees don't drink, some are recovering alcoholics, and some are prone to drinking too much and doing things inappropriate for work

- **A nighttime work event can be awkward** – Some of your employees might have long

commutes, some have kids and might not easily
be able to find a babysitter *(or might rather use
their babysitter budget on date night than on a
company party)*, and some may be caregivers
for a parent or other family member and not be
able to leave them unattended

If your organization's culture is such that none of those warnings
have scared you away, just follow the instructions in the **Celebrate
big work anniversaries at an existing annual event** section on
page 57, but for this event, the speeches will be the primary attraction.

GIVE GIFTS

This is an obvious choice and what most folks think of when they
think of work anniversaries, but it's also deceptively hard.

A gift of some kind is expected on all the fives, and extra especially expected at ten, twenty, twenty-five, thirty-five, forty, forty-five,
and fifty years. (In Denmark and the Netherlands, twelve and a half
years also belongs on that list.) However, organizations that care
about employee experience and workplace culture will give gifts for
all work anniversaries, and they'll make the gifts for the fives nicer.

But beware—the three forces of mediocrity (see chapter 2) are
strongly at play here. The needs to avoid favoritism, to not spend too
much, and to not put in too much effort can prevent the gifts from
being well received, while doing something personalized and meaningfully different for each person is generally too hard for almost all
organizations. However, doing the same thing for everyone sends
the message that employees are interchangeable, which is the opposite of what celebrating work anniversaries is meant to accomplish.

What's an organization to do?!

There's no perfect answer, but below is a quick list summarizing the various categories of gifts that organizations generally give for work anniversaries. They're ordered by how good an idea each one is for the *typical* organization. Your organization may be different from the typical organization, and thus you may disagree with the ratings. When in doubt, keep in mind the three drivers of work anniversary value and the three forces of work anniversary mediocrity from the first two chapters. Then, make the choices that make the most sense for your organization.

Following this list are subsections with more details about each type of gift.

Yes! *(gifts that are generally good ideas)*

- ▸ **High-quality company-branded clothing**
- ▸ **New work equipment** (monitors, chairs, tools, even plants for the home office)
- ▸ **Certificates, framed certificates**

Yes? *(gifts that are generally good ideas for specific kinds of organizations)*

- ▸ **Numbered blocks** (for in-person desk employees)
- ▸ **Numbered pins** (for customer-facing/patient-facing employees)
- ▸ **Numbered stickers** (for employees with mobile equipment)
- ▸ **Whatever your company sells** (if what you sell makes sense for this)
- ▸ **Stock or stock options** (if you give out employee stock)

Maybe *(gifts that can work for some organizations)*

- ‣ **Cash** (if you have a lot of low-income employees)

- ‣ **Famous person shout-outs from a site like Cameo** (if budget isn't an obstacle and utility isn't a requirement)

- ‣ **Someone who knows them well picks the gift** (if you're able to commit to the effort)

Probably not *(gifts that usually aren't worth the money)*

- ‣ **Generic gifts**

- ‣ **Pick-your-own gift catalog**

- ‣ **Gift cards**

No *(gifts that do harm)*

- ‣ **Charitable donations**

- ‣ **Trips**

- ‣ **Alcohol**

- ‣ **Lottery tickets**

YES! – HIGH-QUALITY COMPANY-BRANDED CLOTHING

Company-branded clothing meets the moment. Work anniversaries celebrate the organization's and the employee's journey together, and everyone wears clothes. Done systematically, the clothing can also convey status in a fun way ("I have the gold shirt!"). Also, if done every year it feeds the collector instinct inside many of us. Company-branded clothing has a way of bypassing money judgment too. While it makes sense to do more than a T-shirt for major milestones, even just making them special colors might overcome that.

Other swag can work well or not, depending on what it is and how it's given. Backpacks can be good, but hats are awkward because a lot of people don't wear them. Stuff you give out free at career fairs or trade shows, like stress balls and small toys, are a *probably not*, though if they come along for the ride with clothing they'll generally be well received.

YES! – NEW WORK EQUIPMENT

This works for everyone, but it's especially valuable for remote employees.

Using substandard, old equipment that doesn't work well is bad for morale, just like missing work anniversaries is. You can solve both problems at once!

The key thing is to empower employees by asking the question, "What would make you more productive?" Delivering on their answer demonstrates trust in an inspiring way.

There's a lot that can boost productivity while improving the employee's workday, like an additional or bigger monitor, a standing desk, or an under-desk elliptical exercise machine. Even plants have been scientifically shown to boost productivity. Just make sure you don't force any of these gifts on employees. That's not empowering—give them what they request.

This gift is such a good idea that there's an entire chapter dedicated to it, **Ideas for IT support,** on page 139.

YES! – CERTIFICATES, FRAMED CERTIFICATES

These are the lowest-priced of gifts, especially certificates printed on standard printer paper, but they can be done well, and they successfully communicate that the organization remembered and did something.

Paper certificates are a reasonable option for every work anniversary (not just major ones), and there are many ways to enhance the experience.

First, it's helpful to design the certificate to be unique to the organization. Feature the organization's colors and the organization's logo. If there's anything fun about the organization's visual identity like a mascot, including that makes it better match the moment. Using your organization's design department or paying your design vendor is worth it, since you can do it once and reuse the design (but make sure the design supports long names!).

Another important thing to consider in the design is whether there's a metric that summarizes the employee's contribution over the past year. There isn't a metric for everyone, but it can be really meaningful when there is one. For example, if the job is to give vaccinations at the pharmacy, including an estimate of the number of vaccines administered over the year can help make the employee's impact tangible. Or for a software developer, if the company tracks lines of code written, that could be an interesting metric to include. A customer support representative's certificate could mention the number of calls or the number of customers assisted over the year.

If you're motivated to make certificates even better, design nicer templates for higher years. This is especially useful for in-person employees with desks, as the certificate can both start conversations and convey status. If the higher-year work anniversary certificates are noticeably different, the employee's status rises for all to see.

Should you frame the certificate and/or print it on special paper? If you have the space, time, budget, and available personnel, yes! It makes the gift feel more substantial and it will be even better received. However, if you aren't sure you'll be able to do it consistently for everyone, it's better not to do it for anyone.

And last in this category, there are plaques. These aren't right for every culture, but they can make sense for major milestones at some organizations. Generally, they'll be better for the more stodgy or old-fashioned kinds of businesses and for businesses where employees have a place to display them at work—rarely will employees (or their spouses/significant others, if they have them) be interested in hanging them at home. Some organizations have a "wall of fame" in the office where the plaques are hung.

And as with certificates, the more the plaque can be customized to reflect the organization, the better it will go over. Including the organization's logo and any other organization-related visual is valuable, though graphics will be more expensive, and color is generally not an option. These limits may send you back to doing a really nice certificate in a really nice frame instead, which although not as classic, may still have a stronger impact.

YES? *(FOR IN-PERSON DESK EMPLOYEES)* – NUMBERED BLOCKS

This isn't all that common, but numbered blocks can be a wonderful option, especially for employees who have their own desks and work together in person. If you're not familiar with them, the concept is that you get a block etched or printed with the number of the anniversary on one side and the organization's logo on another side. You can also add things like core values and mission statements to the other sides.

To see examples, just google "work anniversary blocks." It's most common for the blocks to be wooden, with a matching tray, but another fun option is custom Lego blocks.

There are many remarkable things to say about numbered blocks:

- They're not expensive

- They can be classy or quirky, depending on which best fits your organization's culture

- They communicate how long each employee has been at the organization in a far more unusual and fun way than a certificate

- It can be inspiring to give new hires a tray with a zeroth anniversary "welcome" block. The space for future blocks symbolizes the organization's hope for them to be there long term

- They trigger the innate "collector" instinct inside many of us

- They give any kids who happen to visit—not to mention the employee—something to play with!

If you have in-person employees who have a place to put them and you want to give something tangible, strongly consider numbered blocks.

YES? *(FOR CUSTOMER-FACING EMPLOYEES)* – PINS

Just like plaques, pins are classic. Your grandparents might have received a pin for their work anniversary at some point, but pins generally go over poorly these days because they just aren't a part of our culture anymore—no one knows what to do with them. So instead of symbolizing the organization's commitment to its employees, it symbolizes that the organization is out of touch.

There's one exception, though. Customer-facing (or patient-facing) employees in uniform or who are required to wear lanyards will often have a more favorable view of pins because they have somewhere to put them. Displaying them conveys a level of status both with their colleagues and with the customers they serve—and may function as conversation starters that make the employee feel good. This can be especially true in high-turnover industries where longevity stands out and new employees might not be aware of who's been there for a long time.

But every workplace culture is different. If you're giving out pins to customer-facing employees and notice that nobody's wearing them, you'll probably want to have a couple of conversations about how the pins are perceived, which can help you come up with an idea for work anniversary gifts that will go over better.

The tips on certificates and plaques also apply to pin design. The more personalized to the organization the better, though with the small space, you'll need to devote a big percentage of the space to the number and the word *years* so that the pin successfully does its primary job.

YES? *(FOR EMPLOYEES WITH MOBILE EQUIPMENT)* – STICKERS

This option works well at organizations where employees have their own portable equipment and there's already a culture of personalizing that equipment. For instance, many organizations use a single make and model of laptop, and because they all look the same, employees put stickers on them to make theirs recognizable from the others. Stickers can be used to personalize everything from helmets to chairs to flashlights to toolboxes.

As with certificates, plaques, and pins, coming up with an appealing design that is clearly related to the organization makes this more valuable. Use the organization's colors and logo. Maybe make them different in some way for more significant anniversaries—bigger or more elaborate. And as with pins, make sure the number is visually prominent and readable from a distance, since that's the part that conveys the information and status.

The big warning on this gift is that if your organization doesn't already have a sticker culture or employees don't have an obvious and work-related place to put their stickers, it can come off as cheap and childish. If a bunch of your employees don't know what to do with the sticker and end up throwing it away or giving it to their kids, this option isn't working.

The corollary to the above warning is that if this takes off, employees will want replacement stickers when they get replacement equipment. Ideally, you'll do this as part of the equipment replacement process without their having to ask.

And last, you'll probably want to give the sticker with a note or inside a card that says, "Thanks for *sticking* with us!"

YES? *(IF WHAT YOU SELL MAKES SENSE FOR THIS)* – WHATEVER YOUR COMPANY SELLS

Maybe you manufacture recliners, or work for a travel agency, or sell ice cream, or manufacture trendy unisex shoes. If the thing you sell is something that most employees are likely to want or have a use for, it will make for a meaningful work anniversary gift for similar reasons that company clothing is meaningful. The holiday is about the employee working at the company, so giving what the company does—a new recliner, vouchers for plane tickets, free ice cream, or free shoes in the examples above—very much fits the spirit of the holiday. There's also the economic benefit that your budget will go further because you'll be able to buy these gifts at cost rather than full retail price.

Even if you sell something that doesn't make sense to give directly to employees, there may be ways to tie what you do into the gift. Are you a nonprofit focused on nature conservation? You'll probably need a donor to explicitly sponsor this, but giving away nature trips for major milestones would make sense and make for some great photo sharing. Does your company make microphones for professional musicians? Give away tickets to events at venues that use your microphones.

YES? *(IF YOU HAVE STOCK)* – STOCK OR STOCK OPTIONS

This option clearly isn't for every organization. It also clearly isn't for every work anniversary. But for select major milestones, it meets the moment in the way that company-branded clothing does, but at a much higher level of commitment.

It's sort of like getting engaged on the anniversary of your first date: it's a thoughtful escalation of the relationship at a moment when reflection makes sense.

If you can do this for everyone, that's great. If you can't, then it's important to keep it quiet—or you'll be setting up the employees who *won't* get stock options for disappointment. And if you're not doing it for everyone, you absolutely do *not* want to announce it at an all-hands meeting. If for some reason you feel compelled to announce the stock or options grant, don't mention it together with the work anniversary and instead attribute it to exemplary effort, ideally in a way that makes it clear what other employees need to do if they want to receive stock.

MAYBE *(IF YOU HAVE A LOT OF LOWER-INCOME EMPLOYEES)* – CASH

While cold hard cash can feel impersonal, for lower-income employees a cash or cash equivalent bonus for their work anniversary can be well received and may actually be the most thoughtful option.

Pretty much everyone likes money, of course, but the noticeable impact (and thus value to the organization) is bigger for lower-income employees. They're less likely to have savings and more likely to know exactly what the bonus is going to help them pay for, and they'll genuinely appreciate the organization's giving them something they *need* instead of something symbolic. For a higher-income employee, on the other hand, a cash bonus is more likely to just disappear into their existing funds without any special earmarking and thus be less meaningful.

Another reason cash makes more sense for lower-income employees than higher-income employees is that it will be subject to income tax. It's best to gross up your employees' pay to cover the tax for them so they get the full amount of the gift, and the gross-up will be a lower percentage of the total for lower-income employees.

MAYBE *(IF BUDGET ISN'T AN OBSTACLE AND UTILITY ISN'T A REQUIREMENT)* – FAMOUS PERSON SHOUT-OUTS

Getting a famous person to record a short video congratulating your employee on their work anniversary is unique, personal, and likely to be remembered for a long, long time. It's also something your employees can share through their social networks, which is good for the organization too.

If you're not familiar with how this works, certain sites—Cameo is a popular one—act as a kind of talent agency where you can hire actors, athletes, musicians, comedians, and reality TV stars to make a video recording about whatever you want. You choose someone from their roster, fill out a form telling them what you want them to say, and within a week receive your recording. Prices vary according to the celebrity and how long you want the recording to be.

This option can be made even more meaningful than you'd expect by having the famous person say your organization's purpose, slogans, or core values, which is a fun way to strengthen your work-

IDEAS FOR HUMAN RESOURCES

place culture and reinforce employees' sense of being a valued part of something bigger than themselves.

Learning which famous people have significance for their colleagues is also a form of team bonding, which is another benefit. One tip is to avoid the word *celebrity* because many employees will react negatively to it while still having interest in sports figures, comedians, influencers, creators, gamers, and others who are well known in their unique spheres.

One downside to this gift is that you need to put work into choosing a suitable famous person and writing the script for them to record. And while there are many surprisingly affordable talent options, others are quite expensive, which is another complication you'll need to navigate.

MAYBE – SOMEONE WHO KNOWS THEM WELL PICKS A GIFT

The concept here is that the employee's manager, assistant, or best friend at work reaches out to the employee's spouse, family, and/or friends to figure out what they want, up to whatever price limit the organization chooses. The gift can be something physical, or it can be an experience, like tennis lessons or theater tickets. Someone at the organization then figures out how to get the gift and it is presented to the employee, typically by their manager, on their work anniversary.

While this can be really special and appreciated—and gives off a strong "we're a family" vibe—it's also a lot of work. In addition, to make it memorable and to get something the employee wants but hasn't bought for themself, the price limit needs to be on the higher side, especially for higher-income employees. The extra effort and expense required make this approach most suitable for major milestones, like ten or twenty-five years.

This option also generally works best for smaller organizations and/or organizations that pull employees from a close community, where the group bond is especially tight. If you're asking yourself, "How the heck do we reach out to the employee's family or friends?" then this idea isn't a good fit for your organization.

PROBABLY NOT – GENERIC GIFTS

Picking a single generic gift that's given to all employees on specific work anniversaries solves the favoritism problem and reduces the effort needed, but it tends to fail miserably in the all-important *meaningful* department. It signals that the organization doesn't know the employee or care to, and thus it can do more harm than good.

Some of your employees are married while others are single, some have kids and some don't, some are nearing retirement, and some are just out of school—and their interests are going to vary widely. So if you want to give generic gifts, consider the following questions from the perspective of various life situations:

- ‣ What would they actually do with it?
- ‣ When they move, would they pack it or throw it away?

This is in the *probably-not* category because it's really, really hard to come up with a generic gift where those two questions can be answered well for all your employees. What typically happens is the person picking out the item chooses something *they* would want—and doesn't think about it from other people's perspectives—and then the gift is quietly ridiculed, doing more harm than good to the organization's culture.

Let's use the most common of generic work anniversary gifts, the watch, as an example. Suppose your organization has a lot of money and you get everyone a Rolex watch. How many of your employees would truly value that? How many would rather keep wearing their Apple Watch so they can track their health metrics and get phone calls while they're out running? How many don't wear a watch at all and just use their phones to check the time? How many think Rolex is too stodgy and would prefer a Cartier? At most organizations, you will have ended up spending a lot of money on something that's going to sit in a drawer.

One last thing to say on this topic is that if you're absolutely determined to give expensive generic things, you probably don't want to engrave or otherwise put your organization's name or logo on them. Since many people won't actually want the generic gift, they'll look for ways to pass it on to someone else, and branding will make it unregiftable and not even donatable. And if it's expensive, people will find it difficult to throw away, so the employee feels stuck with it as a permanent reminder of how poorly the organization understands them.

PROBABLY NOT – PICK-YOUR-OWN GIFT FROM A CATALOG

A common solution to employees not wanting a generic gift and organizations not wanting to put the effort into figuring out something better is to give employees a catalog and have them choose their own gift.

But this "solution" has its pitfalls. Organizations generally use a vendor who specializes in this kind of thing, and of course that vendor wants to make money, so they cut a lot of corners. The markup may be so high that the organization ends up spending double what they would if they bought the gifts themselves, or the vendor gets the gifts at a deep discount because they didn't sell in retail markets, which makes them unlikely to be popular with employees either. Often the catalogs are outdated, which can make the organization seem even more out of touch—no one wants a DVD player anymore, and seeing one turn up in a gift catalog throws off a weird vibe. The vendor can also make it hard for the employee to choose a gift by having too many options to scroll through and no categorization or search function. In those cases the vendor profits from the unredeemed gifts, and the employee's left with a frustrating work anniversary experience instead of a positive one.

The pick-your-own-gift option is okay at best, but only in an at-least-they-did-something way. An employee might need a vacuum or want a pair of wireless headphones, but that's not really increasing the bond between the employee and the organization. And for this to be viewed positively, you need to go with high-end gifts that a big percentage of employees really want and wouldn't just buy for themselves (which is going to make the vendor markup more painful).

The one exception to this is if you already have an employee rewards points system that allows employees to recognize each other's contributions with points they can use to choose gifts. In that case, automatically giving employees lots of bonus points on their work anniversaries can be okay.

For more on the cultural drawbacks of this approach and some tips for doing as well as possible if you do go ahead with it anyway, see the **Work anniversary vendors and workplace culture** chapter on page 247.

PROBABLY NOT - GIFT CARDS

Giving gift cards is a popular way to avoid the problems involved in letting employees choose their own gifts, but it too has hidden downsides.

Not everyone knows this and not everyone follows the rules, but in the United States gift cards in any amount are taxable as a type of supplemental wage (and in many other countries—see the **Taxes** appendix on page 347). This means that you are required to withhold federal income, Social Security, and Medicare taxes from an employee's gift card amount, and if applicable, you also need to withhold state income tax and possibly local income tax.

So while you can give gift cards, with all the added tax complication you may want to just give the employee a work anniversary bonus. The downside of that, though, is the money will generally just end up in their general budget, whereas a gift card is more likely to be identifiably spent on something special the employee wants.

All that said, if you're going to go ahead with gift cards, food is usually a good choice, especially if you customize which gift card by employee. Some employees may appreciate being able to take a friend or date to a fancy restaurant, some may always bring a to-go cup from a particular coffeehouse to morning meetings, while others would love to grab lunch from the corner burrito place a bunch of times for free. Also bear in mind where the employee lives and how convenient or inconvenient any specific restaurant might be for them.

NO - CHARITABLE DONATIONS

For this option to work, you need to let the employee choose where the money goes; if you don't, the *best* you can hope for is a disappointed employee. It's more likely they'll feel actively disrespected and frustrated that you spent their money without giving them any say in the matter.

So the first drawback is added administrative time and effort, since you have to find out the preferred charity for the employee, then find out how and where to make the donation—though there are vendors that can help with this.

Even if you have all that sorted out, there's a second drawback: many charitable organizations are controversial. Part of the value of work anniversary gifts, from the organization's point of view, is sharing them with other employees and possibly more broadly on social media. Sharing employee-chosen charitable contributions is generally too risky and complicated for that and, by creating discord and conflict, can even damage the sense of teamwork and belonging you're trying to encourage.

NO - TRIPS

There's a fair bit of research that points to experiences being better than "stuff," and it's natural to think how that might apply to work anniversaries. One obvious way would be gifting trips or vacations, but these are so problematic that they end up in the *no* category.

So what are the problems? Well, not everyone likes to travel or is in a life situation where travel is even logistically possible. As mentioned in the after-work events section, if employees have kids or take care of other family members, it may be difficult or impossible for them to go anywhere. Or if the employee is recently divorced or widowed, giving them a trip for two may reinforce feelings of loneliness. True, there will probably be some employees who think this is the best work anniversary gift ever, but it won't be the majority.

Even for those who *would* like it, how do you decide where they go? You're back to either spending the time and effort to talk to their friends and family or just picking a place for them, which may or may not end up being somewhere they want to go. You could give them some sort of travel allowance and have them choose, but that's basically giving them money and might make them wish you'd just done that instead; and now they have to find the time, energy, and motivation to actually schedule the trip, which may be more work than many people are up for.

Probably the best thing is to provide a list of four options, let the person pick, then do the booking for them—but that's still not a great solution and is probably going to cost more money and time than the value it will provide for most of the employees receiving it.

The only exception to trips being in the *no* category is if the trip is somehow related to your business. If you're an airline, a travel agency, or a nonprofit that helps people in faraway places, this can work well for big milestones, as covered in the *whatever your company sells* section.

NO – ALCOHOL

A bigger percentage of your employees than you think: (1) are recovering alcoholics; (2) belong to religions that refrain from alcohol; or (3) just choose not to drink. Giving alcohol as a work anniversary gift to these employees is harmful.

For recovering alcoholics, two of the rules that friends follow are: don't do anything that might tempt them to relapse, and don't draw attention to their situation. Giving alcohol to a recovering alcoholic as a work anniversary gift is tempting them, and giving them a different gift than everyone else—assuming you even know who to do that for—is drawing unnecessary attention to their situation.

For the employees who don't drink for religious or other reasons, alcohol as a gift can be alienating and lead them to feeling like they don't belong at the organization, which is the opposite of what a well-celebrated work anniversary is trying to achieve.

Let employees buy—or not buy—their own alcohol. There are many other work anniversary gifts that your organization can choose to give instead.

NO – LOTTERY TICKETS

This is the only 100%, absolute, under-no-circumstances, don't-even-think-about-it item on the list:

> **Do not ever, *ever* give lottery tickets as work anniversary gifts**

It might sound fun, but think about it. Lottery tickets are the universal symbol of employees hating their jobs and being so desperate to quit they'll waste money gambling for a tiny, tiny chance at getting rich.

Further, the vast majority of employees will lose, which is disappointing, and disappointment isn't the emotion you want them to associate with their work anniversary. And if one of your employees beats the odds, wins big, and quits their job—that might even be worse, as it will make for a uniquely uninspiring, culturally corrosive, and widely shared story.

OPTIMIZE YOUR BENEFITS PACKAGE

Improved benefits are another work anniversary gift option—which you may well already be giving, and you may just need a little celebratory fanfare.

If you go this route, it's important to communicate to the employee that the new benefit has kicked in while you wish them a happy work anniversary *on the actual, exact work anniversary date.* Otherwise the employee may not make the connection, which lessens the effect.

CELEBRATE TENURE-BASED BENEFITS WITH TIME-BASED ELIGIBILITY

Paid paternity leave starts at a year? That's a work anniversary gift! Does their equity vest after three years? That's a work anniversary gift!

Even if something starts at ninety days, that's a ninety-day work anniversary and worth celebrating.

Optimization comes into play when you communicate to the employee that those benefits have kicked in and do it in a warm, personal, congratulatory way, not a minimal, check-the-box, matter-of-fact way.

If you can do it in person, that's amazing, but an automated communication is far better than nothing. It's worth a little extra effort to address the employee by name, wish them a happy work anniversary, and deliver it on their exact work anniversary. If you can't do it on the actual date, do it early rather than late.

GIVE EXTRA VACATION TIME

From an abstract accounting perspective, extra paid time off is expensive compared with typical work anniversary gifts, but an advantage it has over other expensive gifts is that there aren't any tax complications to worry about.

Also, additional time off costs less than the simple calculation would imply for many jobs, because for many jobs the work expands or contracts to fit available time. That is, the employee will find a way to work extra before the vacation or after the vacation, or their colleagues will do the same to cover for the employee who's out.

You can give an increase in vacation time that continues every year after the milestone, or you can give time off that's only good for that one milestone year. If you're giving vacation time just for that one year, communicate that clearly to prevent future disappointment. If you go with only giving the time for that one year but give a lot of it, a helpful way to communicate that it's for that year only is to call it a sabbatical. Sabbaticals will be discussed in the next section.

One idea that sometimes comes up is giving employees their work anniversaries off, but that's not a good option because work is where people *celebrate* work anniversaries. It would be like a kid celebrating their birthday by being away from their family. While in almost every other way it's better for an organization to put its energy into work anniversaries rather than into birthdays, if you're going to give one uniquely personalized day off to an employee, give them their birthday off.

The relative merit of various amounts of vacation or unlimited vacation or increasing vacation after a specified amount of time is a controversial, inconclusive topic beyond the scope of this book. But for our purposes, and in super-generic terms, if longer-tenured employees are especially valuable to your organization because of high training costs, then increasing vacation time with tenure may make sense for you, and if it does, claim full celebratory credit for it on the employee's work anniversary.

Whatever you do, *don't* make it an unannounced, anonymous, and imperceptible change to the per-pay-period vacation accrual amount that kicks in the following January. Make sure there's a clear and clearly communicated connection between the increased vacation time and the work anniversary.

THE PAID SABBATICAL

Do you employ knowledge workers? Is deep knowledge of your organization or industry especially valuable to your organization? Want to go big?

Sabbaticals can be a terrific option. They're attention-getters. They're easy to communicate in the hiring process. Nearly everyone values them. They can support once-in-a-lifetime experiences that make remarkable stories.

A further, subtler benefit is that they force the organization to not be overly dependent on a single long-tenured employee, because other employees will need to figure out how to cover for them. You can even build this into the sabbatical process by having the employee document everything they do and submit it to the manager so they can create a coverage plan. This benefits the employee taking the sabbatical too because less dependence means it's easier for them to take time off *after* the sabbatical.

Paid sabbaticals also just make intuitive sense as a work anniversary gift. After many years at an organization, getting time away will open new perspectives and make returning to work feel like a fresh start.

To lean into the renewal aspect, do a job crafting exercise before the employee leaves. Job crafting is a process of collaborating with an employee to identify what parts of their job they would like to be shifted to others, what parts they would like to put more time into, and what new tasks or responsibilities they want to take on. And if the employee has already submitted the documentation of their responsibilities so you know what others need to cover, you're halfway through the job crafting process. Just schedule a meeting with the employee before they go on sabbatical to discuss which tasks they would like to remain permanently with whoever is covering them. Then discuss how that newly available time could be better spent by the employee.

Then, when the employee gets back from the sabbatical, it will be to a "new" job that they enjoy more and that makes better use of their full potential!

TRAINING

Does your organization offer significant career-enhancing training and give employees discretion to choose what training is best for them?

If training is something you provide and want to promote, use work anniversaries as a trigger to encourage employees to take advantage of what you offer. (Note that this is in addition to—not a replacement for—one-on-one conversations about training between employees and their managers.)

There are a couple of subtle psychological benefits to this. First, it will force you to figure out how to do individualized communication rather than bulk organization-wide announcements. Even if it's the same content, sending it to a single employee with their name on it will make the employee more likely to think it's worth reading.

Second, for many employees, training can come off as one more thing to fit into their schedule. It can be a chore, even a burden. However, in your communication, you can wish the employee a happy work anniversary and position the training opportunities as a *benefit*. And if you want to go all in, come up with an eligibility schedule based on tenure, and position the training as a work anniversary gift!

PAY FOR ONBOARDING COHORTS TO GO OUT ANNUALLY

If your organization is big enough that you onboard new employees in groups so that they go through the same initial orientation and training together, you can support the continuation of that interdepartmental bond by paying for onboarding cohorts to meet up for a meal on their collective work anniversary.

This is an uncommon fringe benefit, but it's especially relevant to candidates as part of the hiring process if you promote your organization's great onboarding experience. It sends a message that you care not just about their making strong, career-enhancing connections at the organization but also about their maintaining them. This will

PART 2: IDEAS BY ROLE

be valuable to a lot of candidates, particularly the motivated, ambitious ones you want to accept your offer.

Very often those employees will have connected on a personal level because they all went through the same uncertainty and vulnerability together. Many times, they'll naturally find each other after they've finished training and form their own informal group, but you can boost that kind of camaraderie by paying for these annual meals. This makes it clear that the organization cares about their joining and what was probably most memorable about starting—the people they started with.

Usually the members of these groups will be scattered throughout the organization, so done at scale, these meals encourage informal networks that can break down interdepartmental barriers and create serendipitous connections that unlock opportunities for the organization.

THE QUARTER-CENTURY CLUB

Another option for promoting interdepartmental interactions at larger and older organizations is to start a Quarter-Century Club, an idea that IBM pioneered in the 1920s.

In case you're not familiar, this one is pretty much what it sounds like: every employee who reaches twenty-five years is inducted as a member. Given the rarity of long-term tenure at most organizations, there's a great deal of prestige around membership. Induction typically involves a sit-down lunch or dinner where an existing member talks about the new inductee and welcomes them to the club.

The Quarter-Century Club generally meets regularly, perhaps monthly or quarterly. For large organizations, it can have separate regional meetings. These meetings are generally organized by Quarter-Century Club members who are elected by the group.

Events are typically meals but can also be fun outings or even trips. Senior leaders who are not members of the club themselves are sometimes invited to speak about what's happening at the organization. The group can choose to tackle initiatives to make the organization better, or they can go bigger and be active in local, regional, national, or global charitable initiatives. It's important for the group to choose the specific initiatives themselves. Forcing the initiatives on them will generally backfire.

A club like this sends the message that your organization is strong, stable, and in it for the long haul. While it can seem extraordinarily distant for a candidate just beginning the hiring process, it will be appealing for stability-seeking candidates who have perhaps been burned by unreliable organizations in the past.

And if your organization is too young to have a Quarter-Century Club, consider a variation like a Decade-Or-More Club or even a High Five Club.

USE WORK ANNIVERSARIES TO ATTRACT CANDIDATES

What makes your organization special to employees? How do you communicate that on your careers page, in your job posts, and as part of your hiring process? Can work anniversaries help you with that communication?

It's hard for anyone to know if they'll truly like one job better than another. Candidates are making a consequential choice that will have an enormous impact on their lives, and they're doing it with very limited information. Humans are designed to trust observable signals more than words. You can tell candidates that your organization has a great culture and cares about employees all you want— but anyone can say that. Candidates will be looking for concrete examples that *show* the organization's commitment to its employees.

Here are some of the things work anniversaries can signal:

▸ **Your retention is high for your industry**. This is best communicated by consistently posting long-tenured employees' work anniversaries to your social media accounts. If you have stats for your industry's average attrition compared with yours, promote them on your career page and in your job posts, and then point candidates to your social media accounts to see for themselves.

▸ **Your organization is diverse**. Again, this is best communicated through social media. In general, any photographs work, but most people will be aware that photos can be staged or curated to make the organization appear more diverse than it really is. If you consistently post about work anniversaries with pictures of the employees, then it will credibly show how diverse your organization truly is.

▸ **Your organization is financially successful**. Communicate financial success and stability by giving uncommonly big work anniversary gifts. Luxury gifts and impressive experiences are the two most typical options.

▸ **Your organization is a careful steward of resources**. Maybe you're a nonprofit that focuses on keeping costs down for the benefit of your cause. Stick to free and low-cost options and communicate that that's intentional and why.

▸ **Your organization values work-life balance**. If your organization values work-life balance, then time off associated with work anniversaries is the thing to promote. Implementing and promoting the sabbatical described in the previous section is a great option.

▸ **Your culture is fun**. If there's something you do to celebrate work anniversaries that's unusual, quirky, or very specific to your organization, promote that. If every team sings a company-specific work anniversary song before dessert at work anniversary lunches, promote that. If you give out custom Lego minifigures to each employee that look like them and then give them a block engraved with their number of years of service every work anniversary, then promote that.

▸ **Your culture is team-oriented**. If your culture embraces teams and teamwork, celebrate work anniversaries with the employee's team. Take team pictures and post them to social media when congratulating employees on their work anniversaries. These will contrast wonderfully with the more typical, boring pictures of a boss and employee looking serious and holding a stodgy framed certificate.

▸ **Your culture is meaningful**. If your organization has a strong purpose, it's best to lean into that purpose during work anniversaries. The work anniversary isn't a celebration of years past— it's a celebration of the date the employee and the organization came together to work on that common purpose. When you post work celebrations to social media, put this idea front and center.

Of course, if none of these sorts of things are true, or if you celebrate work anniversaries with some sort of check-the-box, pick-it-yourself-from-a-catalog approach that's beyond your ability to change, you won't want to bring up work anniversaries as part of the hiring process.

ONBOARDING WITH GREAT WORK ANNIVERSARIES IN MIND

This may not be intuitive, but great work anniversaries can begin on day one, which is also known as *work anniversary zero*.

For no additional budget and minimal effort, the onboarding team can have an outsized impact on the quality of work anniversaries at their organization.

> *If you're serious about a caring workplace culture, onboard with work anniversaries in mind*

Here are the onboarding checklist items recommended in this section:

▸ Take first-day photos

▸ Capture employee preferences

▸ Set recurring work anniversary reminders

▸ Train new managers on work anniversary expectations and set up their work anniversary reminders for their direct reports

▸ Communicate performance review and pay raise timing

TAKE FIRST-DAY PHOTOS

Photos from the past make work anniversaries special, not just for the person celebrating, but also for newer employees who'll see their colleagues in a deeper way.

While the investment in first-day photos takes a while to pay off for work anniversaries, the photos are also useful for introducing employees to the organization through newsletters, social media, and all-hands meetings. Another side benefit is that treating first-day photos as important helps the employee mark the event as special, just like when people get their pictures taken to celebrate birthdays, going to prom, or getting married.

One more thing to note about capturing first-day photos is that it's *free!*

Choose the location for the photo that best captures your workplace culture:

▸ At the front door of the office

▸ At their new desk

▸ In front of something quintessential about your workplace, like a big piece of machinery or a statue of the founder

▸ Is the employee fully remote? Grab a screen capture of them on an onboarding video call (which ten years from now will look amusingly antiquated)

▸ If your organization issues photo identification, take a picture of their new ID

After taking the photos, make sure you store them systematically in a place where other important documents are stored so that they will be migrated every time your organization changes systems, and so you'll remember where to find them if you don't hire often. (Hint: using the employee's name and hire date in the filenames can help you sort and retrieve them.) If it can be somewhere that many people have access to, great, but the most important thing is that the photos be maintained over the years.

CAPTURE EMPLOYEE PREFERENCES

Here's an item for the onboarding checklist that's sure to be more fun than almost all the others, for you *and* for the new employee.

Those of you who have kids may already be in the habit of sending questionnaires to teachers at the beginning of the school year to get to know them a little and to know what kinds of holiday and end-of-year gifts they might appreciate. You can do that as you onboard new employees too!

For those of you who aren't familiar with the concept, the idea is to capture the employee's preferences on a variety of things, which makes it easier to get simple, personalized gifts for them. For example, you can ask them:

- Their favorite candy, fruit, or snack food

- Their favorite beverage (hot and cold)

- Their favorite restaurant near the office
  (for their work anniversary team lunch)

- Their favorite home delivery meal
  (for remote workers)

- Their favorite cake or other dessert
  (not everyone likes chocolate, or even cake)

- Their favorite pizza toppings
  (pizza party with a special pizza just for them)

- Their favorite sandwich, soup, and salad
  dressing (if you celebrate by eating in)

- Their favorite color (for decorations)

- Their favorite sports team
  (tickets? bobblehead?)

- Their favorite band or musician
  (tickets? merch?)

- What kinds of pets they have, if any
  (and what are their names?) 🐾

- Where they like to shop (for gift cards)

- Whether they have allergies or food intolerances

You can capture it on paper and then photograph it, or you can capture it electronically with a Google Form connected to a Google Sheet, or whatever works best for your organization. *The important thing is to make sure the preferences don't get lost.* They, like the first-day photo, should be stored so they're migrated along with other important documents as your organization switches systems over the years.

The preferences should also be included in the work anniversary reminder set up for the employee's manager, which will be discussed in the next section.

And last, unrelated to work anniversaries, you can use the same questionnaire to ask quirky questions, questions about their interests, or the ever popular two truths and a lie, which you can use in your communications to introduce the employee to the organization.

SET RECURRING WORK ANNIVERSARY REMINDERS

If you want work anniversaries to be reliably acknowledged, you're going to need reminders. So setting up recurring reminders of the new employee's start date should be on the onboarding checklist.

The details of where to set the reminder will vary by organization. The three most common types of reminders are calendar entries, scheduled text messages, and scheduled emails. And in many cases it's best to do more than one.

The new employee's manager should get two reminders: one that goes out two weeks before the work anniversary, so they have time to prepare, and one that goes out the day of the work anniversary. The manager's manager might also appreciate a reminder the day of the anniversary so that they can mention it to the employee. And last, anyone in HR involved in any part of the work anniversary process should also get reminders. They'll need a preparation reminder for sure, and in some cases a day-of reminder.

While all the reminders are important, the manager reminder that goes out two weeks ahead of time is the most crucial. In that reminder, include a refresher on what's expected of the manager as well as a link to the employee's preferences that were captured as part of onboarding.

SET UP NEW MANAGERS FOR SUCCESS

If the new employee is a manager, two more onboarding steps are needed.

First, share with the new manager the organization's expectations for how managers celebrate their direct reports' work anniversaries.

Second, provide the new manager with the work anniversary dates of each of their direct reports and make sure to transfer the reminders discussed in the previous section to the new manager.

COMMUNICATE PERFORMANCE REVIEW AND PAY RAISE TIMING

The timing of performance reviews and pay raises was discussed starting back on page 49, where it was suggested that it's best that neither happen on an employee's work anniversary, but from the onboarding perspective *the most important thing is to set accurate expectations.*

If you don't communicate how and when your organization does performance reviews and pay raises, many employees will assume they'll happen on their work anniversary.

This can lead to unnecessary bad feelings and angst when their work anniversary comes and goes and the review and pay raise don't happen. Some employees will speak up, but many more will just stew silently about it.

If all raises take effect the first of the year, let the employee know. If your organization believes that high-quality one-on-ones with your manager eliminate the need for an annual review, let the employee know. If your organization is inconsistent about these things and employees have to advocate for themselves, let the employee know.

DON'T UNDERESTIMATE THE ONBOARDING CHECKLIST!

As you can tell, the onboarding checklist is surprisingly powerful in setting up the organization to celebrate work anniversaries well.

DON'T FORGET TERMINATIONS

This may seem obvious, but whenever an employee leaves, it's important to remove reminders, especially from automatic communications. Getting a congratulatory work anniversary package mailed to your home after you're no longer with an organization can be awkward, especially if you were laid off or fired. And it's far worse than awkward for the family if the employee died.

And on that delicate subject, something you can do that's helpful to the deceased employee's family, friends, and coworkers is to help them shut down or memorialize the employee's LinkedIn account. The employee's death is probably traumatic to many of your employees. If the family fails to shut down or memorialize the employee's LinkedIn account, many of your employees will get work anniversary reminders for the deceased employee every year. That's not going to be great for their mental health.

For information on how to close or memorialize a LinkedIn account, go to:

www.workiversary.com/blog/
how-to-report-a-death-to-linkedin

SET UP THE WORK ANNIVERSARY BUDGET FOR SUCCESS

It's easy to make penny-wise, pound-foolish decisions around work anniversaries. It's so easy that organizations do it all the time.

Here's a story to illustrate my point. Every year, a hamburger bun company hires a new MBA, and every year the newly hired MBA has the brilliant idea that the company can save millions by removing just *four* sesame seeds from its sesame seed bun without affecting customer satisfaction, and they have the research to back it up. But the research only compares the company's buns with the company's buns, not with any other bakery's buns, and it doesn't take long before the company's buns aren't as good as their competitors'.

While the story is no doubt apocryphal, the logical fallacies behind it aren't. In the case of work anniversaries, doing anything less than you did the previous year will go poorly. Eventually you'll end up in the dreaded—but more-common-than-you-might-expect—final minimal state of merely giving a generic certificate printed on standard printer paper for twenty-fifth work anniversaries. That will attract cynicism.

So how do you avoid this?

The best way to prevent damaging cuts to the work anniversary budget is to have it allocated per capita across all departments, just as you do with information technology and office space. In other words, don't make it a line item in the human resources budget. That way HR won't feel pressure to quietly cut it when trying to make the HR budget work.

don't do this

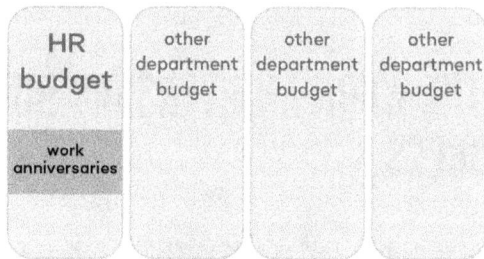

work anniversaries cost allocated entirely to HR

do this instead

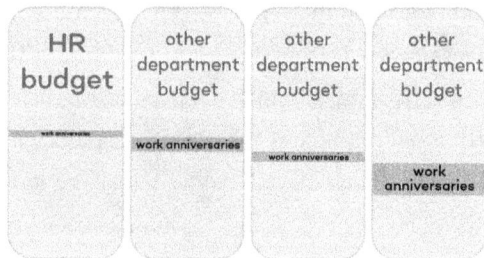

work anniversaries cost allocated per employee

That way, the pressure is more constructively shared throughout the organization. It will be clear to all the senior leaders what they're paying for work anniversaries, and they can weigh in on whether they're getting good value for their money, which will strengthen the program over time, which in turn will strengthen support for the program.

IDEAS FOR HUMAN RESOURCES

Note that if the leaders of other departments object to the budget being tracked this way, consider not having HR do anything at all for work anniversaries. You won't have the support you need anyway, which is the opposite of being set up for success. If it doesn't matter enough for the other departments to contribute, it doesn't matter to your organization. Spend your time, energy, and budget some other way.

ENLIST OTHERS

The human resources team can be the spark, but for truly amazing work anniversaries, many other people throughout the organization have their own parts to play.

The seven chapters after this one are about how other roles can contribute, often in powerful ways. Here are quick summaries to help steer you toward the chapters that make the most sense for your organization:

▸ **Managers and supervisors** – Managers and supervisors are high leverage in that there are usually a lot of them and they're closest to employees. As you get started, think about the managers at your organization who are most invested in being great managers and on the lookout for ways to do it better. Getting them excited first so they can pilot anything you're thinking of doing can create the early wins that make it easier to get others on board. *(page 107)*

▸ **The head of IT support** – Perhaps surprising to many, the person who oversees the budget for computers and any other equipment maintenance and upgrades can play a significant role in making work anniversaries special for employees and productive for the organization. Share the IT ideas from this book with them (or their boss) and see if they're open to implementing any of them. *(page 139)*

▸ **The CEO** – There are many types of CEO, and being supportive of work anniversaries comes easier to some than others. But there are many ways in which work anniversaries can make their jobs easier, which can help them see the value. To whatever extent you can, get your CEO on board with your work anniversary efforts. It will help things go more easily with everyone else. *(page 149)*

▸ **Executive assistants** – CEOs are busy. Sometimes the best path to the CEO is through their assistant. The job of an executive assistant is to help their executive succeed, and there are many ways that work anniversaries can help make that easier. Once you help EAs see how, they can be great allies. *(page 161)*

▸ **Graphic designers** – There are several aspects to celebrating work anniversaries that can benefit from design work that emphasizes the specialness of your organization. You only need one graphic designer, and you only need them briefly, but the higher design quality you get from that small amount of time will help to convey that work anniversaries, and thus employees, matter. *(page 183)*

▸ **The head of marketing** – While involving IT support is always helpful, involving marketing makes sense only for some organizations. The marketing chapter can help you determine if it's right for yours. *(page 195)*

‣ **Fun committees and culture committees –** Not every organization has one of these, but if yours does, enlisting them to help make work anniversaries a positive experience for everyone involved is an obvious choice. *(page 207)*

WHATEVER YOU DO, SET EXPECTATIONS

Disappointment is your enemy. Whatever you choose to do from this chapter, communicating what you do—as part of onboarding, through regular announcements, through scheduled reminders, and so on—is critical to your success.

Your organization probably has somewhere it lists your organization's auxiliary benefits. That's a great place to document what your organization does for work anniversaries. It's also valuable to briefly but clearly communicate what you do occasionally—alongside the all-hands work anniversary announcements or the mentions in the organization's newsletter.

There will always be organizations that do more and there will always be organizations that do less, so you'll have to find the level that works best for yours. If your organization happens to be on the lesser side, avoid making it doubly bad by at least making sure that employees' false expectations don't lead to disappointment.

THE HUMAN RESOURCES CHECKLIST

Human resources plays a central role in enabling great work anniversaries.

- [ ] **Communicate work anniversary dates** – Nothing will happen if no one knows when to make it happen

- [ ] **Overcommunicate the timing of raises and reviews** – Make sure employees know what to expect or not expect on their work anniversary so there aren't disappointing misunderstandings

- [ ] **Celebrate publicly** – Pick the public channel or channels that make the most sense for your organization and set up a process to reliably acknowledge work anniversaries there

- [ ] **Give gifts** – Go through the options listed in this chapter and pick what makes the most sense for your organization and budget for each milestone

- [ ] **Optimize your benefits package** – There are work anniversary-related opportunities both to improve your benefits program and to better celebrate existing benefits

- [ ] **Use work anniversaries to attract candidates** – If part of your employment brand is having an employee-centric culture, don't forget to use work anniversaries as a tangible example that sets you apart

- [ ] **Onboard with work anniversaries in mind** – There are small things you can do when onboarding new employees to make their celebrations more memorable

☐ **Don't forget to handle terminations well** – Make sure you stop anything automatic—in the case of death, consider helping the family shut down or memorialize the employee's LinkedIn

☐ **Set the work anniversary budget up for success** – Whatever human resources does for work anniversaries, allocate the cost per capita across all departments, as with office space

☐ **Enlist others** – Many people outside HR can play a role in work anniversaries—reach out to *and inspire* the CEO, the senior leadership team, the managers and supervisors, the executive assistants, a graphic designer, the IT support team, the marketing team, and the fun/culture committee

☐ **Whatever you do, set expectations**. Does your organization not do anything for work anniversaries? If so, tell employees this up front. That way they'll be less disappointed and less anxious about whether it's just them. Is year one celebrated way bigger than year two? Again, make sure employees know to expect less on their second work anniversary

4

IDEAS FOR MANAGERS AND SUPERVISORS

*Note that this chapter is for anyone directly manag-
ing or supervising one or more employees. You might
be a supervisor, team leader, foreperson, department
chair, or any variety of other sector-specific terms.
For conciseness, I'll use the term manager throughout the rest of the chapter, but I also mean you.*

*This chapter is also for leaders in matrix organi-
zations or otherwise outside the hierarchy, such as
scrum leaders, product managers, project managers,
and program managers, though in that case you'll
need to navigate how to share responsibilities, just
like you do with all other employee management.*

BEING A MANAGER is hard.

There's always so much to do and so many people needing so
many things. Important things take priority over minor things,
and urgent things take priority over important things. It's up to you
to know which is which and deal with it all accordingly.

You're probably doing one or more of these *important* things less often than you'd like:

- **Showing genuine appreciation** for the employees on your team

- **Celebrating the successes** of the employees on your team

- **Making small, caring gestures** that show the employees on your team that their well-being matters to you

- **Having thoughtful career conversations** about your employees' aspirations and how they can make progress toward them

- **Sharing team meals** that boost trust, respect, and team cohesion

You might be understandably worried that work anniversaries are just one more thing that's going to squeeze your already super-squozen time. This is why this chapter focuses on how work anniversaries can make your job easier.

How? For starters, they're a built-in annual deadline for each employee. While in an ideal universe you'd continuously do all the things listed above, having a little deadline urgency to help guarantee you'll do at least some of those important things on a regular basis can be helpful.

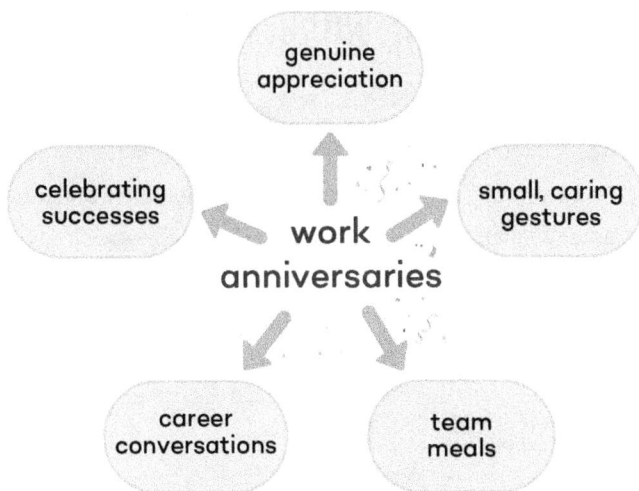

But while work anniversaries are a once-a-year thing, their impact extends throughout the year. For example, to write up a work anniversary thank-you post, speech, or email, you need to keep your eyes open throughout the year for content, which makes you more attentive to the good things happening. Not only will employees notice your increased attention to the positive year-round, but you'll have great material for writing annual performance reviews too!

A theme of this chapter is that while well-done work anniversaries are valuable, so is the preparation for them, so the chapter is laid it out as a timeline, followed by a couple of other topics:

- ▸ Long before the work anniversary
- ▸ A week or two before the work anniversary
- ▸ The day of the work anniversary
- ▸ Messaging tips
- ▸ Skip-level work anniversary conversations

LONG BEFORE THE WORK ANNIVERSARY

There are four things you can do immediately to make work anniversaries better for your team, regardless of when the work anniversaries actually happen. The latter three are valuable *even if you don't celebrate work anniversaries at all!*

SET UP A REMINDER SYSTEM

The most important thing for a manager to do with work anniversaries is *remember* and *acknowledge* them, because sadly, even if all you do is casually say, "Happy work anniversary!" your employees will be getting more work anniversary recognition than many. And you don't want your employee to go home and say they got more acknowledgment from people on LinkedIn who they don't know than from their boss.

Some organizations have a system for reminding managers of their employees' work anniversaries. By all means, encourage HR to do this for everyone, but if they don't, you need to step up. Besides, organization-wide systems sometimes miss things, so even if HR does it, you may also want to do something on your own, just in case.

For each of your direct reports, set up two reminders. One will be before the work anniversary, giving you enough time to prepare whatever you'll be doing. Two weeks is a common amount of time, though some managers prefer less and some more. Then you'll also want a reminder for the day of the work anniversary.

Everyone has a different approach to managing their work, but a common one is to set up an annually recurring task in your task management system for pre-work-anniversary preparation, which you can mark complete once you're prepared. And then, for the day of the work anniversary, add a reminder to your calendar.

Be careful to remember to do this whenever someone new joins your team. If you have any kind of checklist for new hires who report to you, add it to your list.

CAPTURE EMPLOYEE FAVORITES

I also discussed capturing employee preferences in the *Ideas for human resources* chapter, but like communicating performance review and pay raise timing, it falls to you if HR doesn't do it.

The idea is to learn what employees like in a way that will support your doing something small and thoughtful on their work anniversary. Here are some examples of what you can find out from them, but feel free to think up your own:

- **Favorite restaurant near the office** (to take them out to lunch on their work anniversary)

- **Favorite delivery lunch order near their home** (for remote workers)

- **Favorite nice restaurant** (to get them a gift card)

- **Favorite candy or snack** (to drop off the morning of their work anniversary)

- **Favorite cake or baked good** (if you celebrate at a team meeting)

- **Favorite color** (if you decorate their desk)

For managers it makes the most sense to do this in a conversation rather than with a form. You'll be surprised at how much you learn about the person, especially if you ask for the backstory on how any of these things became their favorites.

Important: *make sure you write down the answers.* A convenient place to record it is on their work anniversary reminder in your calendar or wherever else you set up the reminders, but use whatever system works for you.

SET UP A ROUTINE TO CAPTURE HIGHLIGHTS FOR EACH EMPLOYEE

One of the things to consider doing for each of your employees' work anniversaries is to write them a thoughtful, heartwarming note recapping their many contributions, accomplishments, and learnings over the past year and letting them know how much you appreciate them.

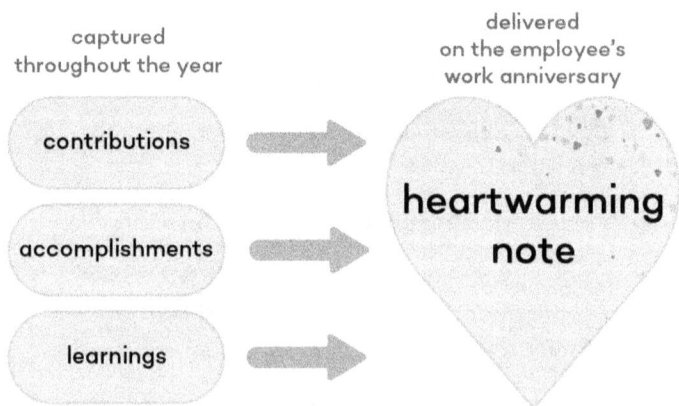

captured
throughout the year

delivered
on the employee's
work anniversary

contributions

accomplishments

learnings

heartwarming
note

It can be hard to do this at the last minute. You'll most likely fall prey to something behavioral psychologists call "recency bias" if you do, and forget some gems from further back in time, so the best thing to do is to make note of them as they happen.

The two key things to have are:

> ▸ **A place** where you capture a list of highlights for each of your employees

> ▸ **A system** for making sure you update the lists regularly

Some managers might like to begin every day reflecting on whether they have something to add, while some may prefer to do this either before or after their scheduled one-on-ones with employees. Other managers have some sort of task management system and can add a recurring task. *How* you do it doesn't matter as long you do it consistently for all the employees who report to you.

What do you write? Anything positive! For each role it will be different. Maybe it's kudos from customers, or big sales, or project completions. Maybe it's a new skill or taking on additional responsibilities. Here's one framework for coming up with ideas:

> ▸ **Contributions** – In what ways can what the employee does be counted? Total sales? Number of customers helped? Number of invoices paid? Number of widgets produced? Number of vaccines administered? Number of other employees trained?

> ▸ **Accomplishments** – Are there any wins or moments that stood out? Big contracts won? Big projects completed? Patents granted? Internal improvement ideas implemented?

Industry awards won? Internal organization awards won? A promotion? Positive quotes about the employee from customers?

▸ **Learnings** – How did the employee improve their capacity to help the organization? Completed training classes? Took on new responsibilities in their role? Came up with new and better ways of doing their job?

While this will take some of your valuable time, the effort is rewarded well beyond work anniversaries because:

> **Capturing employee highlights will make you a much better manager**

Biologically speaking, we're more naturally wired to look for threats and mistakes than things that go right, but that can be demotivating to those who work for us. As you condition yourself to consistently look for the good in your employees, they'll notice subtle changes in how you interact with them. Your focus on the positive will lead you to become a better liked and respected and more *motivational* manager.

COMMUNICATE PERFORMANCE REVIEW AND PAY RAISE TIMING

This last one isn't about getting something good to happen but rather about helping avoid something bad.

This too is covered in the *Ideas for human resources* chapter, but you can't rely solely on human resources for this. First, they might not come through, and if they don't, you're the one who's going to have the problem, not them. And second, even if they do their part, that doesn't guarantee your employees will get the message. Things that matter are best communicated from multiple sources multiple times.

What does this have to do with work anniversaries? In the absence of clear communication about how your organization does it, many employees will expect a performance review and a pay raise on their work anniversary. Even if that's rare in your sector, many employees' expectations will be set by friends or family or their own experience in other sectors.

If your organization has a different timing, like everyone getting a review at the end of the calendar year and raises starting at the beginning of the calendar year, then you need to make sure your employees know so there's no awkwardness or confusion when nothing happens on their work anniversary.

And if you *do* have reviews and raises tied to work anniversaries, communicate that clearly. Let employees know very specifically when to expect communication about reviews and raises—and invite them to speak up if that communication doesn't occur. Employees dwelling on what they should do if they're forgotten and quietly and unhappily doing nothing is far worse for you than if they speak up and say, "Shouldn't my review process have started last week?"

Feedback and money are both powerful forces. When handled poorly, and especially when that poor handling is left unaddressed, they can create a giant invisible motivation-destroying wall between you and your employees.

Don't let that happen. Overcommunicate.

A WEEK OR TWO BEFORE THE WORK ANNIVERSARY

So you've followed the steps in the previous section, including setting up reminders, and you get your first reminder that it's time to prepare for the work anniversary of someone on your team. What do you do?

USE THE FAVORITES LIST

If you're going to use the favorites list, now's the time to prepare. Review the employee's answers to the questions about their favorites. Buy the candy, make sure you have the right color decorations, or get the gift card.

Note that for remote employees this can be more difficult. Don't feel the need to force it. At the chosen price point, if it's hard to find something to do that feels personal and appropriate, it's fine to invest your energy elsewhere, like in the heartwarming note.

SCHEDULE THE TEAM LUNCH

Meals don't make sense for every team, but if they make sense for yours, add it to the calendar. Make a reservation if appropriate.

The goal here is to get as many people from your team there as possible so the employee feels honored and so there's a lot of team bonding.

Another valuable thing to do is to invite people from outside your team who work closely with the employee celebrating the work anniversary. That can go a long way toward supporting interdepartmental understanding and cooperation. Also consider inviting your boss.

Which restaurant? If you've captured employee favorites, then the employee's favorite local restaurant is an obvious choice. Or, if that restaurant is too small to support the size of your group, you may want to choose a restaurant that's able to seat you all at a single table (or multiple tables pushed together). The ideal restaurant will be quiet enough to support easy conversations. A restaurant you can walk to is better than one you have to drive to, especially for office workers who spend most of their time sitting.

While the cost of these kinds of meals adds up, eating together is scientifically proven to build trust and cooperation.[1] That makes this especially valuable for teams that need to collaborate and work creatively together. It also makes including people from outside your team especially valuable when interdepartmental cooperation is important.

If meals are too expensive or otherwise don't make sense for your team, consider sharing a snack in the break room. Make it special by choosing something from the employee's preferences list and personalizing it, like their favorite kind of dessert with "Happy work anniversary" and their name on it.

WRITE A FEW THANKFUL PARAGRAPHS ABOUT THE EMPLOYEE'S PAST YEAR

You may or may not choose to do a small gift, and you may or may not choose to celebrate the employee's work anniversary with a meal, but:

Whatever else you do or don't do for an employee's work anniversary, *definitely* write a few thankful paragraphs about the employee's past year

Thankful paragraphs don't cost anything, and thoughtfully appreciating your direct reports is something you probably want to be doing more of anyway.

If your organization doesn't do anything for work anniversaries, this is the best way to help your employees not resent that. And if your organization does celebrate work anniversaries, this is likely to be the most memorable highlight.

So how do you do it *well*?

As previously mentioned, taking notes throughout the year helps, but even if you didn't, you can scroll through your calendar or through your emails or texts with that employee to remind yourself what happened in the past year. If you have a peer appreciation system, you can look there for quotes. If they're customer-facing, you can look through the customer feedback system for quotes. Then write down the highlights of the employee's key contributions, accomplishments, and learnings. Throughout the paragraphs, repeatedly thank the employee for their efforts.

To make it extra special, get a little personal and say something about the two of you from the past year. If you're sharing the message with a wider audience than just the employee and not everyone who reads it will know the employee that well (like an organization-wide group messaging platform channel), consider including some "ice-breaker" facts about their personal life. If you have relevant photographs, share them along with what you've written. This helps employees get to know and relate to each other, which strengthens connection and belonging.

In general, the more personalized the note, the better. That will convey the message that you put some time and thought into it and genuinely care about the employee.

SET UP A SPECIAL CAREER-FOCUSED ONE-ON-ONE

Some organizations have a formal process for having conversations with employees about their careers, but many don't. If yours doesn't, consider setting up your own personal tradition of having a career-focused one-on-one conversation on each employee's work anniversary. Note that this is not an appraisal or review session where you judge the employee but rather a session where you ask the employee about their career goals and aspirations and truly *listen*.

This can be a terrific way to build trust and boost perceived organizational support. It can also help with retention. As previously mentioned, employees are twice as likely to leave within a month of their work anniversary as at any other time of the year.[2, 3, 4] Some recruiting companies know this and will specifically time their calls to your employees accordingly. Work anniversaries are a natural time for employees to be thinking about their careers. If you step in to support them in their goals, they'll feel less need to look elsewhere for opportunities.

A straightforward approach is to ask them where they'd like to be in one year, five years, and ten years and then look for ways in which the two of you can work together toward making those aspirations a reality.

Another approach—which works both with employees who think about their long-term plans and with those who answer the above questions with shrugs—is job crafting. Here are the basic steps:

1. Before the meeting, let the employee know that you'd like to learn more about their job and their interests—set the expectation that it's possible that nothing will change, saying you'd just like to explore the options—then ask the employee to come to the meeting with a list of everything they put time into as part of their job or would *like* to put time into as part of their job

2. In the meeting, have them go through the list with you and answer any questions you might have

3. Ask them what things on the list they'd like to stop doing or do less of, and what things they'd like to start doing or do more of

4. Spend the rest of the meeting working with them to come up with a plan to make one or more of the changes actually happen— importantly, add an item to the plan for when you'll check in on the plan's progress

And a last idea, which can work alone or alongside either of the above two approaches, is to ask the employee if there's any formal training that would help them advance their career. Then, if it's at all possible, help them devise a plan to make it happen.

CONSIDER PROMOTING THE EMPLOYEE

Promotions on work anniversaries have greater meaning than promotions any time during the rest of the year. The two events reinforce and amplify each other to create a "peak" day the employee is unlikely to ever forget.

Many promotions are triggered by vacancies. In those cases, I don't recommend you introduce an extended delay; but for "increased competency" promotions (like from junior engineer to engineer) where the role is essentially unchanged, timing them with a work anniversary can greatly increase the impact.

It also creates a rhythm for assessing whether to promote an employee so that the question doesn't get overlooked. The need for this kind of promotion can be difficult to notice. There's generally not one magical triggering event when you realize a junior engineer isn't junior anymore, so you might miss it.

So if your organization has promotions for increased competency, think through whether the employee having a work anniversary is ready for one and time the announcement of it with their work anniversary.

THE DAY OF THE WORK ANNIVERSARY

Here's a list of key activities to have at the top of your to-do list when the big day arrives.

ANNOUNCE IT USING YOUR GROUP MESSAGING SOFTWARE

If your organization uses Slack or other group messaging software, post your thankful paragraphs about the employee there. If not, post on the largest relevant channel that has active participation from employees, and preferably multiple levels of leaders above them. For many organizations, that will be the organization's #general channel. Some organizations choose to start a #celebrations channel where work anniversaries share the limelight with birthdays, engagements, marriages, and births. For large organizations, a division or department channel may make sense. But if possible, don't post it for just your team. Your employee probably works with many people outside your team, and you want those people to be able to celebrate the employee too.

After you've posted, direct-message any key executives whose participation you think would be especially meaningful to the employee and request that they jump into your thread with something congratulatory. These executives are most likely not watching group messaging closely and will otherwise miss it—but usually are willing to respond to a specific request.

If your organization doesn't have an active group messaging application, then email can work, but you need to get the distribution list right and beware the risks of awkward reply-alls.

ANNOUNCE IT ON THE BULLETIN BOARD

If your team doesn't communicate electronically and instead uses a physical bulletin board to post notices near the time clock or in the break room, use that space to post a happy work anniversary message.

The message will be even more memorable if you post paragraphs about the employee's past year and add a photo or two.

If you're up for going further, put all those things on a poster and make it a tradition that the employee's coworkers all sign the poster. Then, at the end of the day, present the employee with the poster. They then can either put it in their workspace or take it home. This may seem cheesy and cheap, but with the right team it can be amazing!

ONE-ON-ONE REACH-OUT FIRST THING IN THE DAY

Reaching out live at the very beginning of the workday sends a strong message that the employee is important. It's highly recommended that you set up recurring calendar appointments for each of your direct reports, both so you remember and so other meetings don't get in the way.

If you work in person and can get there physically, that will be most appreciated and can be a wonderful opportunity for you to give them something from their preferences list. Candy, fruit, or a packaged snack is simple. If you're authorized to give them their favorite gift card, that works too, but be aware not to give gift cards outside of an organization-wide program because they're taxable, no matter the amount, and that gets complicated. (See the **Taxes** appendix on page 347 for tax details for your country.)

If you're reaching out electronically, start with a message that says, "Happy work anniversary!" and then asks if they have a few minutes for a call. The main objective of the call is to thank them—not to ask for status updates! Talking about what you just posted on your group messaging platform makes for a meaningful topic. Another winner is to ask them if there's anything you can do to help their day go better.

And make sure you don't forget to reach out to employees who might not be front of mind because they're on client site, are traveling, or are on parental or medical leave.

ANNOUNCE IT AT THE DAILY STAND-UP

If your team does a daily stand-up, congratulate anyone having a work anniversary that day at the start of the stand-up. Sharing your thankful paragraphs goes over well here, as does tossing them a small item from their preferences list, because having everyone learn that they like that kind of candy or chips or gift card helps build team camaraderie.

If your direct reports don't have a stand-up together but they are on a cross-functional project team where they do the bulk of their work, you can do something similar by reaching out to the person who runs the stand-up (scrum leader, product manager, etc.) and asking if you can crash the beginning of the meeting to congratulate your employee on their work anniversary.

HAVE THE SPECIAL CAREER-FOCUSED ONE-ON-ONE

The **Set up a special career-focused one-on-one** section on page 119 covered the details—now you just need to do what you prepared for.

The one day-of tip is that if for any reason you need to move the meeting (and if you have enough notice), it's better to move the meeting to *before* their work anniversary than after. Anything done after the actual date will feel less meaningful.

TEAM LUNCH

Remember, while it's called "team lunch," don't forget the value of inviting people who work with the employee beyond your team.

As mentioned earlier, it's best if the group can all sit at a single table or multiple tables pushed together. A large circular table is ideal because everyone can see everyone else, but a single long narrow table is better than multiple circular tables.

Bring along your boss when you can, and again, people from other departments who work with the person celebrating, if possible.

One option is to have someone share a few words about the person celebrating the work anniversary. Either you can do this and use the paragraphs described in the previous section, or the employee's best friend at work can say a few words. (For help preparing, see the **How to write a great celebratory work anniversary speech** appendix on page 339.)

Another wonderful option is to make it a tradition to go around the table and have everyone share some kind words about the employee being honored. It can be free-form, or there can be a prompt such as:

- ▸ What three words best describe them?
- ▸ What's your favorite memory of them from the past year?
- ▸ Why are you thankful they've been with us for the past year?

This last idea isn't for every team, but consider a ritual, like singing a happy work anniversary song. You can modify the Happy Birthday song, or you can sing "For They're a Jolly Good Colleague" to the tune of "For They're a Jolly Good Fellow." If your group is less musically minded, then maybe right after the meal has arrived and before anyone starts to eat, call out, "Two, four, six, eight! Whose *seven* years with *XYZ Corp* do we appreciate?" and have everyone respond with the person's name. Then say, "Let's eat!"

CHECK IN AT THE END OF THE DAY

This is especially important if your organization has a standard way of acknowledging work anniversaries. Check to make sure that it happened and happened as expected.

While empowering employees and delegating the solving of their problems to them is generally the right call, a forgotten work anniversary is an exception. Don't ask an employee to follow up with HR about a missed work anniversary. That's just too awkward for most people and destroys all the value. Straightening things out with HR is your job in this case. And the good news is that while the employee will initially feel slighted that the organization forgot them, you'll be able to more than make up for that by jumping in and making it clear that they're important to you by doing whatever it takes to fix the mistake.

Another reason to check in at the end of the day is to make sure they're able to leave work on time, or at least to let them know that you realize they can't and you feel badly for them. If at all possible, though, find a way to help them leave on time.

MESSAGING TIPS

Whatever you do for your employees' work anniversaries, here are some general tips to help give your interactions the most value.

CONVEY ENTHUSIASM, *NOT* A DESIRE FOR TASK COMPLETION

The key thing to remember when talking to your employees about their work anniversaries is the importance of keeping the excitement up. Don't let it become a burden or even routine. Remember, for each of your employees, you're celebrating the anniversary of a day that was of central importance to their lives. If you have any employees hired directly out of school, it was an especially big deal for them.

Never do anything unceremoniously. If your organization has managers give out pins or certificates or any other tangible item to commemorate the occasion, never just silently put it on their desk when they're not there and walk away. Stop back again later or leave a note for them to come find you because you have something important for them (just make sure it doesn't sound ominous).

The goal is to convey that they *matter*, to you and to the organization, and that you're genuinely happy to celebrate their work anniversary because you're so thankful they're there.

> You don't want an employee's work anniversary to come across as one more chore you're trying to quickly check off your task list

Another way to convey that the event is important is to take photos, since that's something people associate with celebrations like holidays, birthdays, and other big life events. When you give them their pin/certificate/whatever, take a picture of them with it. That small gesture will give the experience more weight and show that it's meaningful to you as well as to them.

REINFORCE YOUR ORGANIZATION'S PURPOSE, CORE VALUES, AND/OR GOALS

If a work anniversary were only about time, it wouldn't be that special. After all, some people stay at an organization for years and years just because they don't like change or simply can't muster the time or energy to look for something better.

What a work anniversary really commemorates is the time when the employee and the organization teamed up to work together toward a common purpose with shared core values. So when you talk about an employee's work anniversary, the more you emphasize that common bond the more meaningful it will be. For example, saying, "Wow, ten years, that's a long time" doesn't convey much, but "Wow, that's ten years of helping us improve XYZ and making more than 450 customers happy!" shows you're paying attention and supports your organization's mission, goals, and values.

BOOST BELONGING AND PERCEIVED ORGANIZATIONAL SUPPORT

Everyone is insecure about something. For many people, it's their job. As their manager, *you* are where they get most of their information about the organization. Work anniversaries are an opportunity to ease employees' anxiety by reassuring them that they belong—and that the organization is there to support them when they need it.

This is important, not just for the employees' job satisfaction and your organization's retention rate but because many, many studies have shown that organizational support and a sense of belonging boost performance.[5, 6, 7, 8, 9, 10, 11, 12, 13]

WHAT IF YOU AREN'T ENTHUSIASTIC AND APPRECIATIVE?

So far, the advice has been to be enthusiastic, let employees know they've contributed to something bigger than themselves, and make sure they know you're glad they're there.

But what if being enthusiastic about one of your employees is hard? What if they aren't contributing? What if you aren't glad they're there?

The answer may not be easy, but it *is* simple: either come up with a new story in your head so that you are genuinely thankful for them or resolve to part ways somehow. The employee most likely senses how you feel. Life is too short for either of you to endure that kind of tension every day. The employee/manager relationship is a vital one, personally and professionally. You owe it to both of you to get things on the right path.

SKIP-LEVEL WORK ANNIVERSARY CONVERSATIONS

If you're a manager of managers, work anniversaries provide a great context for having skip-level conversations with employees more than one level under you.

For employees who don't get to speak with you one-on-one, this can be the highlight of their work anniversary. The more levels removed you are, the truer this is.

It's also great for *you*. One of the awkward truths of management is that as you climb higher in the organization, you have less firsthand frontline knowledge even as you become responsible for more and bigger decisions. By coming up with a system for regularly connecting with lower-level employees, you'll make more informed decisions.

You'll also be perceived better. You'll build a reputation as a leader who cares about what employees think and who actually knows what's going on. When you make a big decision, you'll be able to use frontline language and give frontline examples to back it up. And because of this, frontline employees will be more likely to give you the benefit of the doubt if they don't fully understand a decision or understand the reasoning behind it.

The above two paragraphs are true about skip-level meetings no matter how you do them, but one powerful thing about using work anniversaries as the catalyst for a skip-level meeting is that it makes it far less threatening for both the employee and their direct manager. If you set up skip-level meetings out of the blue, even if it's merely out of curiosity on your part, it will trigger anxiety for many employees and those employees' direct managers. That just isn't helpful.

A convenient thing about work anniversary skip-level meetings is that the urgency and extra value of a specific date makes it more likely for them to actually happen. It makes it easier to schedule well ahead of time, easier to *keep* the meeting scheduled, and easier to not repeatedly schedule over it.

One more thing to note is that you don't have to have one of these meetings with every employee for every work anniversary. You might be tempted to try if you were recently promoted and feel bad that you're not connected to the front line like you used to be, but the more indirect reports you have, the more impractical that gets. So perhaps meet with everyone hitting five years instead, or everyone hitting ten years. Just figure out how many people you can realistically talk to per year and pick the work anniversary milestones that will get you to that number.

Once you have them scheduled, what do you actually *do* in the meetings? You may have your own approach, and the internet abounds with ideas, but next up are a couple of ideas that work well.

THE GETTING-TO-KNOW-THEM APPROACH

If you're going to be talking with employees you really don't interact with or don't know at all, a natural format is to use the time to get to know them.

Here are some especially interesting open-ended questions that will reveal a lot about what's going on in your organization and gently nudge the employee toward constructive answers:

- ‣ What parts of your job do you enjoy most?

- ‣ What parts of your job do you do best?

- ‣ What was your biggest accomplishment at work in the past year?

- ‣ What are you looking forward to in your job over the next year?

- ‣ Are you being challenged? What challenges would you like to take on?

- ‣ Is anything getting in the way of sharing your opinions and ideas at work?

- ‣ Is there a skill you'd like to learn or training you'd like to receive?

- ‣ Is there anything you need to help you do your work better?

THE QUICK FIFTEEN-MINUTE-BUT-STILL-POWERFUL APPROACH

Not every leader will be interested in the details to be learned from the approach above, and that's okay. If you want to go straight to the most important content at the fastest pace, center the conversation around this single question:

> ▸ If you had a magic wand and could change one thing about our department *(or division or whatever you call what you're in charge of)*, what would you change?

After you get the answer, gently probe into the backstory and find out why the employee responded that way. You may well learn as much about the employee as you do about your department.

Then use one of the following options to conclude the conversation:

> ▸ **Suggest a next step the employee can take to make progress** toward making it happen. This will often be making a connection, saying something like "You know, they think about that a lot in marketing. You'll want to talk to Pat. Let me get you their number."

> ▸ **Suggest a next step the employee can take to research the details** behind their request. For example, if they think your organization should start recycling paper clips, have them calculate how much the organization spends on paper clips each year and find out what a paper clip recycling program would cost. The idea here

is that if their idea doesn't make sense, *they* figure out that it doesn't make sense without your having to say no. This avoids you being the meanie—and figuring it out on their own will teach them to think about things from other angles, which is more valuable than just having someone in authority tell them it's not going to happen. And if their idea is a good one, the employee gains confidence and insight into the business while the department benefits from their work.

▸ **Simply empathize with them**. Acknowledge that you can see how things would be much better if what they imagined were the case. Sometimes people just need to feel heard.

Notice that committing to doing something about their request wasn't one of the options above. You're busy and a lot of people work for you. If you truly can *and will* do something, then you can commit to it, but don't feel pressured to. Actively and sympathetically listening to their perspective is more than enough and more than most employees get from most leaders. Then if you *do* do something, you can always pleasantly surprise them later!

WHATEVER APPROACH YOU USE, DO THIS

Be curious. Stay curious and positive no matter what they say. Listen. Listen a lot.

Try not to say anything other than to ask questions—this is not a time for you to share *your* thoughts, it's a time to listen to *theirs*

You already know what *you think* and sharing it one-on-one with a low-level employee is a poor use of your time. But you don't know what *they think* and finding that out is an excellent use of your time.

Tailor your questions to steer the conversation toward topics that interest you, but remember it's not helpful for you to answer your own questions. If an employee says something you disagree with, don't argue or explain why they're wrong. Definitely don't try to "constructively" share what you think. Instead, ask more questions about why they think that way and try to really see things from their perspective.

Even if they ask you what you think, don't take the bait. Tell them that what you think is that it's good for you to learn from others and redirect them back to talking about what *they* think.

You'll be amazed at what you'll learn!

THE MANAGER CHECKLIST

Half of being great at work anniversaries is great preparation.

- ▸ **Start preparing long before the work anniversary:**

  - ☐ Set up a reminder system

  - ☐ Capture employee favorites

  - ☐ Set up a system for capturing highlights for each of your employees

  - ☐ Communicate performance review and pay raise timing

- ▸ **A couple of weeks before the work anniversary:**

  - ☐ Use the favorites list (*typically only if your team is in-person*)

  - ☐ Schedule a meal (*if appropriate for your team*)

  - ☐ Write a few thankful paragraphs about the employee's past year (*always*)

  - ☐ Schedule a special career-focused one-on-one (*always*)

  - ☐ Consider promoting the employee (*if you have skill-level promotions*)

▸ **The day of the work anniversary:**

☐ Announce on your group messaging platform, the bulletin board, the daily stand-up, or wherever makes sense

☐ Reach out one-on-one first thing in the morning

☐ Go out for a team lunch *(if that makes sense for your team's situation)*

☐ Have a special career-focused one-on-one

☐ Check in at the end of the day

▸ **Other tips:**

☐ Convey enthusiasm, not a desire for task completion

☐ Reinforce your organization's purpose, core values, and/or goals

☐ Help the employee feel secure and confident in their job

☐ Consider setting up skip-level one-on-ones *(if you're a manager of managers)*

5

IDEAS FOR IT SUPPORT

GREAT ORGANIZATIONS EMPOWER employees.

Your organization has a budget allocation per person per year for IT upgrades and perhaps also furniture. For their work anniversary, empower your employees to choose how to spend that budget to make themselves more productive.

Employees generally know best what they need in order to do their jobs well. Maybe an employee has back problems and needs a standing desk to work without pain. Maybe they've started regularly dealing with jumbo spreadsheets and need more memory or a larger monitor. Maybe they travel a lot, and their laptop isn't reliably connecting to the projectors in their customers' conference rooms.

These things can reduce the employee's productivity, and their managers aren't well positioned to help them. Also, these problems tend to grow slowly over time, and without an urgent need it's hard to know exactly when to address them.

Regular planned, proactive check-ins from the IT support team, where an employee can ask for (and get) what would make them more productive—*and timing it to the employee's work anniversary*—help employees not just to work at their full potential but also to feel valued and appreciated. Some organizations will want to do the check-in every year. Others will find it works better every two years or even three years.

An important caveat is that this sort of program should never be a reason to deny employee requests for equipment necessary for doing their job well during the rest of the year. Saying, "You'll have to wait until your work anniversary" will create ill will. The goal of regular check-ins is to proactively surface productivity-enhancing improvements that the employee hasn't yet requested.

IT WILL MORE THAN PAY FOR ITSELF

What I just suggested is probably a big process change from how your organization does things. It will most likely cost you in time, and at first—as you catch up on "debt"—it will almost definitely cost you in money.

The good news is that the benefits of getting IT involved with celebrating work anniversaries this way are backed by quantifiable hard science, which shows that both better equipment and feeling empowered to influence your work environment improve productivity.

Multiple monitors improve employees' memory:

> Researchers from the University of Virginia and from Carnegie Mellon University reported that study participants were able to recall 56 percent more information when it was presented to them on multiple monitors rather than on a single screen.[1]

Larger screens help employees think more broadly and insightfully:

> When using a large display, [participants] engaged in higher-order thinking, arrived at a greater number of discoveries and achieved broader, more integrative insights. Such gains are not a matter of individual differences or preferences ... everyone who engages with the larger display finds that their thinking is enhanced.[2]

Under-desk exercise bikes help employees focus:

> Moderate-intensity exercise, practiced for a moderate length of time, improves our ability to think both during and immediately after the activity. The positive changes documented by scientists include an increase in the capacity to focus attention and resist distraction; greater verbal fluency and cognitive flexibility; enhanced problem-solving and decision-making abilities; and increased working memory, as well as more durable long-term memory for what is learned.... The beneficial mental effects of moderately intense activity have been shown to last for as long as two hours after exercise ends.[3]

Standing desks help with just about everything:

> *The British Medical Journal* published a study showing that standing desks improved job performance, improved work engagement, reduced occupational fatigue, reduced sickness presenteeism,

reduced daily anxiety, and improved quality of life. The only thing tested between the intervention and control groups where no difference was found was sickness absenteeism.[4]

Empowering employees to choose improvements themselves has twice the impact of just doing good things for employees without involving them. (This study also had "lean," "disempowered," and "enriched" control groups, and the empowered group was the clear winner):

> In the lean office, participants invested a low level of effort in their assigned work; they were listless and lackadaisical. In the disempowered office, subjects' productivity was similarly mediocre; in addition, they were very, very unhappy . . . . In the enriched office, participants worked harder and were more productive; in the empowered office, people performed best of all. They got 30 percent more done there than in the lean office, and about 15 percent more than in the enriched office.[5]

There's much, much more research supporting this concept that could be cited, but let's move on to how to get started.

STEP 1 – SET UP THE PROCESS

To get the most out of this approach, it's vitally important *not to miss anyone* and *not to be late*.

That means that the IT team needs to track all work anniversaries and set up reminders to start the process enough in advance to get each employee their updated equipment in time for their work anniversary.

Each IT team will have a slightly different process that works best for them, but these are the general steps:

1. Get an initial list of all employees and their start dates

2. Create a shared spreadsheet listing all the work anniversaries, with columns for:
   - The employee's name
   - Their work anniversary date
   - The IT employee assigned
   - The status (not started, initial meeting scheduled, initial meeting complete, ordered, on site, shipped, delivered)
   - What was purchased
   - Cost
   - Notes

3. Assign IT employees to each of the employees with upcoming work anniversaries

4. Add checking in on the spreadsheet to the standing agenda for your IT team meeting

5. Work with HR to have new employees added as part of the onboarding process

STEP 2 – EMPOWER EMPLOYEES

The IT person assigned to each employee sets up a meeting with them about a month before their work anniversary. Name the meeting something like "Annual Equipment Check-in." In the description, say something like "Congratulations, Jim, you're about to hit your fourth work anniversary here at XYZ Corporation! We wanted to make sure you have what you need to be as productive as you can be. Let's talk about how we can help."

At the meeting, the IT person starts by asking the employee what they think could help them do their job better and writes down all they say. As the IT person gets more experienced at this, they may be able to ask the employee about issues other employees in similar positions have had.

> The core of this program is *empowering employees* to decide what would most help them be more productive

The IT person then needs to navigate any budget constraints. Some organizations may have a policy of getting employees anything they ask for within the overall budget for each category, with a max price per monitor, desk, chair, and so on. Others may have a max amount per employee per year, and an employee going over that amount needs approval. Others may have a list of "always say yes" items and a list of "choose one" items where small items are always fine, but for bigger items employees need to choose one—a large monitor, an under-desk exercise bike, a standing desk—in any given year. It's helpful for the IT person to be transparent about any budgetary limitations and ask the employee what's most important for them.

Sometimes an employee may say everything's fine and they don't need anything. This is great and helps make room in the budget for employees who need more, but to ensure no one feels left out, it's best to have a small number of low-cost options for these employees—a plant, a stress ball or fidget spinner, a company-branded mouse. That way, everyone gets *something* from IT on their work anniversary.

STEP 3 – DELIVER ON THE *EXACT* WORK ANNIVERSARY DATE

Timing matters. Delivering on the actual day of the work anniversary amplifies the sense of meaning and importance that will attach to the gift, so while being late is better than doing nothing, make every attempt to be on time.

If you're not a hundred percent sure you can deliver on the exact day or it's logistically impossible, it's better to deliver early. Then, on the actual day, the IT person sends an email wishing the employee a happy work anniversary and expressing hope that their new equipment is working well.

If something happens and the equipment will be delivered late, then on the actual work anniversary send an email wishing the employee a happy work anniversary, apologizing that things aren't on time, and including a delivery status update.

If the employee chose nothing, reach out on the day, wish them a happy work anniversary, and let them know their budget is rolling over to next year. (Let them know that even if you opt to give them something small, as suggested above.)

STEP 4 – MAKE IT SPECIAL

Another way to amplify the power of this program is to put a little extra effort into making the delivery special.

Can you put a bow on it? Or have it gift-wrapped?

Are you in person, and can you add balloons?

Are you remote, and can you put colorful confetti in the box with a congratulatory note?

bows, wrapping paper, balloons, confetti, and personalized notes all make it special

If you're shipping it directly from Amazon, can you put the little bit of extra effort into selecting the gift option and writing a message wishing them a happy work anniversary?

These things are minor, but they're also not hard. In general, throughout the process you want to avoid making the employee feel like a chore on a checklist.

By putting in a little special flair, you can be a big part of helping the employee feel genuinely appreciated by an organization that deeply values them.

THE IT SUPPORT CHECKLIST

Here are the steps for the IT support team to take to become an integral part of celebrating work anniversaries at your organization while simultaneously noticeably boosting employee productivity.

- [ ] **Get approval** to check in with employees before their work anniversaries to see what would help them do their jobs better—any budget concerns need to be addressed, and HR needs to be aware

- [ ] **Put a process in place** so no one gets forgotten and everyone gets their upgrades on time

- [ ] **Empower employees** by asking them what they need to be more productive and letting them drive the discussion of what would be most valuable to them

- [ ] **Attempt to deliver on the exact anniversary date**, and if it doesn't work out, send them a communication on the exact anniversary date

- [ ] **Put in a little extra celebratory flair**, like a bow or balloons, or at the very least a congratulatory message

6

IDEAS FOR CEOs (AND OTHER TOP LEADERS)

IF YOU'RE A CEO, then you're busy, so this chapter is short.

If you have a trusted executive assistant, there's also the option to stop reading and instead have them condense this to what's relevant to your specific situation. There's even a chapter in this book specifically to help them do just that!

As you read through the chapter, many of these things may seem minor to you, but from the employee's perspective they can be major. Both what you do and don't do carry much more weight for them than for you. A work anniversary interaction with you could easily be the highlight of an employee's day.

WHY WORK ANNIVERSARIES MATTER

If your organization doesn't actually care that much about its employees, work anniversaries probably *don't* matter. If employees are readily replaceable and don't play a part in your competitive advantage or brand promise, stop reading here.

If, on the other hand, engaged employees and a strong workplace culture are key to your organization's success, then work anniversaries are a uniquely *tangible, measurable,* and *promotable* way to strengthen that culture.

Or maybe your organization hasn't had a focus on employee engagement and workplace culture in the past, but you're looking to change that. There's just not a simpler or more cost-effective place to start than how you celebrate work anniversaries.

While they can't do any of these things completely on their own, high-quality work anniversaries can materially contribute to the following objectives (I'm repeating this list from the introduction in case you skipped straight to this chapter):

- **Reduce attrition** by providing a memorable and meaningful experience during the month when employees are otherwise twice as likely to quit[1,2,3]

- **Make it easier to hire top candidates** by providing concrete, easy-to-communicate proof that your organization cares more about employees than other organizations do

- **Improve team effectiveness** by providing opportunities for teams to build trust and understanding through shared celebration of moments unique to your organization

- **Increase skip-level communication** by providing a nonthreatening, easy-to-explain, and hard-to-postpone opportunity for senior leaders to have meaningful conversations with employees multiple levels below them

▸ **Reinforce your organization's culture** by providing regular opportunities to remind employees of your organization's purpose, mission, brand promise, core values, and/or slogans

▸ **Support marketing** by providing a regular stream of photogenic and compelling material for your marketing team to use to promote the quality of your employees to your prospects, customers, and other external stakeholders

Well-celebrated work anniversaries can deliver all that at little cost to your organization.

The HR team and individual managers drive much of any organization's work anniversary program, but this chapter describes opportunities unique to the CEO and other top leaders.

CELEBRATE WORK ANNIVERSARIES AT ALL-HANDS MEETINGS

If your organization holds all-hands meetings where work anniversaries are called out, *you* are the best person to announce them. They'll carry more weight and therefore be more appreciated coming from the most powerful person in the organization.

The simple universal message is to thank those employees for all they've contributed throughout their time at the organization, but if you want to go beyond thanking, then tying work anniversaries to your organization's purpose, core values, or slogans is a great way to increase the cultural impact (we'll talk about how to do that shortly).

If you're long-tenured yourself, you were there and you can remind the organization of how much progress has been made since the people being recognized started. Then turn that into an inspiring message of how much *more* progress everyone can make going forward. You might also be able to throw in a brief personal anecdote from your early time working with them that will make them feel special.

Warning: ideally you'll be familiar with your organization's work anniversary program, but if you're not, there's no need to announce it. Saying things like "I'm not sure what you get for twenty years, but I hope it's something good!" doesn't send the right message.

MAGICALLY REMEMBER WORK ANNIVERSARIES

Even the most casual mentions from the CEO, especially on the actual day of the work anniversary, carry a lot of power. They can become stories employees tell their families and friends and even add to your lore as the CEO who cares so much about employees that you actually remember work anniversaries!

To pull this off, set up some sort of system where you're reminded of work anniversaries before your meetings on any given day. Have HR email you a list of work anniversaries for the day first thing in the morning, or if you have an assistant, work with them to create a regular process where they give you a heads-up. If your organization is small enough, simply set reminders on your calendar.

If your organization has multiple remote locations and you visit them, another powerful way to show employees you value them (while also contributing to your lore) is to know if anyone at a location you're visiting is having a work anniversary that day. Take a little time out from your itinerary to find them, shake their hand, and thank them. The employee will greatly appreciate it, feel especially honored, and share the story multiple times.

SEND A PERSONALIZED EMAIL

This is a powerful idea for longer-tenured CEOs who have known the longer-tenured employees for a while. It takes a little time and effort, so you probably won't be able to do it for every work anniversary, but it can create a truly memorable moment for the big milestone work anniversaries, like the fives or tens, or even less frequent ones for larger, older organizations.

The email doesn't have to be long. You just need to:

▸ Send it on the exact day

▸ Thank the employee for their contributions to the organization's mission, purpose, and/or vision over their time with the organization

▸ Mention a memory from a while back or thoughts on the changes that have occurred since they started, if one comes naturally to you

▸ Invite them to reach out to you if they have anything they want to discuss (*very, very few actually will, but the sentiment will be appreciated by all*)

Again, the key thing is to send it *on the exact day,* or the previous workday if it falls on a non-working day. To pull this off, you'll want to have a reminder system in place as discussed above.

HOLD SKIP-LEVEL CONVERSATIONS

Most CEOs would like to connect with frontline employees and managers more but find that it can be awkward to set up and easy to postpone. How do you choose who to talk to? How do you explain why? How do you bridge the divide in your roles? How can these conversations compete with other urgent tasks?

Work anniversaries can solve *all* these problems!

Simply decide how many conversations you want to have per year and then pick the corresponding work anniversaries that roughly match that count—all the ones divisible by five or ten—or maybe concentrate on new employees and do all the first anniversaries. Then, set up fifteen-minute meetings with those employees on their work anniversaries. Really commit to having as many of the conversations as possible on the actual date of each work anniversary, but if that's not possible, it's much better to do it before than after.

Now, how do you run the actual conversation?

You may have your own approach, but my favorite CEO icebreaker is "If you had a magic wand, what would you change about this organization?" It's worded to pull out useful, constructive feedback in a positive and employee-empowering way without setting up expectations that you'll necessarily *do* something about the feedback—after all, magic wands don't exist. And if you do actually do something, you'll be perceived as being magical!

As employees start to learn that that's what you ask, some will start thinking about how to answer the question ahead of time, and the quality and value of the conversations will constantly improve.

HOLD LONG-TENURE EMPLOYEE BREAKFASTS

If you don't want to do the one-on-one conversations described above, or if you want to reach more employees than you can with that, consider having quarterly, semiannual, or annual long-tenured employee breakfasts (or lunches).

As with the skip-level conversations, first decide how many people you'd like to celebrate at each event and from there calculate which anniversary milestones will be included. The goal is for the group to be small enough so each employee can have the time to talk to you, though not all of them will. For larger, older organizations with at least a handful of employees who have been there twenty-five years or more, a catchy name for this might be "The [your organization name here] Quarter-Century Club."

For maximum impact, add the employee to the invitation on the exact date of their qualifying work anniversary with a congratulatory note welcoming them to this special and influential group.

REINFORCE YOUR ORGANIZATION'S CULTURE

A work anniversary is a naturally recurring communication opportunity where it's especially easy to be genuine. It's the celebration of the date that the employee joined together with the organization to work toward a common purpose, mission, and/or goal. It's when the employee joined the culture, learned the lingo, started acting according to the core values, learned the slogans, and began to deliver on the brand promise. In short, it marks the date they became one of "us."

That makes all your work anniversary interactions inherently compelling times for you to reinforce your organization's purpose, mission, goals, core values, slogans, and/or brand promise, whichever is most important to you.

When it comes to workplace culture, you're especially important. As the figurehead of the organization, you're the one everyone looks to in order to understand how important the purpose really is, or how important the core values really are, or just generally what *is* important.

As leadership expert Patrick Lencioni observed, leadership communication is 75 percent about creating clarity through repetition. Three of his four disciplines of organizational health are "create clarity," "over-communicate clarity," and "reinforce clarity."[4] (The fourth—or rather the first—is "build a cohesive leadership team." Not relevant here, but I didn't want you to put this book down to go look it up.)

Don't miss out on using work anniversaries to create clarity about your organization's culture and steer your organization's culture in the direction you want it to go.

ENCOURAGE THE ON-TIME WORK ANNIVERSARY DELIVERY RATE

Have your head of HR include the on-time work anniversary delivery rate in the departmental metrics they track and publish to the senior leadership team.

Being late or outright forgetting work anniversaries is bad, and this is a rare example of an objective, easy-to-track employee experience metric. It also has the advantage over engagement score and retention in that it's a *leading* indicator rather than a lagging one.

You may rarely or never pay attention to this metric, but just requiring that it be captured sends a powerful message that will improve how well work anniversaries are handled, thereby improving employee experience.

Want to go all in to make sure that work anniversaries aren't forgotten and, if they are, that you'll find out about it? Put a large "bounty" on forgotten work anniversaries. That is, publicly declare that work anniversaries are so important to you that if anyone's work anniversary is forgotten, they get a conference room named after them, or an extra paid week off, or $5000, or whatever makes sense for your organization.

MODEL THE BEHAVIOR YOU WANT

We all know that actions speak louder than words. For CEOs, that's doubly true—or more. Everyone is looking to you to see what you value so that they can behave accordingly.

If your organization has expectations for how managers acknowledge work anniversaries *and you want them to be met,* do what's expected on your direct reports' work anniversaries.

If your organization doesn't have specific expectations of managers, remember that the two most important things for a manager to do are:

- Set up a reminder system for *all* your direct reports' work anniversaries

- Acknowledge every work anniversary in a live conversation on the day of the anniversary or the last workday before weekend/holiday work anniversaries

THE CEO CHECKLIST

Employees are hypersensitive to the CEO's every word and action, and work anniversaries offer an opportunity for easy wins.

USE WORK ANNIVERSARIES TO CONNECT WITH EMPLOYEES

- [ ] Personally acknowledge work anniversaries at all-hands meetings
- [ ] Come up with a system to "magically" remember work anniversaries
- [ ] Set up one-on-one fifteen-minute work anniversary meetings
- [ ] Set up recurring long-tenure breakfasts

USE WORK ANNIVERSARIES TO ENCOURAGE WHAT'S IMPORTANT TO YOU

- [ ] Use work anniversaries to reinforce your organization's purpose, mission, goals, core values, slogans, and/or brand promise
- [ ] Use tracking of on-time work anniversary acknowledgment as a way to measure how well your organization is prioritizing employee experience
- [ ] Acknowledge your direct reports' work anniversaries the way you want managers at your organization to acknowledge theirs

And remember that while many of these things may seem small or even trivial to you, they can have an enormously positive impact on your employees. If you go out of your way to stop by an employee's desk in person, they will excitedly tell others about it!

7

IDEAS FOR EXECUTIVE ASSISTANTS

YOU WORK WITH your executive every day and see all their flaws and quirks and humanness up close, but for many frontline employees the executive is a larger-than-life figure. So how the executive handles work anniversaries can have a big impact on employees, and how *you* help the executive with work anniversaries can have a much bigger impact than you might expect.

Every executive is different, of course. This chapter includes a variety of ideas, not all of which will make sense for working with all executives. As you read, keep your executive's style in mind and choose the ideas you think will work best and ignore the rest.

But note that just because there's something your executive hasn't done before or might not naturally be good at, that doesn't mean that wouldn't be a great idea to pursue. It may be an excellent opportunity for you to use your role to enhance their effectiveness and improve employee perception of them. For example, if they're terrible at remembering dates, prompt them before every meeting if someone in the meeting has a major work anniversary that day. Or if they're not especially good at regularly being thankful, craft thankful emails to employees celebrating work anniversaries on their behalf.

Another thing to keep in mind is that work anniversaries are far from being your executive's top priority at any given moment, so you may not want to hit them with all the work anniversary ideas in this chapter at once. Tossing out a creative work anniversary idea every now and then in your one-on-ones with your executive can keep them interesting. It will mix up their day, and yours too.

If the above paragraph doesn't describe your executive and they're really into the idea of celebrating work anniversaries better, you might want to direct them to the **Ideas for CEOs (and other top leaders)** chapter beginning on page 149. If you support an executive other than the CEO, note that the content in that chapter applies to any executive with a lot of indirect reports—and you can point out that it's good practice for the day they get promoted to CEO.

As a last note, if you're an EA at a small organization, you probably take on responsibilities that would fall to human resources at a larger organization, so you may want to check out the **Ideas for human resources** chapter on page 43.

FIND THE WORK ANNIVERSARY DATES

You can't help anyone with work anniversaries if you don't know when they are. If they aren't readily available to you, reach out to HR:

- ▸ **Request access to your organization's HRIS**
  (human resource information system, sometimes called an employee tracking system) – Most HRIS systems will have a level of access that provides basic employee

information without any of the super-sensitive stuff. This will include start dates, which you'll need for work anniversaries, as well as addresses and phone numbers, which may on occasion be useful for you to know when supporting your executive

‣ If HR won't give you access to the HRIS system, **the next best thing to ask is whether they can set up a report to be sent to you on the fifteenth of every month** – Ask for the report to list all the employees having work anniversaries the following month, along with their hire dates, which is typically straightforward for the HRIS administrator to set up

‣ If HR won't give you access or set up an automated report for you, **ask them to manually pull a list of work anniversaries and send it to you** – New hires won't hit their first work anniversary for a year, so you only need a new list about every ten or eleven months

I don't recommend trying to update that initial list manually yourself by keeping track of new hires, even if you're at a small organization, because there's too much risk that you and HR will end up with different start dates for some employees, which can lead to confusion and disappointment.

If you do get access to the HRIS, find out if it will allow you to export a work anniversary calendar directly into your calendar system. If part of your reminding approach is to have work anniversaries on calendars (which I recommend), that export feature can save a lot of work and keep you from accidentally entering the wrong date.

HELP YOUR EXECUTIVE WITH THEIR DIRECT REPORTS

Your executive is an example to the managers under them: what your executive does sends a message about what they value and don't value.

If your executive is bad at celebrating their direct reports' work anniversaries, then the executive's direct reports will be more likely to be bad at celebrating *their* direct reports' work anniversaries. The problem will keep cascading all the way down to the front line. Conversely, if you can help your executive be *great* at celebrating their direct reports' work anniversaries, you'll create a ripple effect of appreciation and positivity that will be felt throughout the organization.

SET UP A RELIABLE PROCESS

To support your executive in this endeavor, first find out what your organization expects of managers on their work anniversaries. Some organizations will have documented expectations. Others will have unwritten traditions. For still others, it will be every manager for themself and a patchwork of completely different approaches. If your organization falls into that last category, as many do, consider reading the **Ideas for managers and supervisors** chapter starting on page 107.

Once you've figured out what should be done for your executive's direct reports, figure out how much of it you can do without them. Usually you'll be able to do quite a bit of it, sometimes even all of it, so from there all you need to do is set up a repeatable system for making sure everything gets done on time and nothing gets forgotten, which will probably be similar to a number of other areas of your job.

LOOK FOR CUSTOMIZATION OPPORTUNITIES

It's not all about repetition, though. Let yourself be open to opportunities where a small amount of thoughtful customization will make a difference.

For example, if you typically craft emails to be scheduled and sent out from the executive but the next work anniversary is someone the executive has a special relationship with, calling attention to it so the executive can add a personal touch to the email is something both the employee and your executive are likely to appreciate.

As another example, suppose your team celebrates work anniversaries by going out to lunch or dinner and getting dessert, but you know the honoree follows a keto diet. In this case, arranging for a nearby baker who makes keto desserts to deliver a keto cheesecake to the restaurant will make the employee feel noticed and appreciated.

And as a last example, if decorating desks for work anniversaries is one of your responsibilities, then knowing people's favorite colors for the balloons, streamers, and so on can make it more special.

Note that minor customizations are great, but it's important not to make one employee's work anniversary "better"—that is, materially more expensive or time-consuming—than any other employee's, because you'll risk creating negative feelings of favoritism. Only make a work anniversary "better" because it's a bigger milestone, and then treat that milestone the same way for all employees who reach it.

In other words, for work anniversaries to be successful, they need to be consistent and fair. Don't do a big party for one and a cupcake for another—and definitely don't do that because you like one employee better than the other or one is higher paid than the other. In a hybrid work situation where employees generally prefer working from home, giving a special cupcake to employees in the office is fine because it would be weird to ignore them, but that shouldn't be the main way employees are honored.

REMIND YOUR EXECUTIVE AT THE RIGHT TIME

Executives have a lot on their minds. Their jobs are full of stress and complexity. It's the rare executive who's going to remember the work anniversaries of employees multiple levels down in the organization when just remembering everyone's names is a win that's often not won.

Yet a timely in-person acknowledgment of a work anniversary can be enormously powerful in ways that are good for your executive and the organization as well as the employee. That's where you come in.

You can be the cause of some truly memorable moments by scanning both the work anniversaries for the day and the people who'll be in the executive's meetings for the day and then giving the executive a heads-up about any work anniversaries right before the meeting. And by "memorable moments" I mean moments that the employee will mention to their loved ones when they get home and possibly remember for years to come. A lot of executives will come to treasure these moments too. You'll know that what you're doing is working when they ask how they'll get reminded while you're on vacation.

If your organization has multiple locations that your executive visits, that's another opportunity. In these cases, the executive usually flies in and has a bunch of planned meetings with the same people they always meet with. Often they'll want to tour the location and be visible to the frontline employees, but just walking around can be awkward. What *you* can do is look up all the employees at that location who'll be having work anniversaries during your executive's visit and provide your executive with the list. Then, when your executive gets there, they can make a point of finding the employees and visiting each of them on their work anniversary day. Each interaction will only take a few minutes but will be talked about by not only the employee having the work anniversary but also by all the other employees who witnessed it.

I think it's helpful to point out that this works far better with work anniversaries than birthdays, particularly for executives in larger organizations. For many employees, if a powerful person they don't know mysteriously knows an intimate detail about their personal lives and uses it to try to strike up a conversation, it will come across as disingenuous at best and very likely as downright creepy. But work anniversaries don't carry that same creepy baggage. If an executive you don't know remembers your name and hire date, it feels like the executive cares in a very role-appropriate way.

ACKNOWLEDGE WORK ANNIVERSARIES ORGANIZATION-WIDE

This section is most relevant for EAs to CEOs (or whatever title leads the entire organization) at organizations that aren't big enough to have someone specifically in charge of internal communications. If you aren't involved in organization-wide internal communications, feel free to skip to the next section.

ALL-HANDS MEETINGS

Many EAs play a crucial role in organizing a weekly or monthly all-hands meeting for everyone in their executive's organization. If that's true for you, then making sure the acknowledgment of work anniversaries is a standing topic will go over well. Many employees will rarely get mentioned in the meeting, so the day their work anniversary is called out will be extra meaningful. The other wonderful thing is that by announcing work anniversaries, you set up a lot of icebreaking small talk opportunities that can help the employees in the organization connect with each other.

Here are some tips for making the most of acknowledging work anniversaries at all-hands meetings:

- ▸ **Announce upcoming work anniversaries, not recently passed work anniversaries**. Not only does being early have a more positive impact on employees celebrating anniversaries than acknowledging them after the fact, but you may inspire the employees' colleagues to do their own preparation for the day. Announcing ahead of time also subtly influences direct managers to be timely, since they know that everyone *else* knows the exact day. The one exception to this rule is if you have a monthly meeting that falls early in the month. In that case, while a few may end up being announced late, most will be announced in advance. And one last tip here is that if you know a meeting is going to be skipped for whatever reason, announce ahead to cover the time period of the two meetings. If a meeting has to be skipped unexpectedly, either mention the upcoming work anniversaries as part of the cancellation notice sent to everyone or retroactively mention them at the next meeting. *(There's also no harm in doing both.)*

- ▸ **Ask a designer for help improving the work anniversary announcement slides**. Well-designed work anniversary slides will send the subtle but valuable message that the organization cares enough about the employees being honored to put some thought and care into preparation, and that small amount of work will keep delivering value week after week, month after month, year after year. There's a chapter later in this book for graphic designers and a specific section about all-hands slides on page 187 that you might find helpful.

- **Have the highest-ranking person at the meeting announce the work anniversaries.** Even if someone else typically emcees the meeting, having the highest-ranking executive announce the work anniversaries gives them more weight. To support this, provide the person with phonetic spellings of any names that are difficult to pronounce. While people with hard-to-pronounce names are used to hearing their names butchered, that doesn't mean they like it. It can be especially alienating for their names to be mispronounced in front of everybody at a time that's supposed to demonstrate that they matter to the organization. That the employee is already bracing for their name to be mispronounced sets up an opportunity for the executive to blow away expectations when they confidently get it right. Getting it right also subtly signals to everyone that the executive—and the organization—truly value diversity and inclusion.

THE EMPLOYEE NEWSLETTER

Organizations that start to outgrow all-hands meetings will often move to putting out a regular internal newsletter for employees. As with the all-hands meeting, an EA will often be the driving force behind making it happen every week or every month. And newsletters are also a valuable place to announce upcoming work anniversaries.

The tip about the highest-ranking person doesn't apply here, but the other two tips about all-hands meetings have corresponding newsletter-related tips:

- **Announce upcoming work anniversaries, not recently passed work anniversaries**. As with all-hands meetings, this will facilitate inspired colleagues to perhaps do their own preparation for the day while also subtly influencing direct managers to be timely. And again, the one exception to this rule is if you have a monthly newsletter that generally goes out early in the month, when you may catch a few after the fact. Newsletters are skipped less often than all-hands meetings, but if it does happen, be sure to find a way to not completely miss announcing the work anniversaries, even if you need to do it retroactively.

- **Add a little pizzazz**. For newsletters, involving a designer is typically too much, but if you can find something like a not-too-much animated GIF with confetti to make the section feel a little more festive, that's great. Using celebratory emojis is another small touch that can make the section more noticeable and more fun. And finally, consider bolding the employees' names, which again is subtle but sends the message that they're important.

GROUP MESSAGING PLATFORMS AND ORGANIZATION-WIDE EMAIL

If an organization doesn't have a dedicated internal communications person managing company-wide group messaging channels or sending company-wide emails, the task of sending such communications often falls to the EA.

If your organization uses Slack or another group chat tool with standing channels and reaction emojis, it can be an amazing place to announce work anniversaries.

Ideally, each manager will write up something thoughtful and post it the morning of the work anniversary, either in the #general channel or in a #celebrations channel (where babies, weddings, and birthdays will generally also be announced).

If your organization hasn't reached the level of work anniversary recognition where managers are doing that for their reports, your scheduling of generic work anniversary announcements is a big step up from its not happening at all. Seeing something done consistently can become the catalyst that leads managers to get more involved. They may start by simply writing something in a reply thread to your post, but over time that can become such a regular habit—and be so well received by employees—that the manager decides to do more. And even if they don't, at least now they're more involved than they were. (This is yet another example of how your actions can lead to big, long-lasting changes in an organization.)

If you don't have a suitable group chat tool, sending work anniversary announcement emails to all employees may seem like a reasonable alternative, but there are a couple reasons that's not a good idea.

First, replying to everyone can get messy and distracting or worse, as people may forget that what they're saying can be read by others, especially for employees who deal with a lot of email as part of their regular work. Second, a group email creates the expectation of a written response from everyone who receives it, whether or not they know the employee with the anniversary well, rather than the quick "Congratulations!" or emoji that would be more appropriate for most not-that-close work relationships. If you don't use a group messaging platform like Slack and really want to do something, start a newsletter and send out a link to it over email.

ALL-HANDS MEETING, THE NEWSLETTER, AND GROUP MESSAGING, OH MY!

One last note on announcing: don't worry about redundancy—in fact, it can be a good thing. If an employee's work anniversary gets announced at an all-hands meeting *and* in a newsletter *and* in the #celebrations group messaging channel, it sends a clear message that work anniversaries matter. The goal in this case is not efficiency but making the point that employees, and their work anniversaries, matter.

SET UP SKIP-LEVEL ONE-ON-ONES

Conversations with employees multiple levels down in the organization are valuable for any executive who manages managers, but the value increases with the number of employees in the organization under your executive.

The idea of a skip-level one-on-one is that it provides an executive the opportunity to gain a better understanding of what's really happening on the front lines of the organization while also making frontline employees feel that they're valued both by individual managers and by the organization as a whole.

There are a few common reasons why useful information might not reach an executive. In an unhelpfully political organization, every manager will be trying to project a rosy picture intended to make themself look good and so ignore or discount any information that doesn't support that picture. The same thing happens for different reasons in a performance- or efficiency-oriented organization, where managers may demand that employees stifle "complaints" and adopt a can-do attitude for working around problems the managers are unable to fix, which can prevent information about systemic problems from reaching the very people who could actually do something about them. And finally, there's the problem everywhere that information passing through multiple layers of management may be garbled or completely altered by the time it reaches the end of the line, as with the children's game called "whisper down the lane" or "telephone."

THE SKIP-LEVEL ONE-ON-ONE OBSTACLES

While skip-level one-on-ones can solve a clear and nearly universal problem, there are three tactical obstacles that prevent many organizations from having any sort of formal process for them. Work anniversaries are the solution to all three:

> ▸ **Who to talk to since there's not enough time to talk to everyone?** If your company is large enough that the CEO can't talk to every employee on every work anniversary, help

them decide on a consistent approach and make sure it's clear to everyone what that approach is. Gossip thrives in an informational vacuum, so if an executive starts talking to selected employees and no one can make sense of who's selected or why, you might suddenly find everyone talking about layoffs even though none are planned. If, on the other hand, it's well known that the conversation is to commemorate a milestone work anniversary, the problem is neatly solved.

▸ **How to prevent employees from feeling like they're being sent to the principal's office?** This isn't true of everyone, but being asked to speak to someone in a position of power fills many employees with anxiety, taking them back to the days when being summoned by the principal meant being in trouble. Even if they're assured it's "just to talk," the anxiety will be there— after all, how many positive conversations ever started with "We need to talk?" This is easily solved by telling them up front that the executive wants to commemorate their work anniversary by thanking them in person and finding out how things are going. The chronically anxious will probably still worry, but most people will feel a lot more comfortable about the meeting and hopefully even look forward to it.

▸ **How to prevent the meetings from being canceled?** Executives always have a lot going on. Their job is not so much to figure out how to juggle all the balls but to figure out which ones to drop, and skip-level meetings are easy to drop if there's no obvious urgency. But the wonder of work anniversary skip-level meetings is that they have *built-in* urgency. The meeting is clearly most valuable on the day of the work anniversary and less valuable the further away from the day it gets, while canceling it altogether will do substantial damage. By tying them to work anniversaries, many more skip-level meetings will actually happen, *and* you get all the extra value that work anniversaries bring!

SKIP-LEVEL ONE-ON-ONE FORMATS

There are many formats for skip-level one-on-ones, but here are a couple that work well.

The most time-consuming—but also the path to the deepest connection—is for the pair to go to coffee, breakfast, or lunch. If you go this route, choose which milestone anniversaries to include so the executive has no more than one per month. That is, if you declare that the executive is going to meet with every employee hitting a work anniversary evenly divisible by five (or ten or fifteen, etc.), make sure that's only going to be about ten employees in any given year. Most executives will find more than ten to be too much of a drain on their time.

A path on the other end of the spectrum that allows for the executive to meet with more employees is to schedule fifteen-minute work anniversary meetings in the executive's office or as a video call. The most common fifteen-minute format is the "magic wand" meeting, which is described in detail on page 133 in the **Quick fifteen-minute-but-still-powerful approach** section.

Your executive will probably have a clear preference, or geography may limit your options. All the formats are good—what matters most is that the executive enjoys it or at the very least gets something valuable out of it so they're more likely to stick with it.

One more idea to be aware of is that if your executive is conflicted about how many people they'd like to meet with and how much time that would take, you can suggest a program where it's split up among the executive's senior team. This is more work for you, but it also has a bigger impact. More executives will get wisdom from the front line, their group discussions will be greatly enriched, and employee perception of organizational support will improve.

SET UP EXECUTIVE BREAKFASTS

If doing individual one-on-ones just isn't going to work out or you want to do something in addition to them, executive breakfasts can be a great idea.

The idea is to decide how often to do this, and then invite everyone who has celebrated the chosen milestone in that time period to a breakfast with the executive. That is, you could pick quarterly and then invite everyone who celebrated a work anniversary divisible by five over the prior three months.

The group can go out to breakfast, but having it in the office with food catered or delivered can be a lot simpler and often adds more value, as it better allows for conversation and/or a presentation by the executive.

If the executive does want to give a presentation, one direction to take is a review of the pillars of the organization's culture. For organizations that are serious about their purpose, mission, and values, it's common for them to talk a lot about the culture as a part of onboarding but then not to bring it up much with longer-tenured employees. These meetings can be a terrific opportunity for the executive to review the core values (purpose, mission, goals, vision, etc.) or even the current strategic plan. The executive can then lead a discussion that brings any perceived obstacles to the surface and deepens understanding, reinforcing a sense of shared purpose.

Another format for the presentation is for the executive to share a topic that's front of mind for the executive and candidly ask the gathered employees for their perspectives on it. If the company has a strategic plan that lists specific objectives for the year, it might be one of those objectives. Or, if a new challenge has come to light that the organization needs to respond to, that can be the topic.

Whatever the core of the meeting is about, it's important to make sure the meeting starts and ends with the executive expressing genuine appreciation for the gathered employees' contributions to the organization.

You can make these events less stuffy and more fun to talk about by giving them a catchy alliterative name. Some examples:

- Donuts with Dae
- Bagels with Barbara
- Muffins with Makayla
- Scones with Scott
- Coffee with Carlos
- Apple Fritters with Apelia
- Chick-n-Minis with Charlie
- Pop-Tarts with Patty
- Teacakes with Tran
- Grits with Greg

Wikipedia has a helpful list of breakfast foods sorted alphabetically if the right food isn't immediately obvious to you.

SYSTEMATIZE WORK ANNIVERSARY COMMUNICATION

Missing work anniversaries can be worse than awkward, so it's important to come up with a repeatable system to make sure that doesn't happen.

Everyone has their own preferences, but most EAs will want to batch a lot of the work together and get a head start so that they're ready no matter what, even if unexpected events pull them away.

With that in mind, a good approach is to pull the following month's list of work anniversaries on the fifteenth of the month. Then for each anniversary, figure out if there's anything that needs to be done in preparation. Many EAs will have devised a way to add calendar reminders in bulk for the full year, but if you don't have reminders set up for you or your executive, this is the time to do that.

Once you have your list for the next month, send it to your executive with a note about what HR (or whoever is responsible for work anniversaries) already has planned for each of them, and clearly call out if there's anything additional the executive needs to or might want to do. If there's a step they can do for everyone at once, like signing cards that will be mailed out, you can review the upcoming list while they sign.

After that, the two things left to do are to check in with HR (or whoever's responsible) to make sure anything scheduled or planned for the work anniversaries is going as expected, just as you would with any other kind of organizational activity you coordinate.

Finally, remind the executive about each work anniversary, preferably on the actual day unless they need to do something that requires time up front—though, ideally you've done everything for them and already scheduled any communications. If there's something public they need to do that you don't schedule to happen automatically, such as posting a thoughtful message to your group messaging platform, check in to make sure it's done and remind them if it hasn't been.

Depending on your executive, you may want to provide your reminders in writing, either over messaging or by email, so it's clear they received them and weren't absentmindedly thinking about something else while you were talking.

CONSIDER BEING A WORK ANNIVERSARY CHAMPION

Work anniversaries provide abundant opportunities for EAs to have an outsized impact on an organization. Here are just a few examples.

With the simple act of repeated just-in-time reminders about the work anniversaries of people your executive will be meeting with, you can shift the organization's perception of the executive from that of being cold, aloof, and distant to that of being caring and appreciative. The indirect impact of that on performance and the executive's career can be immense. Or if your executive naturally comes across as caring, you'll be helping to amplify that strength.

By simply setting up automatic announcements over Slack or whatever group messaging platform you use, you have the power to shift your organization's culture from thanklessly transactional to warmly supportive. That one act leads a small number of caring managers to thoughtfully appreciate their direct reports, which leads to pressure on other managers to do the same, which leads to all managers doing it and competing to do it best, which leads to happy, productive employees and a successful organization. And all because you started the ball rolling!

By implementing a plan for regular work anniversary skip-level one-on-ones and breakfasts, you're setting up conversations that lead to shared understanding, which both improves working conditions and leads to better executive decisions that meaningfully impact the organization's success.

This isn't for every EA, but at many organizations, there is an opportunity for a so-inclined EA to take informal ownership of making their organization one of the best at acknowledging work anniversaries.

For this to work, you can't be in a position where you're being micromanaged. You'll need autonomy over your discretionary time with the simple expectation to make good use of it. If that's your situation, one of the rewarding things about championing work anniversaries is that it's very visible work that leads to a lot of positive outcomes and thus will reflect well on you (and your executive).

If this sounds like something you might like to do, here are some ideas to explore:

▸ **Take on the task of looking after your executive's direct reports' handling of work anniversaries too** – Remind them of their team's work anniversaries and make sure they're doing what's expected of managers—and if you can, make sure they're supported in their efforts

▸ **Become your organization's "photo historian"** – Take fun photos of employees at work and ask around for photos from the past—after a while everyone will know you're the photo person and will start thinking to share photos with you without being asked, and they all can help make work anniversaries more fun

▸ **Check in with employees at the end of the day on their work anniversaries** – Make sure everything went smoothly—if something didn't, like a gift that typically comes from HR didn't show up, reach out on the employee's behalf to find out what went wrong, and let the employee know what's up

▸ **Go beyond this chapter and read the rest of this book** – You've already read this chapter— only fifteen more to go!

THE EXECUTIVE ASSISTANT CHECKLIST

EAs who love work anniversaries can have an unexpectedly outsized impact on their organization's workplace culture.

- [ ] Help your executive treat work anniversaries the way all managers in the organization are expected to treat work anniversaries

- [ ] Help your executive "magically" remember the work anniversaries of employees who they'll be meeting with or who are at locations they'll be visiting

- [ ] Acknowledge work anniversaries in organization-wide communication channels (*if organization-wide communication is a part of your responsibilities*)

- [ ] Set up skip-level one-on-ones for major milestone work anniversaries

- [ ] Set up yearly, twice-yearly, or quarterly work anniversary breakfasts with everyone hitting milestone work anniversaries in that time period

- [ ] Systematize your work anniversary tasks so that no one's forgotten

- [ ] Consider whether being the organization's work anniversary champion is something you're interested in

8

IDEAS FOR GRAPHIC DESIGNERS

WORK ANNIVERSARIES ARE a wonderful opportunity for a graphic or experience designer to have a direct and lasting impact on the employees around them.

Work anniversaries are "ownable" moments in an employee's journey with the organization. That is, they're prone to changing or escalating the employee's positive or negative emotions toward the organization. One concrete manifestation of this is that employees are twice as likely to leave their jobs the month after their work anniversary than at any other time of the year.[1,2,3]

Your designs will become a part of this key moment of heightened emotion, and the work you do once will continue to impact every employee every year.

THE GOAL

Work anniversaries are a time of reassessment. How has the past year gone? Does the organization appreciate me? Do I respect the organization? Is continuing with the organization a good use of my potential?

For some employees, it's time to move on. They're no longer a good fit for the organization or maybe never were. That's okay, and those employees aren't your target audience. Your target audience is the set of employees who *are* a good fit for the organization and remain with it for many years.

> The goal of work anniversary design work is to build in cues that support the employee's sense of belonging to a unique organization and their sense that they're contributing to the organization doing something that matters

With anything you're designing for work anniversaries, here are three key questions to ask yourself:

- **How can I better emphasize the uniqueness of the organization?** Start by leaning into the brand's colors and logo, but look for opportunities to include other visual elements that make your organization unique too, like an iconic building, product, or mascot.

- **How can I reinforce the meaningfulness of what the organization does?** What's your organization's purpose or mission? What about core values? Are there any slogans that are unique to your organization? If none of those things works for this purpose, are there any goals that could be inspiring? If what you're designing has room, figure out how to include the best of these.

▸ **How can I make a connection between the work anniversary and the employee's contributions to the shared mission?** First, in the wording don't just mention the number of years that have elapsed since the employee joined the organization. Instead, emphasize the number of years *the employee and the organization have been joined together working toward a common purpose.* Second, is there anything concrete that can be said about the organization's progress toward that purpose over the past year or over the entire time the employee has been with the organization? Are there metrics for what the employee contributed or what the organization achieved during that time—or both?

There are a variety of work anniversary items you might be called on to design. Depending on the constraints inherent in the item, you might have more or less flexibility in how you answer the questions above.

THE ITEMS THAT NEED DESIGN

Four work anniversary items benefit the most from customized design: (1) printed certificates; (2) slides for all-hands meetings; (3) numbered gifts such as stickers, pins, or blocks; and (4) branded clothing. Not every organization will have all four of these, but most will have at least one.

PRINTED CERTIFICATES

A printed certificate serves as a completely personalized, tangible reminder of the employee's tenure at the organization, not only so the employee feels recognized by the organization but also to signal the employee's status to their colleagues.

Depending on the work anniversary and your organization, it might be the only gift they receive, or it might be the only *physical* gift they receive. In either case, it will probably be the only gift they receive that has their name on it.

Printed certificates are by far the most fun of the work anniversary design tasks. You get lots of real estate, you can work in full color, and you get to play with size scales and visual hierarchy for an audience who'll look at it from a distance as well as up close.

You also get a lot of elements to potentially include in the design:

- ▸ The employee's name *(triple-check that you have it spelled correctly)*
- ▸ The number of years being commemorated
- ▸ The date of the work anniversary *(and maybe the employee's start date)*
- ▸ The organization's name
- ▸ The organization's purpose, mission, and/or tagline

- The organization's logo

- The organization's colors

- A message of thankfulness and/or appreciation for their contributions to the organization and its purpose or mission over the years

- Signatures of one or more leaders (the CEO, or the CEO and the head of HR, or the CEO and the direct manager)

- Frilly, fancy, or serious-looking stuff (depending on your organization's culture) that provides a sense of importance, usually in the organization's colors, and ideally doesn't distract from the certificate's core message

You can create one template that's used for all work anniversaries, regardless of tenure length, but the certificates will have greater impact—and perhaps be a more fun challenge for you—if they get fancier as the celebrated number of years increases. Regardless, be sure to keep the three questions from the previous section front of mind as you design the template(s).

And finally, to help increase the perceived value of the certificates, choose or recommend appropriately high-quality paper and/or a good frame to really make the design stand out.

ALL-HANDS SLIDES

At organizations that have regular "all hands" meetings, it's common to announce and acknowledge the upcoming work anniversaries. By default, a non-designer will whip up a quick slide with a list of names on it, and it won't be great.

PPTX

PART 2: IDEAS BY ROLE

The objectives of designing the all-hands slides rather than "throwing them together" are to:

▸ Embrace the organization's uniqueness

▸ Convey that work anniversaries matter

▸ List employee names in an easily readable font size and color

If you can also include employee photos, that will help employees learn each other's names, which will build trust and improve interdepartmental cooperation.

Depending on the size of your organization and whether all work anniversaries are acknowledged or just the fives (five, ten, fifteen, etc.), you may need multiple slides. A nice touch is to make the slides more elaborate as the employees listed on them increase in tenure.

A variation to consider is a "work anniversary zero" slide that lists new hires. Since this is a bit of a different purpose, it will generally need some tweaks in design and wording, like adding the word *welcome.*

Another variation to consider is doing a special single-employee spotlight variation for when the longest-tenured employees hit big numbers like twenty-five. The list slides would be shown first, and the work anniversary part of the meeting would end on the slide showing the employee hitting the big milestone. That way, whoever is responsible for work anniversaries at the meeting (or the CEO or the head of HR or however it works at your organization) can say a few appreciative words about and to them while the slide is up.

One last fun thing to consider—but not overdo—is that all-hands slides are the one item in this chapter that supports animation. You won't want to do anything cheesy or distracting, but a little flourish to communicate that this is something special goes over well.

NUMBERED GIFTS

Numbered gifts can be any type of object with the number of years the employee has worked prominently featured on it. The three most common are pins, stickers, and blocks, but if something else makes sense for your organization, go for it (like maybe custom front license plates if you are in a state that doesn't have front license plates, if you employ drivers, and if each driver has a specific assigned vehicle). To make these gifts meaningful, they're typically custom printed or engraved with design elements indicating the organization they're from.

Each type of numbered gift has its own purpose and design constraints.

STICKERS

Work anniversary stickers are most commonly given out at organizations where employees carry identical or similar equipment, like laptops or toolboxes, and have already been putting their own stickers on their equipment so it doesn't get mixed up with everyone else's. In such an environment, work anniversary stickers are an excellent choice.

The first design goal is to create something that's the right scale for the equipment it's most likely to be stuck on, because that will make it more likely for the sticker to be used.

The second design goal is to create something that, from a distance, is readily recognizable to other employees as a work anniversary sticker, with the number of years easily readable. This supports interactions where an employee might say to another, "Wow, Jen, I had no idea you'd been here for fifteen years!" So while it might be fun to make every different number a completely different size, font, and color, it's probably not a good idea.

You'll also want to choose stickers strong enough to withstand typical use. That is, a toolbox sticker will generally need to be sturdier than a sticker intended for laptops.

PINS

Work anniversary pins are most commonly given out at organizations where many employees are customer-facing (or patient-facing or public-facing). The intent is that the people an employee is interacting with will feel an extra level of comfort and confidence when they see that the employee is long-tenured. In turn, an employee can feel inspired to live up to—or surpass—the expectations customers might have of a long-tenured employee.

The primary design goal in this case is to ensure people can tell at a glance that the pin indicates the number of years the employee has worked at the organization. Since pins are generally small, that means most of the design real estate will be dedicated to the number and the word *years*, which limits many of your other options.

If you can get the pin to reflect the uniqueness of the organization, perhaps with color, that's great, but that's a distant second in terms of goals. This may be hard on your design sensibilities, but in terms of effectiveness, an ugly, generic, uncustomized gold pin that just says "5 years" in the largest font that fits is far better than a beautifully complex full-color pin with an abstract overlay of the number five on top of the logo that customers can't read or make sense of.

BLOCKS

Blocks with the work anniversary number printed or engraved on them are most commonly given out at organizations with a workplace culture that encourages creativity and/or playfulness. The intent is to give something simple and fun that represents time in tangible, physical form and calls up happy memories of childhood, when most creative types wished for "more blocks!" for whatever they were building. Also, there's a collector inside many of us, so the promise of more blocks in the future subtly increases their desire to stay with the organization.

The two dominant variations are square wooden blocks and Lego bricks.

For square wooden blocks, you have six sides to work with and are generally dealing with monochromatic dark engraving on a light block. One side needs to display the number of years, in as large a font size as is reasonable. The organization's logo generally goes on another side.

The other four sides can be left blank, or they can be printed with elements from your culture. The challenge is using exactly four sides.

If you have four, eight, or twelve core values, you can do one, two, or three core values per side and it makes a lot of sense. If you have three, six, or nine core values then the fourth side can have a cultural slogan, a marketing tagline, or "Happy work anniversary!"

These blocks are generally given with a matching tray. The tray is a beautiful place to engrave the organization's purpose or mission. If your organization doesn't have a purpose or mission, use the organization's name.

A nice touch when doing wooden blocks is to design a "welcome" block that represents their start date, also known as work anniversary zero, and put the word *welcome* on the side that would have had the number. The employee then gets their welcome block and tray bearing the organization's purpose on their first day, rather than waiting until their first work anniversary to get their first block. This can be a meaningful way to help new or acquired employees feel appreciated and that they belong.

For Lego bricks, you pick the colors of the bricks, what auxiliary blocks will be included, and what will be on the auxiliary blocks. For some organizations, the brand colors will lend themselves well to the bricks, but for others you may be better off going generically multicolor or possibly gray. The most common auxiliary blocks are a base platform and a Lego minifigure customized to represent the employee.

As with the wooden block tray, it's best to print the organization's purpose or mission on the front of the platform, and use the organization's name if your organization doesn't have a stated purpose or mission. For the minifigure, choose the hair and head blocks that best represent the individual's appearance. If the job roles at your organization dress differently, choose the legs and torso blocks that best suit each employee's role; if your organization doesn't have distinctive ways of dressing for different roles, choose the legs and torso blocks that best fit what you know about the individual. A nice finishing touch for the torso blocks can be to put the organization's logo on the front and the employee's first name at the top of the back, like on a sports jersey.

Some organizations will choose to also provide auxiliary blocks. The most common is a set of blocks with each of the core values printed on them. If there are slogans, taglines, or hashtags that are a big part of your organization's culture, they're candidates too.

COMPANY-BRANDED CLOTHING

This is a popular choice because wearing clothing with an organization's logo and seeing other people do the same creates a feeling of belonging and shared purpose and a sense of being a part of something bigger than yourself.

Most vendors who produce branded clothing help customers avoid egregious design mistakes because it's in their own best interest to make sure the clothing looks good. However, as a trained designer, if you know your organization is going to start giving out branded clothing, you may want to see if there's a way you can be involved in reviewing the design before any clothing is ordered. Even tiny improvements can give the item more impact, as they will subtly send the message that the organization cares about quality and that the gift matters.

THE GRAPHIC DESIGNER CHECKLIST

A one-time effort by a graphic designer has lasting, ongoing impact.

The goal of work anniversary design work is to build in cues that support the employee's sense of belonging to a unique organization and their sense that they're contributing to the organization doing something that matters.

THE DESIGN OBJECTIVES:

- [ ] Emphasize the uniqueness of the organization
- [ ] Support the employee's sense of belonging to the organization
- [ ] Reinforce the meaningfulness of what the organization does
- [ ] Highlight the employee's contributions to the organization's purpose

THE KEY DELIVERABLES:

- [ ] Printed certificates
- [ ] All-hands slides
- [ ] Numbered gifts (*pins, stickers, or blocks*)
- [ ] Company-branded clothing (*or other swag*)
- [ ] Anything else your organization customizes for work anniversaries

9

IDEAS FOR
MARKETING

SHARING WORK ANNIVERSARIES externally as part
of your marketing doesn't make sense for every organization,
perhaps not even most organizations. But for the organizations
where it does make sense, it can be powerful.

Work anniversary marketing is primarily social media posts.
Unless you work at a big and/or well-known organization, your posts
with pictures of real people will always do better than your thought
leadership posts. And work anniversary posts are all about real people.

DOES THIS MAKE SENSE FOR
YOUR ORGANIZATION?

These four overlapping questions may seem counterintuitive, but they'll
help you decide if work anniversary marketing is worth your effort:

- **Does experience or longevity reflect well on your brand identity?** Is your product something that has a long time horizon, like insurance or retirement planning? Do your employees deliver a highly technical service directly to customers and need to inspire confidence? Do you have uniquely low turnover in a high-turnover industry, which reflects well on why you're better than your competitors? If the answers to any of these questions are yes, then reminding customers and informing prospects of work anniversaries—particularly the longer ones—will enhance your message.

- **Do your customers have "relationships" with your employees?** Do your customers interact directly with individual employees? If yes, and your employees have uniforms or name tags, then simply finding a way to communicate long-tenured employees' number of years of service (*through custom name tags, pins, or patches*) will reflect well on your brand. Or if your employees interact digitally with your customers, using work anniversaries as an excuse to share personal interests or interesting facts can help deepen the bond between your customers and your organization.

- **Is advertising to your extended community valuable?** Do you sell to people your employees are directly or indirectly connected to? Work anniversary posts on social media tend to draw in employees' networks to cheer them on, which builds your extended network, which you can then cheer on. This generally makes the most sense on LinkedIn for business-to-business companies whose employees use LinkedIn to connect with customers and prospects, but it can sometimes work well for other kinds of organizations and on other social networks as well.

▸ **Do your employees do interestingly photogenic, dramatic, or dangerous things?** Do you restore iconic buildings? Do your employees work in beautiful natural surroundings? Is your product or equipment visibly used at big, well-publicized events? Do your employees work in situations that would scare ordinary people, such as in very high places? Finding ways to take photos of these situations *(with drones?!)* can help your prospects and customers develop positive and memorable associations with your brand.

If you answered yes to any of those questions, read on—because work anniversary marketing is valuable to organizations like yours.

WHERE TO SHARE

The most obvious place to share is your organization's active social media channels, and the rest of this chapter will concentrate on doing those posts well. But if your organization puts out a newsletter to your customers and/or stakeholders, you can also repurpose the social media content into articles there.

PUTTING EXTRA EFFORT INTO EXTERNAL-FACING ROLES

It's important for most people in an organization to not show favoritism in the way work anniversaries are celebrated, and it's absolutely essential for human resources and managers. But for the marketing team, singling out certain employees for additional external recognition of work anniversaries can make sense, *as long as it's done for clearly defined job roles* rather than individuals.

The tips in the next couple of sections require extra time and effort, so if your goal is to build connections between your organization's external-facing employees and your customers, it may make sense to focus on specific roles, like your customer service reps, consultants, or sales reps.

If you can do posts for everyone, that's better, but don't let that extra effort get in the way of recognizing your external-facing employees well. And if you do choose to publicly celebrate only specific roles, it's helpful to communicate that choice to the organization along with the thinking behind it.

INDIVIDUALIZE YOUR POSTS

There's a lot of value in creating posts that convey genuine appreciation for the employee being honored. There will always be pressure to streamline the process, but don't let efficiency drive you to the point where work anniversary posts noticeably come across as just another thing to check off your organization's task list. That will destroy the value of doing the posts in the first place.

Here are some ideas for keeping work anniversary posts feeling personal and genuine:

- **Do an individual post for each employee**. That is, *don't* do a list of everyone celebrating work anniversaries for the whole week or month, as that will be less compelling to individual employees and their networks. If you don't have the resources to pull this off and need to do a single post for everyone celebrating in a particular week or month, that's still better than not doing anything. If you choose weekly, post early on Monday. If you choose monthly, be sure to post early on the first of the month.

- **Do it on the day!** If you can pull off posting for each employee, you can further optimize the value by posting on the exact day, preferably early in the day, to give their network an opportunity to send timely congratulations. As mentioned in other chapters, late is better than nothing, but if you can't do it on the actual day, early is better than late. And while photos of employees receiving their gifts on the day are best, if you're using existing photos instead, you can make this step easier by scheduling the posts ahead of time for the exact day.

- **Don't schedule multiple work anniversary posts for the exact same time**. If you have more than one, and especially if you have quite a few, drip them out one at a time throughout the morning with random amounts of time between, in order from least years of service to most, to give the impression you're working on them in between.

- **Include a photo**. This is so important that there's a whole subsection on it below. If you do decide to include multiple people in a single post, include multiple photos.

- **Tag everyone in the photo**. This will make it more likely their connections will see and engage with the post. Tag the person celebrating the work anniversary first.

▸ **Include a quote**. It can be from the employee, reflecting on their time there, or from a leader or other employee complimenting them. For customer-facing employees, positive customer feedback can work well.

INCLUDE PHOTOS IN YOUR POSTS

This might be obvious, since most people in marketing are aware that images boost social media engagement, but not everyone does it.

There are many options, which vary in how compelling they are and how much effort they take. Unfortunately for you, the most compelling images require the most effort, so choose the most compelling option *that you'll be able to reliably do for every work anniversary.* It's important that you not put more effort into some than others or, if you do, that you do so consistently, with more effort expended for longer-tenured employees.

Here's the list of options in order from best to worst:

▸ **A photo of them receiving a gift that morning** (logistically challenging but amazing!)

▸ **A photo of them that captures some of their work personality** (perhaps depicting them doing their job: driving the truck, running the training class, at their desk, on the ladder, in the hospital hallway, etc.)

▸ **A photo at a recent fun event** (axe throwing? rage room? bowling?)

- **A group photo**
  (ideally with an arrow added, pointing at them)

- **A simple headshot photo of them**

- **Any photo of them**

- **A "happy work anniversary" graphic bearing their name and the number of years of service**

- **A generic "happy work anniversary" graphic**

- **No image** (not recommended)

Also, don't devote a lot of pixels to boilerplate organization-focused content. The work anniversary is about the employee, so make their photo big!

To boost exposure, it's important to tag all the people in the photo as mentioned in the previous subsection. If there are multiple people in the photo, tag the employee having the work anniversary first, but tag everyone. The other people are probably in the photo because they're close to the honoree, and tagging them will boost engagement with the post.

OPTIMIZE YOUR POSTS

These are small tips that help increase the value of your posts:

- **Include the hashtag #thankyou** – This is simple and endearing—think of it as the opposite of the harmful practice of including a call to action (*more details below*)

- **Include your organization's purpose or tagline as a hashtag** – This is also endearing, and it's a small way of showing that your organization views work anniversaries as a way to celebrate working together toward a common purpose rather than just time passing

- **Encourage employees to repost and engage** – Consider reaching out via group messaging or email to employees close to the work anniversary employee to let them know the post is live so they can like, share, and comment

- **Send posts out early in the day** – This gives everyone more time to respond with a timely "Happy work anniversary!" throughout the day

THOUGHTS ON MONETIZING

This might be hard, but don't include a call to action, such as "we're hiring" or "buy from us." That comes off as inauthentic and creates the impression that your organization just wants to squeeze more money out of employees rather than genuinely cares about them.

So if there's no call to action, then what's the value? These are the three objectives:

- **Brand building** – The posts can give prospective customers, clients, patients, etc. a positive impression of your organization and attract potential hires who are good fits for the organization

- **Employee-customer connection** – The posts can help create trust between prospects and salespeople, or help customers have a deeper understanding of their support rep or consultant

- **Network building** – Posts about people generally attract more engagement than strictly promotional posts—if you're advertising-driven, the work anniversary posts can grow your followers and *then* you can run separate targeted ads through your now-bigger network

If the above bullet points aren't compelling enough for your organization's situation, it's better to *not* post about work anniversaries than it is to post about them with a call-to-action payload.

BEYOND WORK ANNIVERSARIES

This is a little outside the scope of this book, but if posting about your work anniversaries on social media makes sense, other kinds of employee posts might make sense too.

Some additional ideas:

- **Employee promotions**

- **New hires**

- **Sales meetings with clients** (tag the clients too)

- **Trade shows or other industry events** (with photos of tagged employees)

▸ **The organization's holiday party, summer picnic, or any other employee event**

▸ **Photos of the employees volunteering** *(if you offer paid time off for volunteering)*

Important: remember to tag everyone in the photo!

EXAMPLES

For examples of good work anniversary posts, check out the retweets from the @workiversary X account (or follow the account). If you want a broader view of both good and less good posts, check out the liked tweets from the @workiversary X account.

X.COM/WORKIVERSARY

THE MARKETING CHECKLIST

This isn't for every organization. But if work anniversary marketing is a good fit for yours, it can be uniquely valuable.

- [ ] Decide if work anniversaries are valuable to your organization's marketing efforts
- [ ] Decide which social networks and/or newsletters you'll share to
- [ ] Decide which work anniversaries you'll promote (everyone's or specific external-facing roles? every work anniversary or just bigger milestones?)
- [ ] Decide what type of images and/or other content you'll put in each post
- [ ] Write and design what the posts will look like
- [ ] Figure out who'll do the operational work to make it happen
- [ ] Make sure you have a backup person—because missing or late work anniversaries are bad bad bad—and ideally a written procedure for how to do it

10

IDEAS FOR FUN COMMITTEES AND CULTURE COMMITTEES

FUN AND CULTURE COMMITTEES go by many names. Yours probably isn't called a fun committee *or* a culture committee. But whatever the name, if you're part of a group of people enthusiastic about their mission to make their organization a better place to work through activities, culture, and/or communication, this chapter is for you.

From here on, I'll refer to the group as the fun committee, but everything in this chapter also applies to groups focused primarily on the organization's culture rather than specifically on fun.

That is to say, culture is fun, and fun is a wonderful way to embed culture.

TAKE AND ORGANIZE PHOTOS

When people think of making work anniversaries better, they usually think of making the work anniversary better for the person being honored. While that's great, it's valuable to think bigger. Work anniversaries can also be improved for those witnessing the work anniversary.

One of the valuable roles of a work anniversary is serving as an excuse for the organization to share details about the employee being honored. This allows other employees to get to know the honoree better, and it provides loosely connected employees with icebreaking topics they can use to strike up conversations. This helps build trust and team cohesion, which leads to higher-performing teams.

The outgoing, enthusiastic types who are drawn to being part of the fun committee will probably be well represented at the organization's social events and most likely won't mind jumping into the middle of an interesting situation and saying, "I'm with the fun committee, and we need a picture of *this*!"

While it can be good to have lots of people taking photos at these events, one person will need to oversee collecting, organizing, and publishing them. Here are the options:

- Someone who's friendly with everyone just asks around for people to send them their best photos—when anyone on the committee needs work photos, they go to this person

- Apple Photos shared albums can be a good solution if everyone in your organization has an iPhone, but if they don't, you risk excluding people

- Another option is to work out a way of capturing and sharing photos using Google Drive,

OneDrive, Dropbox, or whatever cloud-based file
sharing application your organization uses

▸ There are also some special-purpose solutions
designed for this that you might want to explore,
like Greenfly, Cluster, and DropEvent, but they
all have limitations, and none of them have
especially large market share

DECORATE DESKS

For in-person employees at the same location, decorating people's
desks for their work anniversaries can be a lot of fun. It's also great
for making employees feel special and for facilitating conversations,
since anyone passing by the decorated desk will be likely to congratulate the honoree.

This is obviously not a remote-friendly option, so if you're a
remote-*only* organization, skip to the next section.

But if you're a hybrid organization where some people work in
person and others are remote, still consider this. This is the one exception to the work anniversary "no favoritism" rule. Being an in-person
employee can be lonely and underappreciated these days, and let's
face it—it takes people more effort to get dressed and travel to the
workplace every day than it does to stay in their pajamas and walk
to their computer desk. Giving your in-person employees an extra
perk by decorating their desk in a fun way once a year is an acceptable acknowledgment of that extra effort.

So how do you do it well?

The most common approach is to have a large box of supplies.
Some supplies are mostly reused, like signs, banners, banner flags,

balloon weights, balloon sticks, pom-poms to hang from the ceiling, swirls to hang from the ceiling, window clings, and fringe curtains. Other supplies need to be periodically restocked, like balloons, streamers, and confetti. A couple of people are then put on desk-decorating duty. Ideally, they do it after the honoree has left on the day before the work anniversary or before they arrive on the day of the work anniversary.

Rather than just blowing up balloons, organizations that are really into it may prefer helium balloons and either have their own helium tank or go out and buy helium-filled balloons. Note that a small percentage of the population is allergic to latex, which is what many blow-up-able balloons are made of, regardless of what they're filled with. If you're concerned, get mylar or bubble balloons instead.

Another extra-effort approach is to match the decoration color theme to the employee's favorite color. Of course, this requires a bigger supplies box and a way of finding out and tracking the employee's favorite color, but it does make it feel much more personal.

Last, and least fun for most people, it's important to take the decorations down that night. The general convention is to let the employee know to take home any of the decorations they want to keep, because anything left at the office will be discarded that night—and by *discarded,* I mean that the cleanup crew gets to take the balloons home to their kids.

SIDEWALK CHALK

This is a much better idea in, say, Arizona than it is in Seattle, Syracuse, or San Juan, but greeting an employee on their walk into work with sidewalk chalk messages wishing them a happy work anniversary will generally go over well and often will result in amused-grin selfies shared on social media.

As with decorating desks, the tricky part is doing it between the time the employee leaves the night before and arrives the next day on their work anniversary. For extra credit, use the employee's favorite colors.

The wrinkle is, of course, the weather. A cute way to handle precipitation is with a backup portable chalkboard that always says, "As with weddings, rain (or snow) on your work anniversary is good luck!" and allows you to wish the employee happy work anniversary in chalk on a smaller scale inside in an amusing way.

If you do happen to be in Seattle, Syracuse, San Juan, or anywhere else it rains all the time, you may want to purchase a portable sidewalk message board sign and write "happy work anniversary!" messages on that. They're generally less than $500, and the fun committee may be able to come up with other creative uses for it as well.

WRITE IT ON YOUR ORGANIZATION'S SIGN

Does your organization have an outdoor sign that allows you to convey customized messages? Whether it's an old-style analog sign where you slide in the physical letters in a message under your organization's name, or a digital sign where you rotate various images through, the fun committee can decide which work anniversaries to include—all of them, just the fives, or whatever makes sense for your organization. The key thing is that whatever you choose, don't miss any. (Disappointed employees aren't fun.)

HELP OUT WITH LONG-TENURE EVENTS

At a lot of organizations, it's the fun committee that knows how to throw the best parties. If this is the case for yours, consider taking over or helping with the various work anniversary "parties" described below.

WORK ANNIVERSARY CEO BREAKFAST

The CEO breakfast is a—you guessed it—breakfast, usually catered or delivered, which may happen once, twice, or four times a year and to which all employees who hit major milestones in the past three, six, or twelve months are invited. The CEO thanks them all for their contributions and speaks about the organization's culture and/or some current concern for which they'd like the long-tenured employees' input.

While executive assistants often organize these events, some fun committees will be well positioned to take them over and make them more … fun!

You'll find a lot more detail about these breakfasts in the **Set up executive breakfasts** section on page 176.

THE QUARTER-CENTURY CLUB

I think the name says it all, but just in case: this is a club specifically for employees who've been with the organization for twenty-five years or more. Younger organizations might have a Decade-Or-More Club (for employees who've been with the organization ten or more years) or a High Five Club (for employees who've been with the organization five or more years).

These clubs are usually self-organizing, with the events set up by elected members of the club, but there are situations where the fun committee is well positioned to help the events be more ... fun!

Read more about these kinds of clubs in the **Quarter-Century Club** section on page 88.

WORK ANNIVERSARY GALAS

Some organizations will have annual or semiannual evening events after work specifically targeted at major work anniversary milestones. Each honoree can bring a guest, there's generally a formal dinner, and the main attraction is speeches about the honorees.

For these events to be successful, employees have to want to attend them after hours more than anything else they might do with their time outside of work. That's where the fun committee can come in by making these events more ... fun!

Read more about these events in the **Set up an after-work event just for work anniversaries** section on page 62.

EMBED WORKPLACE CULTURE INTO WORK ANNIVERSARIES

If your fun committee's mandate relates to your organization's culture rather than fun, this section is for you.

This book has advised repeatedly to avoid simply acknowledging time passing and instead celebrate the employee and the organization working together toward a common purpose.

Or, looked at another way, work anniversaries can be thought of as a celebration of belonging. And what does the employee belong to? The unique culture of the organization.

Both of these angles point to how powerful it can be to make sure the organization's purpose, mission, vision, and/or core values are all prominent parts of the employee's work anniversary. The slides at the all-hands meeting can call out the purpose. The framed certificate can call out the organization's core values. The CEO can send an email thanking the employee for helping to make the vision a reality.

If you have a culture committee, you know that an important part of making a culture stick is embedding it in ongoing processes like hiring, onboarding, conducting performance reviews, and even firing. If you forgot to include work anniversaries in that list, you're not alone, and this is your cue to put a small team together to see what they can do.

TRAIN MANAGERS

This is another idea for fun committees that embrace workplace culture.

This book contains suggestions for a lot of practices that a manager can do to make work anniversaries more special for their employees, and the fun committee can take charge of embedding those practices throughout the organization by making an initiative of upgrading how managers handle work anniversaries. The steps are straightforward:

1. Read the **Ideas for managers and supervisors** chapter starting on page 107

2. Decide which of the practices described in the chapter are a good fit for your organization

3. Pilot the practices for a few months with one or more members of the fun committee who are managers

4. Encourage those pilot managers to put together a presentation promoting their experience to other managers in the organization

5. Deliver the presentation at the next all-managers event

Does your organization not have all-managers events? They're really valuable and can be fun. Starting them up could be another initiative of the fun committee.

Generally, all-managers events are periodic long lunches that all managers in the organization are invited to. One or more managers are called on to share things they're doing that are working well so that the other managers can adopt the same practices. For smaller organizations, a powerful ending is to go around the room and have each manager share one thing they're going to do differently that they learned in the meeting. For larger organizations, the expectation can be that each manager shares electronically.

ADVOCATE FOR BETTER WORK ANNIVERSARIES

The best fun committees are made up of enthusiastic employees who are trusted by their colleagues and listened to by the leaders of the organization. They're generally more motivated by the organization's best interests than they are by engaging in petty politics, looking good, or avoiding blame. Because of this, they're in a unique position to speak truth to power when appropriate.

Many, if not most, work anniversary programs are mediocre at best. They often elicit quiet sighs and eye-rolls. In many cases they're so poorly done that they're downright demotivating. But who's going to tell the company that the Tiffany bowl with the company name and logo on it that they give to everyone is unanimously loathed and a big waste of money?

The fun committee—that's who! Sure, some long-ago boss or boss's spouse thought it was "lovely," but it's time to do something employees will actually *like*.

Things may not be as bad as that example at your organization, or maybe they're worse. Maybe the issue is that the organization doesn't do anything at all, or maybe your organization is constantly trying new things, many of which don't work. Whatever the situation, the fun committee can be the conduit between the front lines and management when something isn't coming across well. They can also advocate for successful department-specific work anniversary practices to be replicated throughout the rest of the organization and enact real, positive change.

THE FUN COMMITTEE CHECKLIST

Work anniversaries are an opportunity to inject more fun into your organization while simultaneously strengthening your workplace culture.

- [ ] Take, organize, and publish photos
- [ ] Decorate desks
- [ ] Announce work anniversaries with sidewalk chalk or on the organization's updatable sign
- [ ] Help out with events for long-tenured employees
- [ ] Spearhead the embedding of workplace culture in work anniversaries
- [ ] Train managers
- [ ] Advocate for better work anniversaries

11

IDEAS FOR FRONTLINE EMPLOYEES

> *"It had long since come to my attention that people of accomplishment rarely sat back and let things happen to them. They went out and happened to things."*
>
> *—Elinor Smith*[1]

WHAT IF YOU don't fill any of the roles covered so far? Do you want to shrug and say, "Not my problem?" Or do you want to prevent your friends at work from having mediocre work anniversaries? Do you want to avoid having a mediocre work anniversary *yourself*?

As Rosamund Stone Zander and Benjamin Zander so eloquently put it in *The Art of Possibility*:[2]

> You can lead from any chair

You don't need the CEO or HR or any of the managers at any of the levels above you to give you permission. You can make work anniversaries where you work better, and you can start right now.

LEAD BY FIRST KNOWING YOURSELF

Great leaders are great because they serve others. To serve others well, you need to know yourself enough to avoid inadvertently undermining your own efforts. So before you decide to lead the movement to improve work anniversaries for those around you, check in with yourself to see if you're truly ready.

USE WORK ANNIVERSARIES AS AN ANNUAL OPPORTUNITY FOR REFLECTION

One thing that anyone can do to make their own work anniversary meaningful, without being dependent on anyone else, is to use it as a time for reflection.

Ask yourself these questions, and maybe even write out the answers so you can not only clarify your thoughts but also read them next year to see how far you've come:

- What opportunities did I get in the past year?
- What projects have I worked on?
- What were the interesting moments/memories?

- ▸ What were the wins?

- ▸ Who did I meet for the first time?

- ▸ Who did I get to know better?

- ▸ How's my relationship with my manager?

- ▸ Am I working at my full potential?

- ▸ Do I feel like I'm part of something meaningful?

- ▸ Am I still inspired by the organization's purpose?

- ▸ No job is perfect, but all things considered, should I stay or should I go?

If you've lost your connection with your organization and it's time to go, there's no need to read any further. Focus on figuring out the next steps for making that happen rather than focusing on how to improve your colleagues' work anniversaries.

But if you're unsure of whether to stay or not, one way to decide is to do the Uncle Ry gift test. That is, ask yourself if you're willing to give Uncle Ry gifts. If you aren't, you should probably consider finding another job.

So what's an Uncle Ry gift? I'm glad you asked!

GIVE UNCLE RY GIFTS

In the story "Uncle Ry and the Moon," by Jon J. Muth, from his children's book *Zen Shorts*, we learn that Uncle Ry "always gives presents on his birthday." Elementary schools in the United States embrace the same spirit by encouraging students celebrating a birthday to bring in gifts for their classmates instead of the other way around.

You can follow in the footsteps of Uncle Ry (and millions of kindergartners) and flip the traditional script: rather than expecting to *receive* on your work anniversary, view your work anniversary as an opportunity to *give*.

This can have such a powerful ripple effect that you may find the tradition spreads throughout the organization once you get it started. For instance, though the originator is lost to history, Microsoft employees celebrating a work anniversary are expected to bring in and share a pound of M&M's for every year they've worked at Microsoft. That's about ten standard-size bags for every year.

And there are entire countries where this idea has taken root in a big way. Giving on your work anniversary is the cultural norm in countries such as Austria and the Netherlands, where employees are expected to bring in a work anniversary cake to share with their colleagues at teatime.

Why would you want to give on your work anniversary rather than receive? After all, the day is supposed to be about *you*, right? Well, neuroscience, psychology, and religion all agree that unhappiness comes from self-centered expectations and feelings of entitlement, while *happiness* comes from generously giving.[3, 4, 5, 6, 7, 8, 9]

If you've built up in your mind what a work anniversary *should* be and what others *should* do because it's *your* work anniversary, you'll be unhappy when it falls short. And no matter who you are or how many people read this book, some—possibly most—of your work anniversaries won't meet your expectations.

Thus, the path to true happiness on your work anniversary is, to paraphrase the Roman philosopher Cicero (as popularized by John F. Kennedy):

Ask not what *others can do for you* on
your work anniversary, ask what *you can
do for others* on your work anniversary!

LEAD BY EXAMPLE

If you've reflected on your job and are committed to staying but work anniversaries aren't handled as well as you'd like at your organization, then let's get started!

FIND OUT THE WORK ANNIVERSARIES OF THOSE YOU WORK WITH

Start by making a list of the people at work who matter most to you. Who helps make your job easier? Whose jobs do you make easier? Who brightens your day? Who would you miss if they left? Make sure your list has at least ten people on it. Get to twenty if you can.

Next, find out the work anniversaries for each of them. You can ask them directly, but that's less fun for everyone than you just "magically" knowing. There are a variety of ways to find out:

- ▸ Figure out when the employee was hired by looking up an old email or group messaging platform message

- ▸ If your organization mentions work anniversaries in a newsletter, look up old newsletters

- If your organization publishes work anniversaries on an intranet, wiki, or somewhere similar, look them up there

- Reach out to HR and say you like to acknowledge work anniversaries and ask where you can find these dates for your colleagues

If HR says that there isn't a place where you can access them, ask if they can let you know the ones you're looking for. If you're committed to improving work anniversaries for everyone at your organization, tactfully suggest to HR that they publish work anniversaries somewhere so people other than you can join in on spreading the love.

SET REMINDERS

Don't expect yourself to simply remember everyone's work anniversary. You're probably already trying to remember so many birthdays, meetings, holidays, and other event dates that there's just too much risk you'll forget one.

You most likely have a way of reminding yourself of things, in which case just plug into that. The two most common approaches are:

- Put a recurring annual reminder event on your calendar

- Put a recurring annual to-do item in your to-do list

If you don't use a calendar or to-do list, you can post a list in your workspace, but in that case you'll need to figure out how to ensure you don't forget to look at it regularly.

ACKNOWLEDGE THE WORK ANNIVERSARIES OF THOSE YOU WORK WITH

You can help make work anniversaries memorable for your coworkers by connecting with them in a meaningful way. As I've mentioned in most other chapters, it's best to do so on the actual day, but if you can't, it's better to be early than late.

Stop by their desk, stay after the meeting, or catch them in the break room and congratulate them. If you and/or they work remotely, initiate a video call. Here are three powerful topics of conversation:

- **Let them know what makes them special** – Tell them the three words you think of when you think of them or otherwise share the unique ways they stand out from the rest of the team

- **Remind them of interesting or memorable moments the two of you shared** – What will you never forget? What did you do together for the first time in the past year? What happened that was funny? What happened that was touching?

- **Share why you're thankful they're with the organization** – Describe how different your life would be without them, describe how different the lives of others in the organization would be without them, or maybe point out a specific skill that makes them especially helpful

We don't have conversations like that enough. If we all had them more, we could cure impostor syndrome. It can be awkward to start them out of the blue, but a colleague's work anniversary is the perfect opening.

You can make these conversations even more impactful—and your relationships stronger—by actively collecting thoughts for work anniversary conversations throughout the year. Jot down notes year-round and you'll amaze coworkers with your recall at their next work anniversary.

For each of the ten to twenty people on your work anniversary list, ask yourself these questions:

- ▸ How do I connect with them on a human level?

- ▸ How do I support their passions?

- ▸ When will I talk to them next?

- ▸ What question can I ask them about what they care about most?

This next suggestion isn't for everyone, but if you enjoy tracking things, use a spreadsheet to create a grid of each month of the year and your ten to twenty work anniversary connections—and then commit to learning one new thing a month from each connection and putting it in the spreadsheet.

However you do it, making connections takes some time and initiative, but you'll find that the internal network it builds will greatly help you succeed at your current organization and beyond and make your work life—and the work lives of those around you—more fulfilling.

USE LINKEDIN'S WORK ANNIVERSARY FEATURE TO MAINTAIN YOUR NETWORK

Acknowledging work anniversaries doesn't have to be limited to the people you work with at your organization. LinkedIn makes it extremely easy to congratulate people who work at organizations all over the world.

Admittedly, LinkedIn's work anniversary feature is often derided, and there are good reasons for the derision:

> ‣ Getting a single-button-click "Congrats on your work anniversary" message from someone you barely know feels very disingenuous

> ‣ Getting a sales pitch from someone you don't know that's disguised as a work anniversary congratulations message is an annoying waste of your time

> ‣ LinkedIn often doesn't know that someone has died and will dredge up sad feelings every year when it asks their colleagues to wish the dead person a happy work anniversary (if this is happening to you, see the **Don't forget terminations** section starting on page 98 for information on how to let LinkedIn know someone has died)

But even with those drawbacks, the LinkedIn work anniversary feature exists for a reason and can work well if you know how to use it. It's an easy way to help you maintain the weaker connections in your professional network. Conversations with those connections will spark thoughts and ideas that help you in your current job, and if for any reason you need to find a new job, a strong extended network will help you do so quickly.

Any time someone you know uses the LinkedIn feature to wish you a happy work anniversary, know that means they feel some sort of connection to you and have at least some interest in you. They may have sent you a generic message, but they did think of you. If they're clearly trying to sell you something, ignore them, but if they're a former colleague, strongly consider replying to them that it's been a while and asking if they'd like to schedule a video call to catch up. Post-pandemic, this is a lot easier than it used to be, and an option most people appreciate.

You can also use LinkedIn's work anniversary feature to initiate conversations. Any time you see that someone in your extended network is having a work anniversary, consider sending them a message. LinkedIn also now has a page that lists all the upcoming work anniversaries in your network, so you don't have to passively rely on seeing notifications.

Don't send the canned "congratulations" message, though. Instead, say that when you saw they were having a work anniversary, it reminded you that you haven't been in touch for a while and let them know you'd like to reconnect.

> **It's easier to rekindle a friendship
> than to make a new one**

Sure, there may be a lot of people you're connected with on LinkedIn who you don't want to invest time in, *but don't let that get in the way of reaching out to those you do.*

WHAT ABOUT MAKING BAKED GOODS?

This option isn't for everyone. In fact, it's not a good option for most people.

But on the right co-located team it can be really special, and it's something that the CEO or HR or even the manager just can't do. Think about how weird it would be if they did!

For this to be a good idea for you, generally *all* of the following need to be true:

- You love baking

- You're on a small, co-located team

- You know the members of your team well enough to know who has what allergies and who loves/hates what

- You're organized enough to know ahead of time about every upcoming work anniversary *and not miss any of them*

- Your life is stable enough that you can consistently put the time into baking something for every work anniversary

- There's someone on the team who's willing to be your backup if something unexpected happens and you can't bake something for someone's work anniversary

If you can check all those boxes, I would highly recommend using your talent on work anniversaries rather than birthdays. Work anniversaries get much less attention, so your efforts will be much more appreciated. Also, bringing attention to some people's age can feel awkward for them, whereas bringing attention to their time at the organization doesn't.

ARTWORK IS THE REMOTE VERSION OF BAKED GOODS

Making food for others and eating together are deeply wired connection rituals that don't have a simple replacement in the remote world. The closest analog (so to speak) is digital artwork.

Are you an illustrator? A caricature artist? A comic artist? Do you do calligraphy? If you do any kind of artwork that lends itself to creating something personal for a work anniversary, it's likely to be well received and shared across social media.

As with baking, even if you can do it, that doesn't mean that you should, and generally *all* of the following need to be true:

- You love creating the artwork

- You're on a small enough team that you can easily handle the time commitment

- You're organized enough to know ahead of time about upcoming work anniversaries *and not miss any of them*

- Your life is stable enough that you can consistently put the time into creating work of similar quality for every work anniversary

- You're disciplined enough—and inspired enough—to have the artwork completed well ahead of the work anniversary so that if something unexpected comes up, the recipient will still get their gift on time

The great upside to this, in addition to making the other members of your team happy, is that your work will get more exposure. The downside is that it's hard to maintain the discipline to do it regularly and for everyone. If you do decide to go this route, I'd highly recommend that you make it clear that your commitment is only to do it for the next year so that everyone gets one. A different option is to be clear that you only do it for work anniversaries divisible by five, which will keep the workload much lower.

THE MANAGERS CHAPTER IN THIS BOOK ISN'T JUST FOR MANAGERS

Now let's think bigger. Do you want to be a manager someday?

You don't need permission to start practicing right now.

Sure, walking around giving people orders won't turn out well, but that's not what great managers do. Great managers appreciate, encourage, and empower their employees, and work anniversaries are an opportunity to appreciate and encourage. (You can empower once you're promoted.)

> If your manager isn't doing the things in the *Ideas for managers and supervisors* chapter, you can start doing them

This isn't for everyone, as it's extra work your organization may not care about, but it's great practice for ambitious employees who one day want to be managers, either at their current organization or at their next one. (If you want to jump in right away, the chapter starts on page 107.)

LEAD BY ENROLLING OTHERS

As is the theme in this chapter, you don't have to wait until you have an official leadership position to practice leading.

> **Leadership is having a vision and inspiring others to contribute to that vision**

You don't have to be limited to leading your peers. You can also lead those above you in the official hierarchy. You can lead your manager. You can lead *their* manager. You can lead the CEO. You can lead the heads of IT and marketing.

Here's a simple (not easy, but simple) model of leadership:

- **Develop a vision** of how the world could be better than it is today

- **Make that vision concrete** and easy to see by finding examples, mocking up pictures, or doing a small-scale pilot

- **Figure out who can contribute** to making the vision real

- **Figure out concrete next steps** that other people can take to make the vision real

- **Inspire** those people with your vision and ask them to take those next steps

- When people decline to help, consider using that as feedback to **improve your vision and next steps**

There are many variables, such as where your organization is starting from, who you have the best access to, and what you're most enthusiastic about, but if you have the enthusiasm, you can find ideas in this book for other roles and work on getting other people involved in doing them.

THE FRONTLINE EMPLOYEE CHECKLIST

A true leader doesn't need an official hierarchical position or title to start leading.

- ☐ Make a list of the people you care about most at work
- ☐ Find out the work anniversaries of those people
- ☐ If the previous step is hard, encourage HR to make it easier
- ☐ Set a reminder for each work anniversary
- ☐ Deliberately build your relationship with each person on your list
- ☐ Acknowledge the work anniversary of each person on your list with a heartfelt conversation about what they mean to you
- ☐ If you'd like to be a manager someday and your manager isn't acknowledging work anniversaries, consider taking on that responsibility yourself
- ☐ If you love baking, you work on a co-located team, and you're able to take on the commitment, consider baking for your colleagues' work anniversaries
- ☐ If you do a form of artwork that lends itself to custom pieces celebrating work anniversaries and can take on the commitment, consider doing custom artwork for your colleagues' work anniversaries
- ☐ If you'd like to be a leader someday, consider figuring out how to enroll others in improving work anniversaries at your organization

THAT'S IT FOR PART 2!

Now read on to learn how to orchestrate the tactical ideas of Part 2 into a wholistic approach to strengthening your workplace culture.

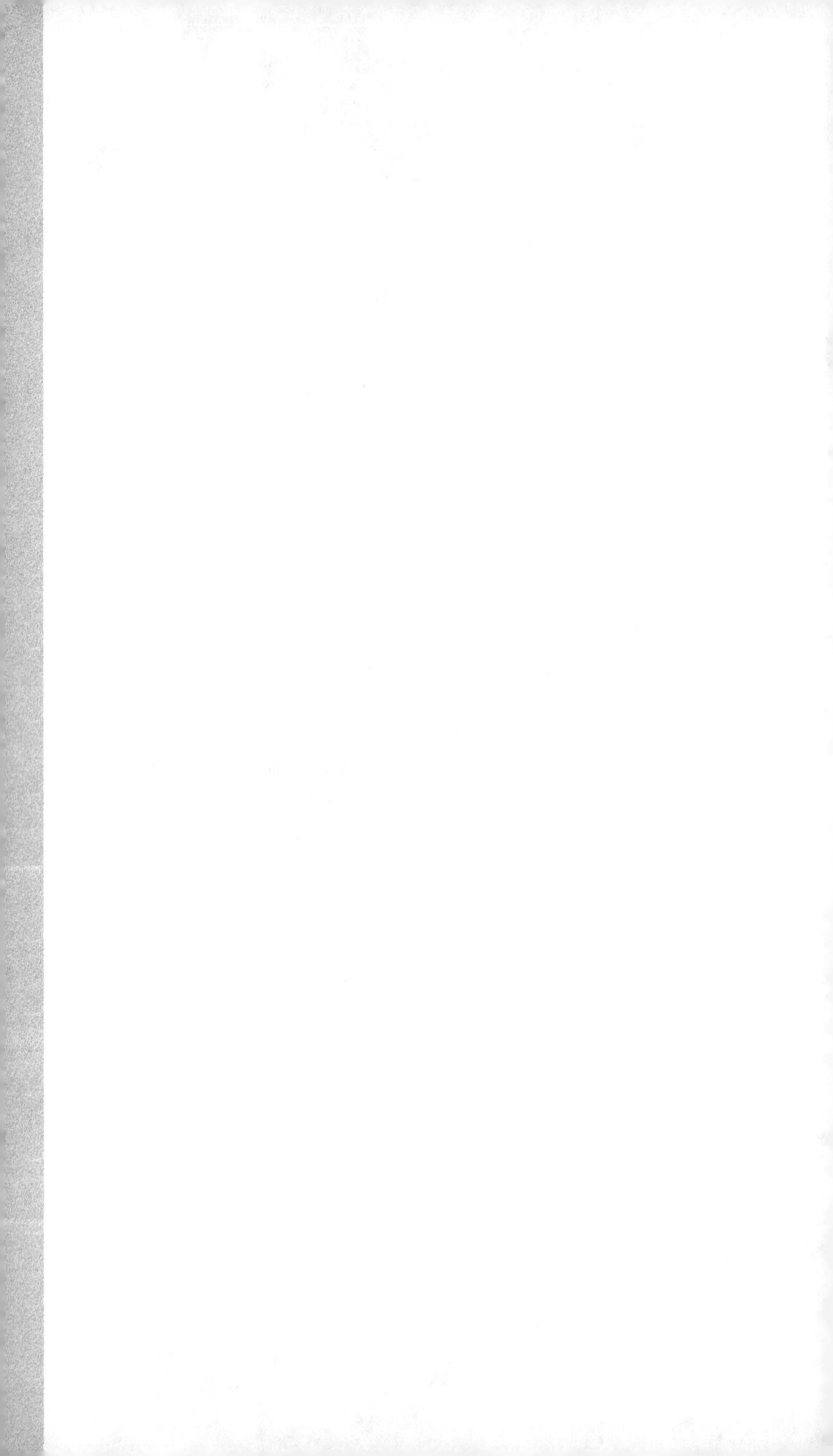

PART 3

IMPROVING
WORKPLACE CULTURE

IS FAST-PACED WORKING and innovation crucial to your strategy? Or does your strategy rely instead on meticulous quality and reliability? You'll want very different employees in those two cases.

Does your business thrive on outgoing social connections or on deeply intellectual risk assessment? Again, different kinds of employees are needed in those cases.

Whatever is important to your organization's success, if your organization's workplace culture can naturally attract the right talent and repel the wrong talent, you'll have an advantage over your competitors.

The problem is that "workplace culture" is a big, nebulous, complicated concept. How do you create a culture?

> Work anniversaries can play a
> significant role in helping you craft
> an intentional workplace culture

Work anniversaries are usefully tangible and measurable, unlike many other aspects of workplace culture. They're also intertwined with many other aspects of workplace culture, and they can make any hidden shortcomings visible, which makes those shortcomings easier to address.

The great thing is, this isn't about spending a lot of money unless you want to signal that your organization pays employees above market. Most organizations, however, will want to signal something else. Maybe your organization is caring. Or maybe your organization is geeky. Or team-oriented. Or maybe what your organization *does* is especially meaningful. All of these can be signaled by the choices you make in how you acknowledge work anniversaries.

Like Part 1 of this book, these chapters will be primarily of interest to OD nerds, I/O psychology geeks, and more generally the curious types who always want to understand the how and why behind things.

Here's what you'll find in this section:

12

WHY WORK ANNIVERSARIES ARE BETTER THAN BIRTHDAYS

OKAY, BABIES ARE AWESOME and becoming a parent is a big deal, so in the broadest sense birthdays are better, but what the chapter title would say if this weren't too long is:

> For an organization, it's much more valuable to invest time and money celebrating work anniversaries than it is to invest that same time and money celebrating birthdays

Birthdays can have baggage. For some, it's about coming to terms with aging. For others, it's related to how they were treated as kids. For many employees, birthdays are fun, but for many other employees they're just not.

Birthdays also have a lot of competition. Organizations will rarely do birthdays better than families and friends, and if they do, that's awkward in a different way.

On the other hand, any baggage that work anniversaries have is most likely related to previous employers, which gives you the perfect opportunity to shine and reinforce the message that joining your organization was a good choice!

Also, it's rare that family or friends from outside work celebrate a work anniversary or even know when it is, so there's not much competition.

Thinking bigger, work anniversaries have more power for an organization than birthdays because they're uniquely about the relationship between the organization and the employee. They're celebrating the moment the relationship began.

Still not convinced? Think of it this way:

> **Parents are to birthdays as organizations are to work anniversaries**

Without the parents, there's no birthday. Without the organization, there's no work anniversary.

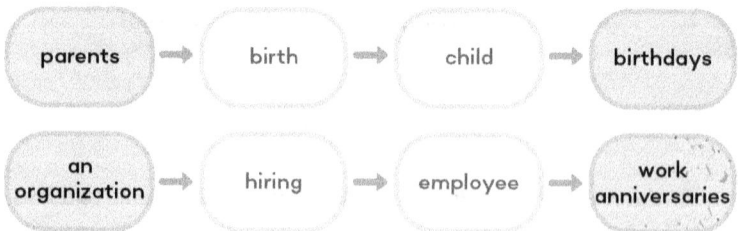

parents	⇒	birth	⇒	child	⇒	birthdays
an organization	⇒	hiring	⇒	employee	⇒	work anniversaries

One final complication to note for organizations serious about inclusivity is that Jehovah's Witnesses do not celebrate birthdays, because they believe that such celebrations displease God.[1] Assuming there isn't a cake with candles that grant wishes, they don't have similar beliefs about work anniversaries.[2]

Sure, you may not have any Jehovah's Witness employees, and if you do someday, they'll find a way to graciously sidestep employee birthdays, but why set up that division and sense of separateness when you can just put your energy into work anniversaries?

THE DAY OFF

This was mentioned earlier in the book in the time-off section, but it's worth repeating because it's important and might be unexpected after reading the previous section:

> Do not give employees their
> work anniversary off

At first thought, giving employees their work anniversary off seems like a nice, effortless way to do something nice for the employee, but a little further reflection reveals the awkward complication: if you give the employee their work anniversary off, they won't be with the people for whom the day is most meaningful and who'll most want to celebrate with them.

If you want to give an employee a special day off, giving them their birthday off makes a lot of sense for the same reasons that giving them their work anniversary off doesn't: birthdays are more appropriately spent with family and friends.

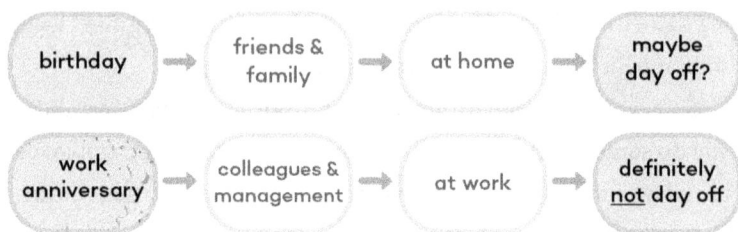

birthday	→	friends & family	→	at home	→	maybe day off?
work anniversary	→	colleagues & management	→	at work	→	definitely not day off

Need more evidence that it's better to give birthdays off than work anniversaries? At organizations that don't give either of these days off, some employees will use their vacation time to take their birthdays off. No one ever uses vacation time to take their work anniversary off.

All that said, there's nothing wrong with making sure the employee leaves on time on their work anniversary, or maybe even a little early.

EFFORT AND EXPENSE

Your organization's time and money are limited. It's better to prioritize work anniversaries over birthdays. As a simple example, if you currently give out $25 gift cards for both birthdays and work anniversaries, stop giving out birthday gift cards and increase the amount of the work anniversary gift cards to $50.

Going back to the parent/child analogy, it would be weird for parents to treat their adult children's birthdays the same as their adult children's work anniversaries, and even weirder for them to put *more* time and money into their adult children's work anniversaries.

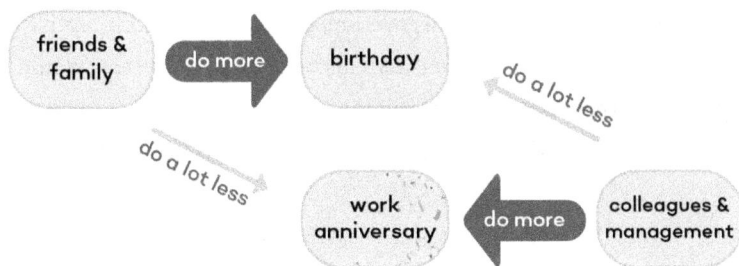

Yet many organizations do more for their employees' birthdays than their work anniversaries—and it *is* weird.

It's nice when a parent or someone else outside work acknowledges a work anniversary, just like it's nice for an organization to acknowledge an employee's birthday, but focus most of your money and effort on celebrating your employees' work anniversaries.

TAXES

At this point, you're convinced that work anniversaries are better than birthdays (at least for organizations). Welcome to the team!

But there's one last amusing comparison point between work anniversaries and birthdays.

In the United States, there is a special tax exemption for money spent on the fifth work anniversary and every five years after that. In the United Kingdom, the special tax exemption is for every tenth work anniversary. This leads many American organizations to only celebrate the fives (five, ten, fifteen, etc.) and many British organizations to only celebrate the tens (ten, twenty, thirty, etc.).

Imagine a country where a government gave parents tax incentives to buy birthday presents for their kids once every five years. Would parents in that country ignore all the other birthdays?

Likewise, you shouldn't ignore any work anniversaries, either.

CHAPTER SUMMARY

Work anniversaries and birthdays are not the same.

- **Birthdays are for the employee to celebrate outside of work** – Don't feel the need to do anything other than offer a simple acknowledgment, though it's a nice gesture to give your employees their birthdays off if you want

- **Work anniversaries are for the employee to celebrate at work** – Put the bulk of your organization's time and effort into celebrating your employees' work anniversaries rather than birthdays (but don't give them the day off!)

- **Don't let your country's tax laws dupe you into ignoring your employees** – Celebrate every work anniversary, even if there's not a tax exemption

13

WORK ANNIVERSARY VENDORS AND WORKPLACE CULTURE

I F YOU'RE READING this chapter, you're likely convinced that better work anniversaries would make a difference at your organization. Yay!

But, you're busy, you already have a grillion competing priorities, and you wonder, "Can't I just outsource this to someone?"

Among larger organizations with big budgets, it's popular to hire a vendor that automatically sends employees a link to a catalog of generic items they can choose from for their work anniversary. They just click on something, enter their address, and a week or two later their "gift" arrives.

This is appealing to many organizations because they can check off celebrating work anniversaries without putting in any effort themselves. The vendor handles everything. No one at the organization had to get involved at all!

Remember from Chapter 2 that reducing effort is one of the forces of mediocrity? This is an example of that force in action. But while this solution is great at reducing effort, it's simultaneously expensive and bad for workplace culture.

Here's the experience:

1. The employee gets a generic email—that is, if your IT team remembered to set it to not go to spam. If it does go to spam, the vendor wins (see #4a below).

2. The employee clicks on a link and scrolls through an online catalog of generic items that have nothing to do with the organization or the work. Sometimes there are weirdly anachronistic items like DVD players, presumably from when the program was originally set up, which makes the organization seem out of touch.

3. The employee often struggles to figure out what to pick. Often the items have strangely different price points (though there are no prices listed), so the employee tries to optimize their gift by picking something worth "the full amount." Another common phenomenon is that there are lots and lots of options and they're not organized in any way. It starts taking a long time to choose something. The email came to the employee's work email, so it's typically work time, and the employee starts to feel pressure to get back to whatever work they were doing.

4a. Often what happens next is that the employee just gives up and doesn't pick anything. This is great for the vendor! In many cases, you paid the vendor per employee up front, and if the employee doesn't pick something, that's more profit for the vendor. The vendor is indirectly incentivized to make the process difficult for your employees.

4b. Another possible outcome is that the employee just picks something that they don't want but that could be useful or maybe even regifted, like a small appliance or tools.

5. Assuming they pick something, the final step is to enter their address. Yes, the process ends with a final reminder that the employee is so unimportant that the organization couldn't bother to remember their address, which they clearly have for payroll and benefits purposes.

You can probably tell I'm not a fan. But there are a few tips you can use if you're going to disregard my advice and go ahead with this approach:

- Make sure your contract is set up so you don't pay for gifts that aren't chosen and delivered

- Make sure the vendor allows you to upload all the address information needed to deliver the gift to each employee

- Ideally, only go with a vendor that allows you to send personalized messages from the employee's manager and a standard message from the CEO

- Go with high-end gifts–for the catalog approach to be perceived positively, you need to have gifts that a big percentage of employees really want and wouldn't just buy for themselves

What if you get that this isn't a good idea? What's the alternative?

If you want the gift to contribute to your connection with the employee and the broader workplace culture, a little more time and effort are needed.

There's a whole section in the **Ideas for human resources** chapter called **Give gifts,** which starts on page 63. For purposes of strengthening workplace culture, here are some of my favorite gift ideas:

- **Company-branded clothing** – Note that this option can be completely outsourced to a vendor and that a company-branded fleece is much more meaningful than a mid-priced vacuum *(page 65)*

- **A "numbered" gift** – Choose the option that's appropriate to your workforce and custom-designed to really lean into your unique culture—the options are framed certificates *(page 67)*, blocks *(page 68)*, pins *(page 70)*, and stickers *(page 71)*

- **Whatever your organization sells** – This is a great option available to organizations that sell to consumers *(page 72)*

- **Team lunch** – Let the employee choose the restaurant and take along the people who work with them, including people from beyond their immediate team—it's also valuable to bring a framed certificate that calls out the organization's purpose and/or mission, and present it at lunch *(pages 116 and 125)*

Each of these options encourages a connection or feeling of belonging between the employee and your organization.

Of course, there are many other options too. The question to ask is:

> **If the employee worked at another organization, could they still get this gift?**

If you give an employee a gift that they could just as well get if they worked at another organization, the gift isn't doing anything for your workplace culture.

For an updated list of workplace-culture-aware vendors, check out the vendor guide at:

WWW.WORKIVERSARY.COM/VENDOR-GUIDE

CHAPTER SUMMARY

Using work anniversary vendors to automate work anniversary gift-giving is the generic, no-effort option. This is great for handling two forces of mediocrity—avoiding favoritism and limiting effort—but you'll pay a high price both directly and indirectly.

Work anniversary vendors' solutions generally don't reinforce your organization's purpose in the minds of employees or build your employees' sense of belonging to your organization. And often they come across as insincere, which hurts employee perceptions of organizational support.

If you're going to go ahead with a vendor that will automatically deliver work anniversary gifts, here are some helpful questions to ask as part of the selection process:

▸ **Is there any way to offer gifts unique to our organization or to the employee?** If the answer is no, this investment isn't going to do anything to strengthen your culture

▸ **Do we only pay if an employee makes a selection and gets a gift?** If the pricing is based on employee count rather than delivered gifts, the vendor will have no incentive to create a good experience for your employees, and the only gift you'll be giving is frustration

▸ **Can the manager send a different, custom message for each employee along with their gift?** If the answer is no, the gift will be judged purely on its cost and utility—this isn't great because you'll be paying a lot of markups to the vendor and a lot of employees won't need any of the gifts you're offering

Great alternatives to work anniversary vendors include giving company-branded clothing, numbered gifts, whatever your organization sells, and team lunches.

14

WORK ANNIVERSARIES AND THE POWER OF CULTURAL UNIQUENESS

THINK ABOUT BROADER, societal-level cultures. Think about one that you are especially drawn to. What is it about the culture that appeals to you? It's the parts that are *different*. What makes the culture unique is what makes it special.

To value belonging to something, there needs to be something to belong to. And for something to exist, it has to stand out from everything else. Quirkiness is good. Having your own lingo and traditions—and in general doing endearing things that don't necessarily make sense—creates an identity that employees can belong to.

For example, if you work at a midsize accounting firm that's just like a hundred other midsize accounting firms, employees may find it pleasant enough but won't feel a strong sense of belonging, because there's not a strong cultural identity. But if that accounting firm has a sports team in every corporate league from softball to water polo to kickball to roller derby, there's going to be a culture. They'll have a team name, like the Ledger Lions or the Number Ninjas, and someone at the firm will volunteer to be the mascot at games. Suddenly this is an accounting firm that stands out.

Accounting firms don't need sports teams, and this accounting firm won't be a good fit for everyone, but for the sporty accountants, it's easy to see how they'll feel they've found the organization where they belong.

If you want to create a strong workplace culture, it needs to be unique, and work anniversaries can help.

Whatever uniqueness is embedded in celebrating work anniversaries will be consistently reinforced throughout the year every time an employee has a work anniversary. Also, unlike other approaches to uniqueness that are essentially declarations, like speeches by CEOs about core values or strong brand messaging, work anniversaries inherently call for the participation of every employee in the culture. Work anniversaries are a celebration of the connection between the employee and the organization. If that connection is celebrated in a unique way, the employee is pulled more deeply into the organization's culture.

A lot of ideas in this chapter are wacky. A lot of people reading this will think, *Our employees would ridicule us if we did anything like this!* That's a sign that you have a weak culture. Doing ridiculous things together bonds people. It allows them to signal that they value being in the group and standing out from people who aren't in the group.

If you're just getting started building the uniqueness of your culture, find early supporters and easy wins that can be built on. There's usually more success to be found in sparking enthusiasm from a small group and then growing it than in taking immediate widespread action.

INVENT A UNIQUE WORD

The easiest and best place to start your work anniversary uniqueness journey is with the word you use for "work anniversary." This will strengthen your culture. Science shows that unique slang or lingo can "establish or reinforce social identity or cohesiveness within a group."[1]

The basic approach is to take a word that uniquely identifies your organization and combine it with the suffix *-iversary*. The word that identifies your organization will most often be the most distinct part of your organization's name. For example, the Swigg Group would go with *Swiggiversary*.

For organization names that end in a vowel sound, the vowel will take the place of the *i* in *iversary*. For example, a company named Vaco would use the word *Vacoversary*, and a company called Webenza would use the word *Webenzaversary*. The same is true for organization names that end in *-er*. So a company named Zuper would use the word *Zuperversary*.

Sometimes the unique word from the name will be shortened such that one or more of the leading syllables are dropped. For example, a company called Automattic might use the word *Matticversary*, and a company called NextRoll might use the word *Rolliversary*.

Some organization names aren't especially distinct, like say, Office Process Solutions or a company in Sacramento, California called the Sacramento Plumbing Company. In this case, if acronyms are commonly used to refer to the organization, they provide a solution. For these two examples, this would lead to *OPSiversary* and *SPCiversary*.

What if your organization name isn't unique and you don't have an acronym? Or you just don't like the way it sounds combined with *-iversary*?

Another option to consider is the term used for employees at your organization. Not every organization has its own unusual term, but many do, and sometimes they lend themselves to a creative alternative. For example, at the Vanguard Group, they lean into a nautical metaphor for their culture and call their employees *crew*. Thus, *crew-iversary* is an option for them. Or, more generically, at a coffee shop the word could be *baristaversary*.

If you don't have success with the term used for employees, the next stop is your marketing. This generally works best with consumer-facing brands that have invested in their marketing and perhaps even have an iconic logo or mascot.

For example, B&G Foods could celebrate *Jolly-versaries* in a play on their well-known Jolly Green Giant mascot. In a move helpfully driven by insider knowledge, Pringles could use the word *Julioversary*, since the oval-headed mustachioed mascot of theirs is named *Julio Pringles*. And in an example of a more abstract approach mentioned elsewhere in this book, T-Mobile is strongly associated with their unique use of the brand color magenta and uses the word *Magentaversary*.

If at this point you haven't found something unique, you have work to do to adopt unique language around your organization. These next suggestions are probably going too far, but maybe consider renaming your organization, coming up with a special name for employees, and/or doing some brand identity work.

One final note is about hyphenating. Most of the examples above did not use a hyphen but a couple did—crew-iversary and Jolly-versary. If your invented word has a distracting string of letters where the distinct word and suffix come together, then a hyphen will help. In crewiversary, *wive* just looks weird and introduces pronunciation uncertainty. Or, if the invented word puts letters together that just never go together in English words, like the *llyve* in Jollyversary, then a hyphen will again make it look less weird and help people pronounce it.

EMBRACE RITUALS

Rituals are actions or behavior that, at least for the most part, are unique to your organization. They're things that don't make sense or have a rational purpose, since, after all, if they made sense or accomplished something, other organizations would do them too and they'd just be common business practices.

Signing up for vision insurance makes sense, lots of employees at lots of organizations do it every year, and it's not a ritual. Putting umbrellas in the bucket thingy by the door on rainy days makes sense and it's not a ritual. Shredding documents with sensitive customer data is not a ritual.

Ritual is associated with the unusual, and with moments of change in a person's life. Dimitris Xygalatas, a leading researcher into the science of ritual and author of *Ritual: How Seemingly Senseless Acts Make Life Worth Living*, writes:

> Ritual is a true human universal. Without a single exception, all known human societies – whether past or present – have a range of traditions that involve highly choreographed, formalised and precisely executed behaviors that mark threshold moments in people's lives.[2]

There is a large body of research showing that rituals, while often appearing senseless (or what is amusingly referred to scientifically as "causally opaque"), in fact provide a lot of prosocial benefit. These benefits can be categorized into three categories:

▸ **Rituals reduce anxiety**. Rituals are especially common in highly uncertain situations such as gambling, athletics, and living in war zones. How does this relate to work anniversaries? Many employees are constantly anxious about the safety of their jobs. Rituals related to their sense of belonging at the organization can ease that anxiety.

▸ **Rituals build community**. Research shows that time invested in ritual strengthens social cohesion and a willingness to sacrifice for others in the same group. Work anniversaries strengthen the social bond at work, making employees more likely to view themselves and their coworkers as part of a team. This is an indirect but more effective way to overcome diversity and inclusion challenges than simply saying, "Differences shouldn't matter." Instead, rituals positively amplify the sense of belonging to a common identity, the organization.

▸ **Rituals improve performance**. This is true for both individuals and teams. Since rituals ease anxiety, they make room for individual employees to take on harder tasks that would otherwise not fit in their "anxiety budget." And since rituals build community, team performance is enhanced through an increased willingness to put the best interests of the group ahead of individual desires.

Ready to explore how you can start building ritual into your work anniversaries? Be forewarned—it's going to get … weird.

DO THINGS THAT DON'T MAKE SENSE

Doing things that don't make sense doesn't usually come naturally to businesses. Most organizations are always pursuing efficiency, and an obvious path to increasing efficiency is eliminating things that have no obvious causal effect on desired outcomes.

But when it comes to work anniversaries, the line between sense-lessness and efficiency isn't that obvious. Being efficient is *inefficient*. To put it another way:

> **Being completely efficient completely ruins a work anniversary**

That is, if you totally automate the process and have an outsourced fulfillment warehouse ship everyone the same generic gift you bought in bulk at a great discount, you'll save a lot of time and money, but the outcome will be useless at best and is likely to be demotivating to many.

That said, the goal isn't complete randomness either. Here are some indirect goals that well-celebrated work anniversaries can communicate:

- The employee is appreciated and respected

- The employee's colleagues will be there for the employee in times of need

- Optimism about the employee's future with the organization

To get you started, imagine that at your organization each employee's manager gets them their favorite candy or snack on their work anniversary. How can you make handing it over a fun ritual? The most efficient thing would be to just drop it on their desk whether they're there or not and go back to work, but we're looking to do something that's *not* that.

How about if the manager hands it over with two palms-up hands, reminiscent of Japanese business card exchanges? Or maybe the manager kneels and bows their head as they hand it over? Or maybe the employee kneels as the manager recites a short, standard swearing-in type of speech, expressing being honored to be their manager and thanking them for the past year? Whatever you choose, go all in with that one. Be over the top with it. Believe it to be *wrong* not to do it that way. Have employees refuse to accept the candy or snack unless the ritual was followed precisely.

Or maybe your organization runs more through cross-functional teams and the manager role isn't that important. In that case, how about having every employee on the work anniversary employee's team stop by the employee's desk or at a particular spot in the break room to leave a message on a Post-it note? What if people take the ritual so seriously that employees who won't be there that day or who work at another location send their Post-its to a colleague who'll be there so that they magically appear anyway? What if at the end of the day, the manager (or HR) comes along and puts all the Post-its in a frame and gives it to the employee?

What if there are hurdles to getting into the office on the first day of your new year with the organization? Maybe you need to do the chicken dance every time you cross the doorway that day, even if nobody else is around. And if you forget or get caught trying to skip it, you'll have to go back out and come in again. Or maybe you're not allowed in the door unless you're wearing the work anniversary crown that your team made for you—and you're expected to wear it all day. If not a crown, how about a sash? Or maybe once you're in the door, there's a sacred line of gaffer's tape on the floor and you jump back and forth over it once for every year you've been with the organization while counting them out aloud? (Or tap your foot on either side if jumping is physically difficult or painful for you, or wheel back and forth if you use a wheelchair—there's always an inclusive alternative.) Or maybe before you can start your day, you need to have your picture taken holding a garishly decorated three-foot by three-foot "Happy work anniversary!" frame around your head.

Or maybe there are too many entryways into the office and/or there's no one at a front desk, and so the ritual happens sometime during the day. Maybe it's that the employee is surprised at a random time during the day, with one colleague firing off a confetti popper at them and another conspiring colleague taking a photo of their face at their most surprised moment. Then maybe there's a public collection of all the photos, either online or IRL.

Other approaches are needed for remote workers, of course. What if on your work anniversary you start your day on a videoconference call with your manager and everyone else who can attend witnessing you recite the organization's sacred work anniversary vow? What if it not only involves reaffirming working toward the organization's purpose or mission and living the core values but also rhymes, and for extra luck you can rap it? Or maybe on your work anniversary you're expected to make a homemade sign with the number of years being celebrated attached to a Popsicle stick and you hold it up at the start of every video call you're on that day? Or maybe there's a plush work anniversary walrus that gets physically mailed from employee to employee and is expected to show up on videoconference calls with the employee on their work anniversary?

For hybrid organizations, a fun ritual is to set up a fifteen-minute video call any morning there's a work anniversary. On the call, start with spinning a spin-to-win prize wheel that lists a variety of work anniversary gifts. In-person employees can get what they win right away, and remote employees have their prizes sent to them—though some prizes don't need to be sent, like the afternoon off.

After the prize wheel, you can re-create some of the magic of in-person meals by borrowing the approach of having everyone on the call go one by one and say something kind about the employee celebrating their work anniversary. As was mentioned on page 125 in the section on team meals, the kind words can either be free-form or follow prompts like:

- What three words best describe the honoree?

- What's your favorite memory with the honoree from the past year?

- Why are you thankful the honoree has been with us for the past year?

There's also lots of fun to be had in coming up with your own ideas. Get creative, but always ask yourself these questions:

- Does this ritual honor the employee?

- Does this ritual express that, as a group, we stick by each other?

- Does this ritual point to optimism about the future?

A great work anniversary ritual doesn't need a yes to all three questions. It just needs one strong yes and for the answer to the other two question to not be, "It's the opposite of that."

BELIEVE IN MAGIC 🦄

The idea of magic is as old as humanity, but we're always coming up with new ways to believe in the impossible. Sure, there's Santa Claus, but there's also the Elf on the Shelf. You can create new work anniversary magic for your organization!

One of the special powers of magic in supporting work anniversary rituals is that it allows employees to playfully, but firmly, confront employees who aren't following the rituals. The more outlandish the ritual, the better a bonding experience it can be—and the more likely you'll run into one or more people who'll feel really awkward doing it and try to get out of it.

But if some sort of future good luck is attributed to the ritual, an employee can be admonished for risking everyone's future by refusing to join in. And the more specific the luck is, the better. It's not general "good luck" that's at stake—it's good luck with new hires, or next month's sales, or not forgetting to come off mute when talking, or not forgetting to go on mute when you should.

Did someone make a mistake while performing a ritual? No matter how minor, make them do it again to avoid calamity! Is the employee claiming that what they did was close enough? Remind them that President Obama had to be sworn in a second time because one word was said out of sequence. You can also quote Greg Craig, White House counsel at the time, and say they need to do it again "out of an abundance of caution."

Want to up the stakes? Make more nonsensical rules! Like maybe the three-by-three "Happy work anniversary" frame grants luck for the following year *as long as you don't turn it upside down*. And if you do turn it upside down? Well, everywhere that picture is posted, *you'll* be upside down!

But there's more to magic than granting luck.

Do you give gifts for work anniversaries? Can they come from a mythical being? If you have a mascot, that's the obvious choice. If not, how about an animal with a silly name like Wally the Magical Work Anniversary Warthog? (Or something else that's alliterative with your distinct name for work anniversaries.)

Another fun way to include mythical beings is with desk decorating. Similar to Santa and the Easter Bunny, you can attribute desk decoration to the Work Anniversary Fairy, whom *no one has ever seen*. The more elaborate you are with this, the more fun it will be. Create a backstory for this mythical being or talk about what the lore says will happen if they're ever spotted.

These are just examples. The options are limitless.

MAKE UP ORIGIN STORIES

Whenever someone new is first involved in doing something that doesn't make sense, they'll generally ask why.

Here's the wrong answer: "Someone in HR read a book about work anniversaries and arbitrarily came up with this useless thing for us to do so that we could fool our brains into trusting each other more."

Here's a generic one that's better: "Because no [insert your type of company here] company that has done this regularly has ever gone out of business!"

But if you can get more creative and come up with something unique to your organization, that's the best. If your organization has a mascot, tell a story about them. And if your organization doesn't have a mascot, maybe this is the impetus it needs to create one.

Are there bad days in the organization's history? Can they be *playfully* blamed on the fact that a ritual wasn't done or was done the wrong way?

Conversely, are there especially good days in the organization's history, like the day it was founded, the day the first customer signed, the day the really big customer signed, or the day you received regulatory approval? Can any or all of these days be attributed to proper performance of a ritual?

SING

Not every organization will go here, but if your organization tends to attract a big enough percentage of employees who are happy to sing in front of others, work that into your work anniversary gatherings.

Sing together? Am I serious? Yes. Researchers have found that singing causes people to bond together more closely and more quickly, and it also lowers aggression, improves mood, and makes people more cooperative.[3] Singing has long been a big part of human culture and of people working together. Neuroscientists even have reason to suspect that humans developed the ability to sing before the ability to speak evolved.[4]

Sing what, you might ask? You can sing "Happy Birthday" with your special word for *work anniversary* substituted for *birthday*. Or you can sing "For They're a Jolly Good Colleague" to the tune of

"For They're a Jolly Good Fellow." But—for all the marbles in the great game of work anniversary workplace cultural uniqueness—if at some point someone in your organization writes a work anniversary song specifically for your organization and it catches on, that's a story to tell for years to come!

CHAPTER SUMMARY

Strong cultures are unique. Work anniversaries are a powerful opportunity to both showcase and enhance your workplace culture's uniqueness.

- **Invent a unique word** – Never say "work anniversary"—instead, create your own word for a day that can only be celebrated at your organization

- **Embrace rituals** – Rituals ease anxiety, build community, and improve performance—work anniversaries lend themselves to rituals

- **Do things that don't make sense** – The core of what makes a ritual a ritual is that it's doing things that don't have a rational purpose, which is not easy for most organizations—this chapter had some thought-starters to get the ideas flowing

- **Believe in magic** – Citing magic allows employees to playfully but sincerely confront employees who don't join in the rituals, which helps maintain their integrity and adds to the sense of belonging

- **Make up origin stories** – It's natural for humans to ask why, and when they ask why your organization does things that don't make sense, be ready with a good story

- **Sing** – Singing bonds people together—if you're all-in on workplace culture, sing at work anniversaries

15

USING WORK ANNIVERSARY METRICS TO MEASURE WORKPLACE CULTURE

ONE OF THE big challenges with workplace culture is figuring out how to best quantify it. How do you know what's working and what isn't? How do you know what to stop doing or what to do more of? How do you know when what you've done is good enough and it's time to move on to other concerns?

DON'T USE EMPLOYEE SURVEYS TO MEASURE WORKPLACE CULTURE

When people are looking for ways to measure workplace culture, they almost invariably settle on employee surveys. There are hundreds of employee survey vendors who'll happily nod their heads and take money to do this "measuring."

However, anyone on the inside of the employee survey industry (as I was for over a decade) will point out that employee surveys don't produce objective measurements.

Don't get me wrong—I think employee surveys are invaluable. I recommend that every organization run one at least once a year. But the value doesn't come from viewing the survey as a tool for objective measurement. Instead, viewing employee survey results as objective measurements can actually *destroy* the benefit of running an employee survey.

CAMPBELL'S LAW

To understand why employee surveys don't work for measurement, start with Campbell's Law. It's an adage named for Donald T. Campbell, a leading social scientist from the mid-1900s, that says:

> The more any quantitative social indicator is used for social decision-making, the more subject it will be to corruption pressures and the more apt it will be to distort and corrupt the social processes it is intended to monitor.[1, 2]

Employee surveys are a social indicator. If you start treating them as objective measurements of your workplace culture, you're using them for social decision-making. That means you'll "distort and corrupt" your workplace culture.

The classic example is deciding that you want your employees to be more "engaged" and so you hire a vendor to measure engagement. Then you find out the percentage of your employees who are engaged is disappointingly low. What's the solution? Add it to your managers' scorecards! Tie their bonuses to it! You get what you measure and reward, right? And you want to be a people-centric organization, so you'll use the score to drive promotions too! Problem solved.

Except employee survey scores aren't like the number of widgets produced per hour or monthly travel expenses or quarterly revenue. At the most literal level, employee survey results are just a summary of a collection of circle clicks from a form on a web page. The circle clicks are intended to represent an employee's *self-reported perception* of a set of abstract concepts, like appreciation of or confidence in their manager. But because of the nebulousness of all that—not to mention the fact that humans aren't particularly good at accurate self-reporting—there's *a lot* of room for distortion.

So what happens if you do add engagement to your managers' scorecards and tie their bonuses to their departments' engagement scores?

First, managers will start getting nervous at employee survey time. Instead of looking forward to it as a time when they can get feedback to help make them better managers and address any issues their reports might be having, they'll start to dread it as a time when they might lose money.

Then they'll start acting weird toward their employees. They'll selectively encourage employees to respond to the survey based on how positive the manager thinks the employee is. *Positive Patty?* The manager will remind them over and over about the survey. *Negative Ned?* Nope, no reminders for them. The manager may even go so far as to tell employees that they should all respond positively for the good of the department's funding and, implicitly, their jobs. If for some reason they can't respond positively, the next best thing they can do for the group is to not respond at all. If any employee has concerns about the workplace that they want to share, they should bring those concerns directly to the manager, not express them in the survey.

Pretty soon you're not measuring what you were measuring on the first survey. Instead, you're measuring your managers' willingness and ability to influence how their direct reports click on circles. Managers who are disliked by their employees will still do poorly because their influence won't work. Managers who don't understand the game and encourage all employees to respond candidly, well, they won't do great either. The managers who'll do the best are those who are most political and manipulative.

So you'll promote them because you tied promotions to engagement as reported on employee surveys. Very quickly, as predicted by Campbell's Law, you'll have distorted and corrupted your culture by encouraging political and manipulative behavior and rewarding it with increasing power. Those who are repulsed by this sort of culture or are bad at playing the game will leave, and your remaining workforce will be composed entirely of scheming, power-conscious managers and complicit frontline employees who all care only about what's best for *them*.

If you still aren't convinced, then okay, I give up. I won't try to convince you anymore. Instead, I'll give you a useful tip before you skip the rest of this chapter: rather than using manager bonuses to boost your engagement scores, directly tie *employee* bonuses to their department's engagement score. Make it so that if an employee responds negatively on a survey, neither they nor anyone they go to lunch with get bonuses. Guaranteed to work!

All right, sorry for the sarcasm, but this is important. *Don't hurt your workplace culture by misusing employee surveys.*

REFERENCE BIAS

Maybe you're thinking that Campbell's Law won't apply to you, that your organization is immune to this kind of Machiavellian maneuvering and corruption, so you can safely use employee survey scores to track engagement. You'll just be ultra-clear that employees should be completely candid, and you'll never make the mistake of tying bonuses to survey scores.

Well, there's another problem beyond Campbell's Law called *reference bias*. And while reference bias always plays a role in any self-reporting tool, it can be especially problematic during culture transformations, which is exactly when you most need measurement to see how you're doing.

Reference bias is the mechanism by which people choose how to respond to survey statements where they're asked how much they agree or disagree with a particular statement.

Responding requires the employee to assess the concept being asked about at their current organization. To do that they'll compare their current organization with other organizations they're aware of. The problem is that employees can't provide a universally calibrated response. Instead, they provide a loose impression of how the workplace compares with whatever comes to employees' minds as they take the survey.

For example, if you ask an employee how efficiently the organization operates, the employee will think about other organizations they're familiar with—maybe past places they worked, maybe where their spouse or family or friends work now, maybe just somewhere that's been trending on social media. And, importantly, they'll also think about how their current organization has been in the past. Then they'll assess how their organization *now* compares.

This seems reasonable at first, and if the average reference point stays stable, the phenomenon can be ignored. But during a time of cultural change, the reference point is *not* staying stable.

The following actions will all make your scores go down because you're *raising* the average reference point:

> ▸ **Merely drawing attention to a problem by making it a focus area** – This one is tragic because each of the steps is clearly good on its own—but put them together and it all goes wrong. Imagine you score low on something on the employee survey, such as appreciation, so you decide it will be an organization-wide focus area. As part of this, you tell everyone the organization scored low on appreciation and is going to focus on getting better. Well, now a bunch of people who didn't think that hard about whether or not they felt appreciated before say to themselves, "Huh, really?" They talk to their family and friends and find out their spouse/brother/BFF feels much more appreciated at their job. Now you have a lot of people feeling like they could be better appreciated. Then let's say actual objective appreciation (if there is such a thing) really does improve because everyone's making an effort. The previously ignorant people now have a higher standard, so the improvement doesn't actually affect employees' perceptions. The people who wanted change probably want more change than happened, and they use their imagined future as a reference point, so they also respond to the improvements less than enthusiastically. What just happened? You focused on appreciation, you successfully encouraged more appreciation in the organization, and your appreciation survey score went *down*. That's reference bias at work.

- **Actively promoting that the organization needs higher standards in a particular area** – This is common when a new CEO comes in. They have a vision for what the organization could be, often based on their knowledge of their previous high-performing organizations, and they communicate that vision to everyone in the company. Employees are excited about it, but survey scores go down. *What just happened?* It's a lot faster to communicate the vision than to make it happen, so the new higher standards promoted by the CEO—which haven't been implemented yet—became the reference point. Reference bias again.

- **Hiring employees from higher-performing organizations than you have previously hired from** – A big part of culture transformation is often swapping out a number of employees. Those who no longer fit with the new aspired-to culture are encouraged to leave. New employees who are better fits are brought in from other organizations. But on your next survey, the new employees respond more negatively than the previous employees who had accepted the culture the way it was. *What just happened?* As with the example above, the problem here is that change takes time. The new employees are comparing your culture with that of the well-run organization they just left. Yep, reference bias.

There's one last example related to workplace culture transformation that isn't exactly reference bias but is related. Culture transformation often happens under duress. It's common that some hard choices are being made about layoffs and increased work expectations. Culture transformation will also set up a situation where some employees just don't fit with the new culture. They won't be happy about that.

In a situation like this, a new CEO may be making all the right calls on what needs to be done to right the ship, but in the beginning employees will remember how things used to be when the organization was blissfully ignoring the impending crisis. With that as the reference point, the employee survey scores will go down. Now, in this case the survey scores are accurately reflecting that things are getting worse for employees, but the similarity to the other examples is that what's driving employee survey scores down is good for the organization in the long run. So again, survey scores are not serving as a reliable metric.

THE VALUE OF EMPLOYEE SURVEYS

If Campbell's Law and reference bias are new to you, at this point you might be saying to yourself, "Wow, if that's all true, what good are employee surveys anyway?"

I'm going to answer that by talking about parenting school-age kids.

Now many of you will be saying, "I don't have school-age kids, so that doesn't help me." But please bear with me and read the next two sections. It will all make sense in the end.

Note: One of my editors recommended that I cut this section. Admittedly, there are many reasons why this section of the book could be a bad idea:

- ▸ This isn't a book about parenting
- ▸ No one likes unsolicited advice
- ▸ A lot of the people reading don't have kids at all

- While I have three school-age kids, I can make no legitimate claim to being especially good at parenting—depending on the moment, you'll quite likely be able to find multiple people at my house who think I definitely *shouldn't* be giving advice on parenting, and one of them will be my wife

But I'm going to do it anyway.

RICK'S ADVICE ON TALKING TO SCHOOL-AGE CHILDREN ABOUT SCHOOL

Specifically, I'm going to give you advice on having great conversations with a child about school. If you don't have children, you can play along by imagining how amazing it would have been if your parents treated you this way. If you have preschool children, your time will come. If your kids are grown, maybe this is something you can use with grandchildren.

The core of the advice is three simple steps:

- **Assign a positivity number to every conversation about school** – That is, at the end of every conversation with your child about school, reflect on how positive they were about school and assign a corresponding number from zero to ten

- **Record and track the number over time** – You may want to record it in a spreadsheet, but just scribbling all the numbers in the same notepad will work too—the purpose is simply to be able to calculate weekly average scores

- **Set a goal for the number** – Be ambitious and let your kid know what you're expecting—maybe for the first week or two you both need to get used to tracking, but after that, let your kid know you're hoping they'll be at a positivity level of ten in every conversation

At this point, you might be thinking, "Ten? Every conversation a *ten*?" I get it, it's ambitious, but you bought this book because you trusted me to be able to help you solve hard problems, right?

Here's a tip that will guarantee success:

- **Tie your kid's allowance to the goal** – That is, just let them know that any week that they aren't at a positivity level of ten, they won't get their allowance

Soon every conversation will rate a ten! Do you not give your kid an allowance? I'd recommend you start just for this purpose. Their education is worth it!

Now you might be thinking this is all well and good, and you see how it could work, but maybe I don't understand how busy you are. Being a parent is hard, and there isn't much time for anything extra. I get it. And, luckily for you and your child, I have three time-saving tips:

- **If you get distracted during a conversation, don't ask them to repeat what they said** – There's really no need—you'll still be able to assign a positivity score from your general impression of what they were saying based on the parts you were paying attention to

USING WORK ANNIVERSARY METRICS TO MEASURE WORKPLACE CULTURE

- **If you get really busy, stop having conversations about school until you have time again** – You can just use the scores you had from before you got busy—if you don't have the conversations, then there are no bad scores!

- **If your family is going through tough times, *definitely* stop having the conversations.** Maybe someone close has died or is seriously ill, or a parent loses their job, or a natural disaster happens, or maybe the family has to move for reasons beyond their control—while the allowance tip works wonders most of the time, situations like these can put a lot of stress on your kid and lower your scores even if you're tying the score to their allowance—to make sure your score doesn't dip below a ten, stop having conversations about school until circumstances return to normal

Voila! Now you have a kid who's positive about school 100% of the time!

WAIT, *WHAT?* ARE YOU SOME KIND OF MONSTER?

By now, I hope you agree with my wife that I shouldn't give advice about parenting.

I mean, that advice was *terrible*.

Conversations with your kids about school are important and valuable, and when they're positive, that's a good sign. So it kind of seems like having more positive conversations would be good, but it turns out that that's a really bad thing to focus on.

You're not actually having the conversations because you want them to be positive. The conversations where your kids are positive are in fact less valuable than the conversations where they share frustrations, struggles, and worries. The real reason you're having the conversations is to support their doing well in school and ultimately to help them successfully navigate the world, whatever success means to them.

And if that's the goal, the behavior I was advising is likely to have the opposite effect. If you followed the advice, your kid would quite likely start to feel that you don't really care about them at all, that what you care about is some dumb number that lets you pretend everything's fine. Not only will this hurt your communication with your kid about school, and thus your ability to help them, but it will also damage your overall relationship with them.

> **So, please please *please* don't follow
> the advice in the previous section**

But if that advice is so bad, why did I put it in this book? My guess is you've figured that out by now …

IT WAS A METAPHOR!

Talking to kids about school is my favorite way to illustrate the true value of employee surveys and how not to destroy it, as well as why the surveys don't work as accurate measurement tools.

The progression that parents talking to kids about school are looking for is something like this:

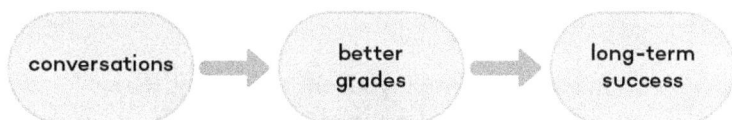

conversations → better grades → long-term success

In the business world, this roughly corresponds to:

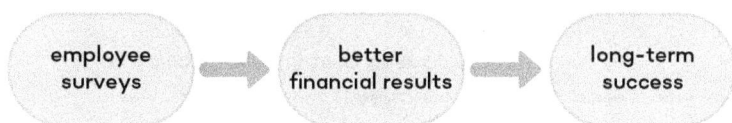

employee surveys → better financial results → long-term success

At work, the deep goal you're working toward is the long-term success of the organization, whatever success means to your organization—widgets sold, species saved from extinction, customers satisfied—just like parents' goal is the long-term success of their kid after graduation. Progress toward the goal is measured in concrete financial results, which equates roughly to the measuring of grades.

And that leads us back to employee surveys, where people with more positional power ask people with less positional power what they think of how things are going, like a parent asking a kid how things are at school.

What makes this metaphor work so beautifully is that it makes what to do and what not to do much clearer:

> ▸ **Don't focus on the overall positivity of employee survey results**. Just as with conversations about school, that's not the point. The point is opening up communication so you can support the employees in overcoming

any obstacles they're facing. If you were really focused on figuring out how to measure the quality of the conversation, then figuring out how to measure candor might be the most important thing.

▸ **Don't tell your employees that you want them to be positive on the survey**. Asking your employees to be positive on a survey alienates them by sending a message that you don't genuinely care about their experiences and you just want to be able to pretend everything's fine.

▸ **Do tell your employees that you want them to be candid on the survey**. Telling an employee you're looking for candor shows that you're a strong leader who can handle honesty and is prepared to use it for the betterment of the organization and the people who work there.

▸ **Don't quietly ignore your employee survey results**. This is equivalent to being distracted and blankly staring at your kid while they talk about school. It demonstrates a fundamental lack of respect and harms long-term relationships.

▸ **Do publicly thank employees for taking the survey *immediately* after closing the survey**. This lets employees know that you value what they had to say and that you take the survey seriously. (And do it immediately—as in a conversation, the longer the pause, the more awkward it gets.)

▸ **Do focus on what the employee survey results tell you about opportunities to remove obstacles to your organization's long-term success**. That is, don't focus on appreciation because the score is low. Instead, focus on how unappreciated your customer success team is feeling because a combination of low morale and high turnover is leading to worse customer interactions with the team, which is leading to lower customer satisfaction, which is leading to lower renewal rates, which is bad for the long-term success of the organization. That will put your focus on how to solve the problems rather than how to improve the scores.

▸ **Don't skip your annual employee survey.** As with the family going through tough times in the metaphor, it's common to *not* survey because the organization is especially busy or something bad happened recently, like layoffs. Busy, difficult, or lean times are when you most need to keep the communication channels open with frontline employees. If running an employee survey is too hard when you're busy, find another survey provider that makes it easier.

Alright, now that I've spent a lot of time on how *not* to measure culture, what do I recommend that you use? (Hint: the title of this chapter might give you a clue.)

USE WORK ANNIVERSARY METRICS TO MEASURE WORKPLACE CULTURE

Yes, there is such a thing as work anniversary metrics!

One way to think about work anniversaries is as a mirror that shows you how much your organization actually values employees. For those who care enough to go a step further, they can also be a bathroom scale, the fancy kind with all the body composition measurements.

Each of the work anniversary metrics described in this section is much less "gameable" than anything you can ask on an employee survey. That is, these metrics are much less prone to the unintended consequences of distorting and corrupting your workplace culture. Also, to the extent that they are gameable, there's another metric that will expose that.

Each of the following metrics work together as part of a pair. The first metric of each pair is some sort of *quantitative* measure that reports how much of something is happening. The second metric is a *qualitative* measure that makes sure the first metric is not being achieved at the expense of quality.

Note that these metrics do assume you're implementing several of the recommendations from earlier in the book, so if you're not, only some of these metrics will apply to you (though I'm also hoping this section inspires you to implement more of the recommendations).

Here are the six pairs of work anniversary metrics:

BELONGING TO THE ORGANIZATION IS MEANINGFUL

The first metric makes sure work anniversaries happen. The second makes sure the first metric isn't achieved by cutting so many corners that work anniversaries are no longer relevant.

> ▸ **Percentage of work anniversaries celebrated on time** – If the employee is meaningful to the organization, the organization can figure out how to reliably celebrate work anniversaries on time

- **Percentage of employees who actively display evidence of their most recent work anniversary** – If the organization is meaningful to the employee, the employee will feel honored to display a recent reminder of their connection to the organization, such as displaying their work anniversary certificate or block at their desk, wearing their pin, or wearing company-branded clothing in virtual meetings or at in-person events

EFFICIENT EXECUTION MATTERS

These metrics rather amusingly measure efficient execution by measuring the efficient execution of helping employees with efficient execution.

- **Percentage of employees who received requested IT upgrades on time** – A big part of the magic is delivering the upgrades talked about in the IT section *on the work anniversary*—without this measurement, it would be easy for the upgrades to be perceived as not urgent and be repeatedly delayed

- **Employee rating of how well the IT upgrade process went** – While on-time delivery is a goal, you don't want it to be at the expense of a great experience for employees—you want it to be on time *and* great, but in the end the *great* is what matters most

MANAGERS GENUINELY APPRECIATE THEIR EMPLOYEES

These metrics will measure management commitment to appreciating employees as well as possibly identifying pockets of manager overload.

- **Percentage of employees who received a public heartfelt message of appreciation from their manager on their work anniversary** – Tracking this metric sends the message to managers that this is an important part of their job *(if you want to go a step further, pick a "best of the month" and publicly cheer the manager for the effort they put into it)*

- **Average number of team messages or emoji reactions made in support of manager work anniversary messages** – This will measure the quality of the interaction that was kicked off by the heartfelt message—this isn't a direct measure of the quality of the message, as the total will be conflated with the popularity of the employee, but in aggregate and over time, it will reflect the degree to which the culture is embracing appreciative positivity

SENIOR MANAGERS ARE WELL CONNECTED WITH FRONTLINE EMPLOYEES

These will measure senior management commitment to valuing the perspectives of frontline employees.

▸ **Number of work anniversary skip-level meetings completed** – Tracking this metric sends the message to senior managers that this is an important part of their job

▸ **Employee rating of how well the skip-level meetings went** – This metric exists in part to make sure senior managers aren't inflating their numbers by meeting with employees without really listening to them—but more important, the frequent feedback will help the senior manager improve how they interact with employees in more general settings too

EMPLOYEES ARE ENABLED TO WORK AT THEIR FULL POTENTIAL

This is especially important because being enabled to work at full potential is highly correlated with engagement.

▸ **Percentage of work anniversary job crafting exercises completed** – This is a measurement of both the employee's willingness to start the exercise and the manager's support of completing the exercise

▸ **Employee rating of the job crafting experience** – This will help expose situations where managers aren't seriously working to figure out how to evolve the employee's responsibilities

EMPLOYEES SEE A LONG-TERM FUTURE WITH THE ORGANIZATION

These metrics will have some predictive value of attrition, but if an employee is already actively searching for a better job, going through this process won't make sense.

- **Percentage of employees who reviewed their long-term career plans with their managers as part of their work anniversaries** – This points to whether employees think they even have enough of a future that it's worth putting the effort in

- **Employee rating of the long-term career plan experience** – This metric will expose any managers who are just "checking the box" and not actually having genuinely supportive conversations

WORK ANNIVERSARY METRICS AREN'T FOR EVERYONE

Using employee survey data to measure workplace culture is clearly the much more common path. It's not going to be easy to show up in a meeting with your boss and say that you read about a much better way to measure workplace culture in a book about work anniversaries.

But if you happen to be at an organization that embraces innovation and is interested in finding a better way, I strongly believe this is that better way. If you're ready to get started, reach out to my company, the Workiversary Group. Because you'll be at the cutting edge of working on our mission to dramatically improve the work anniversaries of the world, we'll help you with work anniversary metrics *at no charge.*

CHAPTER SUMMARY

While employee surveys are great skip-level conversation starters between leaders and employees, they don't work well as measurements of workplace culture due to Campbell's Law and reference bias. But work anniversaries *can* work well as measurements of both quantity and quality, as shown in these twelve metrics:

topic	quantity metric	quality metric
Belonging to the organization is meaningful	% of work anniversaries celebrated on time	% of employees who actively display evidence of their most recent work anniversary in their workspace
Efficient execution matters	% of employees who received requested IT upgrades on time	Employee rating of how well the IT upgrade process went
Managers genuinely appreciate their employees	% of employees who received a public heartfelt message of appreciation from their manager on their work anniversary	Average # of team messages or emoji reactions made in support of manager work anniversary messages
Senior managers well connected with frontline employees	# of work anniversary skip-level meetings completed	Employee rating of how well the skip-level meetings went
Employees enabled to work at their full potential	% of work anniversary job crafting exercises completed	Employee rating of the job crafting experience
Employees see a long-term future with the organization	% of employees who reviewed their long-term career plans with their managers as part of their work anniversaries	Employee rating of the long-term career plan experience

16

ACQUISITIONS AND WORK ANNIVERSARIES

THERE'S A LOT TO THINK ABOUT when your company is acquiring another. Work anniversaries aren't at the top of the list. They probably aren't even on the list.

That's fine if the acquired company was primarily purchased for a reason other than the employees. Maybe the value of the acquisition is the assets of the acquired company, or maybe they have a mature product that can be more effectively cross-sold by your existing sales force. If employees leave the acquired company, no big deal—it can even help you meet cost-saving targets. In that case, it may be most cost-effective to let the cultural side of things unfold however it does by default.

If that's your situation, skip this chapter.

But if, on the other hand, the value of the acquisition is in the employees, then the workplace culture side of the post-acquisition integration takes on a lot of importance. Perhaps the acquired company is expected to bring innovation back to an older company that's been experiencing slower growth, or the acquired company is being acquired precisely because the kinds of employees they have are hard to hire and this is a cost-effective way to bring them on.

In these cases, the hearts and minds of the acquired employees need to be won over. And while work anniversaries clearly can't do it all, they can play a vital role. Unlike speeches, they're a direct interaction with the acquired employees. They're also tangible, and they're not especially or necessarily expensive. Employees who haven't fully made up their minds to stay on can be nudged in the right direction by thoughtful work anniversaries, especially if your organization does it better than the acquired organization used to.

Conveniently, doing this well isn't difficult.

Start with the work anniversary dates. For purposes of benefit eligibility *and* celebrating their work anniversaries, import the hire dates that the acquired company was using for their employees before the acquisition. *Do not use the acquisition date as a hire date.* From the acquired employees' perspective, the acquisition date isn't a day to celebrate—it's a day forced on them, a day they had no say in, and a day that filled them with anxiety. But using their original hire dates symbolically demonstrates respect for the acquired company's history.

Speaking of benefits, be sensitive to how your benefits package might be perceived as worse than the employees' old benefits package at the acquired company and look for ways to help the acquired employees adjust to the changes. As part of this, think of work anniversaries as a benefit. Find out what the acquired company did for work anniversaries and decide if anything they did makes sense to bring across to your company as a whole.

The next step is to think about how you'll acknowledge the acquired employees' work anniversaries. If you've embraced the ideas in this book for embedding your culture in how you celebrate work anniversaries, an acquired employee's first work anniversary with your organization will serve as a great reminder of what's valued in your workplace culture. Even more powerful, the acquired employee's first work anniversary with the combined company will serve as an important ritual that helps them transition from feeling like they still work for the old ABC Inc., which was acquired by XYZ Inc., to feeling like they now fully belong *to* XYZ Inc.

However, just quietly adding them to your work anniversary program would probably be a little weird. That first year, many employees will feel it awkward that they're being honored as part of an organization they've barely gotten to know yet.

The best way to make it less weird is to acknowledge the situation. Essentially, you want to give them a heads-up that their work anniversary is going to be celebrated as though they'd been part of the new organization all along. Then explain that this makes sense because they were a big part of making the acquired organization the highly valuable organization it became and thank them for all they've done for both organizations, before and after the acquisition.

There are many variations on the best format for conveying this to the acquired employees. The most personal approach is to have an email come from the CEO the day before each acquired employee's first work anniversary with the new company. Scaling back in ambition, you can send it in bulk to all the acquired employees after the acquisition has taken place. If getting it to come from the CEO is difficult, it can also come from someone other than the CEO, generally the head of HR or the COO.

As with all the advice in this book, whatever you do, craft the experience so it shows that you care about the employees and aren't just trying to check off a box.

CHAPTER SUMMARY

If the acquired employees are a key component of the value of the acquisition, you'll want to get cultural integration right to maximize the value of the deal. And work anniversaries are an important part of cultural integration.

- ▸ For work anniversaries and everything else, honor the acquired employees' original hire dates—*never* use the acquisition date

- ▸ Find out what the acquired company did for work anniversaries and upgrade your program so that what you do is noticeably better than what they did, or at the very least not noticeably worse

- ▸ Treat the acquired employees' first work anniversaries with the acquired company as:
  - ▸ an opportunity to remind them of your culture
  - ▸ an opportunity to encourage them to feel like they genuinely and fully belong to the new combined organization

THAT'S IT FOR PART 3!

Now read on to learn how to put it all together to improve your work anniversary program with a simple three-part framework.

IMPROVING YOUR WORK ANNIVERSARY PROGRAM

EITHER THROUGH A LOT of reading or through a lot of skip-ping ahead, you've almost reached the end of the book! Con-gratulations!

Now that you have a headful of new work anniversary knowl-edge, or are at least aware of what knowledge is available, you might be asking yourself:

> How do I get started improving my
> organization's work anniversary program?

There are three concrete components of celebrating a work anni-versary:

1. acknowledging employees
2. giving gifts to employees
3. strengthening the organization's culture

If you want to improve your work anniversary program, it's just a matter of examining each of these three areas and deciding if you want to do something more or something different from what you're currently doing.

This afterword will look at work anniversaries through this lens and point you back toward key parts of the book related to each of these three components.

ACKNOWLEDGING

Human resources can send an automated email on the day of the work anniversary, and they can publish work anniversaries in the newsletter or on the intranet, but the best acknowledgment comes from people in the management chain above the employee.

The absolute most important acknowledgment is from the employee's direct manager or supervisor. The first step is for them to know about work anniversaries, which is covered in the subsection

Remind managers on page 48. For ideas on how they can acknowledge employees well, see the **Ideas for managers and supervisors** chapter on page 107. Then consider what your organization will expect from managers and provide training to ensure everyone's working from the same playbook. After the initial training, embed material related to work anniversaries in your new-manager training.

Acknowledgment from the CEO or other senior leaders is also impactful. For hints on doing this well, check out either the **Ideas for CEOs (and other senior leaders)** chapter on page 149 or the **Ideas for executive assistants** chapter on page 161.

And last but not least, acknowledgment from colleagues is highly valuable as well. To do this reliably at scale, you need to set up an environment where employees are aware of each other's work anniversaries. For help with this, review the sections **Communicate work anniversary dates** on page 43 and **Celebrate publicly** on page 55.

GIVING

The simplest rule of meaningful work anniversary gift-giving is:

> **Don't give something anyone could get at any other organization**

For ideas on what your organization can give, see the **Give gifts** section on page 63.

An especially valuable approach is empowering employees to choose what they need in order to be more productive at work, which has its own chapter: **Ideas for IT support** on page 139.

And for ideas about small gifts that can come personally from the manager, check out the subsections **Capture employee favorites** on page 111, **Use the favorites list** on page 116, and **One-on-one reach-out first thing in the day** on page 123.

STRENGTHENING CULTURE

The simplest, most valuable thing you can do to use work anniversaries to strengthen your organization's culture is to make sure your organization has a clear, well-communicated purpose, then reference that purpose every time a work anniversary is acknowledged in any way—by a manager, by the CEO in the all-hands meeting, in the newsletter, on Slack, wherever.

For more on the value of communicating your organization's purpose, check out the **Purpose** section on page 13.

Going a little broader to include the other two drivers of work anniversary value, check out the entire chapter **Why work anniversaries are so valuable** on page 11.

Then, if you're ready to go all in on strengthening culture, check out **Part 3: Improving workplace culture** on page 237.

THE POWER OF THE INTERSECTIONS

Finally, while it's helpful to view a work anniversary program as being made up of three components, the best programs consciously make sure that the three components all overlap.

This diagram shows the intersections of the three components:

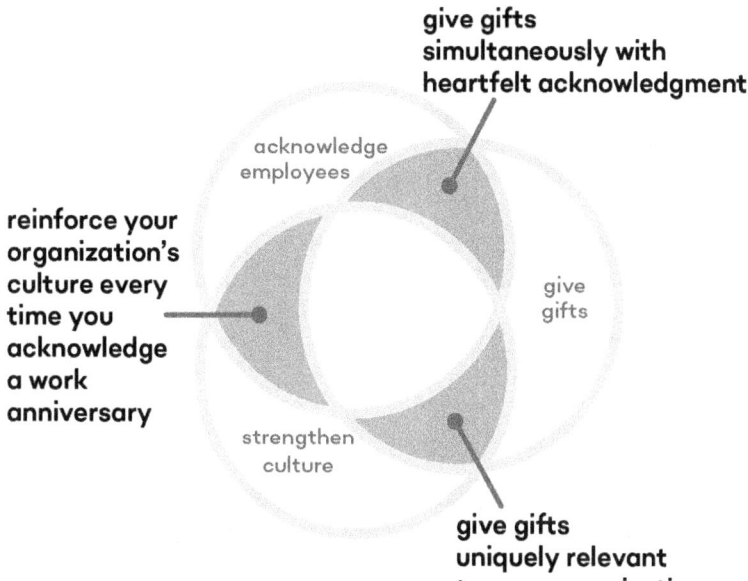

Looking at the intersections reveals that the best gifts are: (1) unique reflections of the organization's culture; (2) given together with acknowledgment of the employee's contributions over the past year; and (3) presented with a personalized message of recognition from the employee's manager.

It's best to avoid gifts that are: (1) random gifts the employee can get anywhere; (2) just dropped off on an employee's desk when they're not there; or (3) shipped by a work anniversary vendor without a personalized message from anyone.

THE WORK ANNIVERSARY PROGRAM CHECKLIST

As you consider improving your work anniversary program, it's helpful to think about these three components:

☐ **Acknowledging** – Remind managers about their direct reports' work anniversaries ahead of time and on the day, encourage your CEO and other senior leaders to embrace work anniversaries as communication opportunities, and make sure work anniversary dates are broadly communicated

☐ **Giving** – Don't give something anyone could get at any organization—instead, use this book to review the many options and choose what makes most sense for your organization

☐ **Strengthening culture** – Tying the organization's purpose to work anniversaries is the most important part of using work anniversaries to strengthen your organization's culture, but if you want to go deeper, this book includes many more suggestions

To create a new work anniversary program or improve an existing one, simply decide what you want to do in each of those three areas, but remember that none of the three components stands alone. For a truly standout program, look closely at where the components intersect.

APPENDICES

THE FIRST FOUR appendices are alternate ways to organize related content together that was otherwise spread throughout the book, which will be helpful for some readers.

The final two appendices go into more depth than made sense as part of the flow of the rest of the book, which will again be helpful for some readers.

TOP TEN MISTAKES TO AVOID

DON'T LET THE FEAR of making mistakes prevent you from taking action.

That said, having some fear of the following ten common mistakes is healthy.

#10 ASKING FOR GLASSDOOR REVIEWS IN WORK ANNIVERSARY EMAILS

Imagine getting a generic automated email acknowledging your work anniversary that has a request for you to leave a Glassdoor review if you like your job.

Really? They want you to take the time to write up something positive and heartfelt about the organization when they couldn't be bothered to do the same about you, and when the little gesture they did make was accompanied by a self-serving request?

Don't be the company that did that.

The work anniversary moment is about the employee, not the organization. And in the same spirit, don't try to sell your company's widgets or promote your hiring page on social media posts celebrating the employee either.

#9 GIVING LOTTERY TICKETS

This was already mentioned in the gift-giving section, but it's so bad it made this list too.

Don't ever give lottery tickets as work anniversary gifts.

They're pretty much the universal symbol of poverty and desperation, not to mention hating your job so much you'll snatch at even the most infinitesimal chance of striking it rich so you can leave. Besides, the vast majority of employees will lose, which makes for a lot of disappointment. If an employee does win big and quits, it can spread dissatisfaction and envy—hardly the emotions you want employees to associate with work anniversaries.

#8 SENDING WORK ANNIVERSARY GIFTS TO FIRED EMPLOYEES

Firing employees (or being fired) is awkward enough. Don't make it worse.

Somewhere, your organization has a termination checklist. If any part of your work anniversary program is automated, make sure that *turning it off* is a step on the termination checklist.

And note that while sending gifts to employees' homes is the worst, turning off other automations is important too. If you send automatic emails, they're going to get forwarded to whoever is now standing in to cover their former responsibilities, which can also be awkward, especially if the person getting the emails doesn't understand or agree with the firing.

#7 FORGETTING THE PERSON WHO RUNS THE PROGRAM

Those who give need taking care of too.

If you're the manager of the person who runs your organization's work anniversary program, you need to make sure you know how they do that and put a reminder on your calendar to do that for *them*.

Don't let them be the only person in your organization not recognized on their work anniversary!

#6 DOING MORE WHEN PEOPLE LEAVE THAN ON THEIR WORK ANNIVERSARY

What message are you sending if you celebrate the people leaving more than you celebrate the people staying?

Do you go out together when people leave? What if you did that for every year (or at least every five years) that they stayed? Do you put a lot of energy into retirement parties? What if you redirected that energy into twenty-fifth anniversary parties instead or at least gave them equal attention and care?

#5 USING A PHOTO THE EMPLOYEE HATES

The goal of celebrating work anniversaries is to trigger positive emotions, not embarrassment. If you post photos of employees as part of acknowledging their work anniversaries, make sure each employee is okay with the photo you're choosing.

You already have some process for getting all the photos, so make part of that process checking in with each employee about how they like the photo. Or, if you want to avoid this step, use their LinkedIn photo, since that's something they chose themself and made public.

And more broadly, avoid *anything* that will truly embarrass them. It's okay if they're a little shy about getting so much attention, but don't say things about them that they wouldn't want to be shared or force them to make a speech they're not prepared for or anything else that might make embarrassment the most memorable emotion from their work anniversary.

#4 COMING ACROSS LIKE YOU JUST WANT TO CHECK IT OFF YOUR LIST

Work anniversaries are about acknowledging the value of the employee's contributions to the organization for one or more years, so the goal is for the employee to feel like they matter and that the organization cares about them.

If the people involved in celebrating the work anniversary appear uninterested, hurried, and generally as if they care more about marking the task done than honoring the employee, they may do more harm than good.

On a related note, beware automations and time optimizations. Sure, if you get everyone plaques *without* their names or number of years it'll be easier, but is it even worth it at that point? And yes, you could send automated emails, but is there any meaning in that?

#3 GOING OVER THE TOP FOR ONE EMPLOYEE BUT NOT FOR OTHERS

Employees are sensitive to any sort of work anniversary favoritism, so the same effort should be put into all employees. Bigger milestones can of course be celebrated in a bigger way than smaller milestones, but every employee reaching a specific milestone should be treated the same. This includes the CEO, who should not receive any special treatment.

I get it—some employees are more valuable than others—but that is best expressed through salary and bonuses and any other recognition system you have, *not through work anniversaries.*

#2 GETTING THE DATE, NUMBER OF YEARS, OR NAME WRONG

There are only three pieces of information you really need to celebrate someone's work anniversary: (1) the date; (2) the number of years; and (3) the employee's name. It's important to get them right.

The goal of celebrating a work anniversary is to make the employee feel like their time at the organization has been valued. If you get the date, number of years, or their name wrong, you destroy your chance of achieving that goal.

If you're using a template for anything, it's better to start from the blank template each time rather than from the last one you did. Starting from someone else's is the path to getting the number of years wrong and not noticing. But even with the template, you need to make sure you replace all the parts that need to be replaced. Blank templates have been sent to employees, and this is bad. Check the certificate (or whatever it is) at least three times, and have someone else check it too. It's easy to be blind to your own errors.

Also, if you're announcing someone's name, make sure you know how to pronounce it. And whatever you do, don't pre-apologize that you're going to say the name wrong. Say it confidently. Even if it's a little wrong, that's more okay than announcing to everyone that you're going to get it wrong because you didn't bother to find out how to get it right.

#1 DOING NOTHING

There are a surprising number of ways to do nothing:

- Doing nothing at all for anyone

- Putting the work anniversary program on pause

- Forgetting someone (*even just a single person*)

- Ignoring people who are out on parental or medical leave

- Not reaching out to employees who are traveling or on-site with clients

- Being late, which from the employee's perspective looks like you did nothing until you do something, which will be *after* they've already had all the negative thoughts you want to avoid

Not everyone thinks about their work anniversary, but many people do. For those people, when nothing happens their heads are filled with some variation of the thought, *I spend a third of my life here and they don't care that I exist.*

Sometimes people's friends remember but the organization doesn't. Ouch.

But whoever you are and whatever your role at your organization, there's some idea in this book you can implement, and you can find a way to do it for *everyone, on time.*

As mentioned in the **Ideas for CEOs (and other top leaders)** chapter, if you want to make sure you don't forget, put a large "bounty" on forgotten work anniversaries. That is, publicly declare that work anniversaries are so important to your organization that if anyone's work anniversary is forgotten, they get a conference room (or machine or whatever makes sense for your organization) named after them, free food in the company cafeteria for a year, *and* an extra paid week off!

TOP TEN IDEAS FOR REMOTE EMPLOYEES

Thanks to COVID-19, many more organizations now support remote workers to some degree or other. In the early days, how best to adapt remote work anniversaries was far from the top of the urgent-things-to-figure-out list, but as we get further into the post-pandemic world, now is the time.

If you skipped straight to here, know that this isn't the only content for remote employees. Almost the entire book applies to both in-person and remote employees. The principles underlying great work anniversaries apply no matter where your employees do their jobs.

But if you're looking for a super-condensed set of ways to approach work anniversaries for remote employees, here it is!

#10 MAKE WORK ANNIVERSARY DATES DISCOVERABLE

Make it so that any employee can look up the work anniversary of any other employee.

Work anniversary dates are often communicated casually at in-person workplaces. If you know a friend's work anniversary is coming up, you might ask the HR person about it when you bump into them. Or maybe you'll overhear someone else wishing an acquaintance a happy work anniversary, so you decide to, too.

Those interactions don't happen in a remote environment, but when you have many remote employees, you're more likely to have a trafficked intranet or wiki you can use to make a list of work anniversaries available to everyone in the organization.

Read more in the **Communicate work anniversary dates** section on page 43.

#9 SET UP A REMINDER SYSTEM AND BE ON TIME

Whoever is involved in acknowledging work anniversaries needs reminders ahead of time so they can acknowledge the work anniversary *on the actual day.*

Remembering on time is especially important in a remote environment because it's easier for an employee to feel forgotten and isolated and not have any way to resolve that feeling. It's less awkward to casually ask your manager about a forgotten work anniversary when you bump into them in person than it is to text them about it, force a phone conversation, or mention it while you're on a team video call. In person, you can also more easily mention it to a friend, who then quietly mentions it to the manager, who then "remembers" later in the day.

HR folks can read more in the **Remind managers** section on page 48.

If you're responsible for onboarding, check out the **Set recurring work anniversary reminders** section on page 96.

Managers can read more in the **Set up a reminder system** subsection on page 110.

#8 COMMUNICATE PERFORMANCE REVIEW AND PAY RAISE TIMING

In the absence of clear communication about the topic, many employees will assume that both reviews and raises will be tied to their work anniversaries.

If your organization has a different approach, or even if your organization *tries* to do reviews and raises on work anniversaries but is sometimes late, it's critical to communicate that to employees. Otherwise, many employees will interpret being forgotten as a sign that they're not a good employee, that the organization doesn't care, or both.

This is true for all organizations, but it's especially true for organizations with remote workers for the same reason that organizations need to work harder at communicating with remote employees about *everything*—that is, it's harder for remote employees to pick up information informally and easier for them to stew over perceived slights.

HR folks can read more in the **Communicate performance review and pay raise timing** section on page 97.

Managers can read more in the manager-specific **Communicate performance review and pay raise timing** subsection on page 114.

#7 JOB CRAFTING

Job crafting is the practice of periodically checking in on whether an employee's responsibilities match what's best for them and for the organization. The basic process is for the employee to make a list of everything they do and then discuss with the manager the things they like and don't like on the list. The manager then collaborates with the employee to figure out how work can be redistributed across the organization to make some of those changes.

In an in-person environment, job crafting can happen organically as employees see what others are doing and pick up subtle cues about who likes and doesn't like what. Managers are sometimes able to just intuitively shift work around so it better matches each employee's interests and skills.

But in a remote environment, that's much harder to get to happen organically, so putting in some sort of regular job crafting check makes sense. You could do it any time, but work anniversaries are a natural, easy-to-remember, and hard-to-postpone time.

Read more in the **Set up a special career-focused one-on-one** subsection on page 119.

#6 ANNOUNCING AT THE ALL-HANDS MEETING

This is straightforward, and maybe you're already doing it, but if you're not, announce work anniversaries at all-hands meetings. Hearing about a work anniversary in an all-hands meeting will give remote employees a warm "excuse" to reach out to a colleague and keep up connections in a way that can be difficult in a remote environment.

More details are in the **Do shout-outs at big meetings** subsection on page 56.

Details specific to CEOs and other top leaders are in the **Celebrate work anniversaries at all-hands meetings** section on page 151.

Content specifically aimed at executive assistants is in the **All-hands meetings** subsection on page 167.

#5 SKIP-LEVEL CONVERSATIONS

Organizations that rapidly transitioned from in-person working to remote working noticed an interesting trade-off: employees' relationships with those they worked most closely with became stronger, while their relationships with those they interacted with more peripherally became weaker.[1]

By definition, a manager-of-managers' relationship with the employees who work more than one level below them is going to be weaker than more direct relationships. Remote working just makes it harder. Thus, I would claim that skip-level meetings, while valuable in all organizations, are *especially* important in remote organizations.

But skip-level meetings can be intimidating for timid employees and easy for busy leaders to cancel. Scheduling a skip-level meeting on an employee's work anniversary mitigates both these problems. For the employee, there's now a clearly positive reason for the meeting, while for the leader, there's now a reason why the meeting is more valuable now than later, and there's a noticeable cost to canceling outright.

Middle managers can read more in the **Skip-level work anniversary conversations** section on page 130.

CEOs and other high-level executives can read more in the **Hold skip-level conversations** section on page 154.

Executive assistants can read more in the **Set up skip-level one-on-ones** section on page 172.

#4 AN EMAIL FROM THE CEO

For CEOs who aren't going to have many skip-level conversations, just an email thanking the employee can be a good option.

Unless your organization is tiny, this will only be for major milestone work anniversaries (like those divisible by five), but knowing that the CEO noticed will go a long way for those work anniversaries. The key points are that the email comes directly from the CEO on the exact day and that it thanks the employee for their contributions to the organization's mission, purpose, and/or vision over their time with the organization.

More details are in the **Send a personalized email** section on page 153.

#3 A FEW HEARTFELT PARAGRAPHS

A core goal of celebrating a work anniversary is to help an employee feel seen and valued. No gift, whatever the price, will ever do this as well as three or four thoughtful, sincere paragraphs from their immediate manager or supervisor about the employee's contributions to the organization over the past year.

This is especially powerful for remote employees. Remote work can be isolating, especially beyond the most immediate coworkers. Posting these paragraphs about contributions on a public group messaging platform helps employees learn about each other and provides an easy opening to start a conversation or reconnect with a more distant colleague.

Conveniently, remote organizations are more likely to have a better group messaging platform like Slack, which provides an amazing place to publicly post these paragraphs. Both the reaction emojis and the conversations that will be sparked will be heartwarming for the employee.

Read more in the **Write a few thankful paragraphs about the employee's past year** subsection on page 117 and in the **Set up a routine to capture highlights for each employee** subsection on page 112.

#2 EMPHASIZE SHARED PURPOSE

A big challenge of remote work is the potential for it to devolve into a lot of isolated people doing tasks at a quantity or quality level just barely good enough to not get fired. The best way to counter this is to inspire employees to want to do more than the minimum.

In an in-person environment, this can be accomplished through team camaraderie, but that's hard to do remotely, especially for employees in roles that work mostly independently rather than collaboratively, such as salespeople or call center representatives.

The remote-friendly alternative is to inspire employees through organizational purpose and regular reminders about their contribution to that purpose. As in many other areas of workplace culture, work anniversaries alone won't accomplish this, but they're a great opportunity to supplement your other efforts. As was said throughout the book, the crucial thing to celebrate about a work anniversary is that it commemorates the amount of time that the employee and the organization have teamed up to work toward a common purpose or mission with shared core values.

A full discussion of the role of purpose in work anniversaries is in the **Purpose** section on page 13.

#1 EMPOWERING EMPLOYEES TO CHOOSE PRODUCTIVITY-ENHANCING UPGRADES TO THEIR HOME OFFICE

The concept here is to reach out to employees a month or so before their work anniversary and ask what would make their home office more productive—so you can deliver what they asked for on the actual day.

This is especially valuable for remote working environments because they vary so much from person to person. What each employee needs in order to be more productive can be wildly different. You won't know until you ask, and the productivity improvements can be enormous.

The full details are in the **Ideas for IT support** chapter on page 139.

TOP TEN WORKPLACE CULTURE RECOMMENDATIONS

Workplace culture and work anniversaries are deeply intertwined. If you don't have a strong workplace culture—and often even if you do—the best thing you can do to improve your organization's work anniversaries is to improve your workplace culture.

One of the biggest problems companies face when they commit to improving workplace culture is being able to see clear, definitive results. But by combining a focus on work anniversaries with workplace culture improvement, your efforts become *visible*.

While these items are on the list because they contribute to making work anniversaries better, each item is a great idea in its own right, regardless of whether or not you're trying to improve work anniversaries.

#10 GIVE EVERYONE PAY RAISES AT THE SAME TIME OF YEAR

It's far better to give all your employees raises at the same time than to associate them with work anniversaries and scatter them throughout the year. Here's why:

- Budgeting is simpler *(assuming you do them at the start of the budget year)*

- It's easier to make good decisions about allocating limited money, including not arbitrarily giving some people smaller raises because they happened to be scheduled during a quarter when revenue was lower than expected

- It's easier to identify and correct pay inequity

- Any disappointment employees might feel about their raise will be tied to the raise process and not to their work anniversary—and the decision to join the organization that their work anniversary commemorates

More details are in the **Communicate performance review and pay raise timing** section starting on page 97.

#9 CLEARLY COMMUNICATE ALL THE FACTORS THAT DETERMINE PAY RAISES

A big part of pay raise disappointment comes from a poor understanding of the reality of pay raises. Many people think that pay raises are all about performance, when that's only one factor of many.

You can't eliminate pay raise disappointment entirely, but you can reduce it by helping employees better understand the factors that go into pay raise decisions.

The first factor is the financial health of the organization. If the organization doesn't have the money to give out raises, then there won't be raises, period. A more awkward but still common situation is that if the organization isn't meeting the financial targets it set with its investors, there will also be a lot of downward pressure on raises. In other words, the organization can be profitable but still limit raises because those profits aren't enough to meet the commitments made to investors.

The second factor is the strategic importance of the area or division the employee works in. In times of growth for the organization, raises may be more forthcoming on the innovation team. In lean times, key members of teams working on major cost reduction projects will fare better.

The third factor is the employment market for the job. The price an employer has to pay to hire another employee to do the job will have a substantial impact on an employee's raise. An employee with stellar performance who can be easily replaced for less money than they're currently paid is going to be limited in the raises they can expect to receive, while an employee with acceptable performance who has a rare skill or knowledge that will be very hard to replace will be more likely to get a notable raise.

Ideally, an organization will be using one or more benchmark salary surveys to inform their pay decisions *and* be transparent with each employee about the comparison data used for their specific position. Transparency about the financial health of the organization and its role in pay raises, or annual bonuses, is also helpful.

Putting it all together, if an employee wants a significant raise without having taken on new, higher-paying responsibilities, they need to (1) work at an organization that's beating financial expectations; (2) work in an area of the business that's of strategic importance; (3) fill a role that would be difficult to replace; and (4) not already be paid more than most employees in their position.

While there are companies that will try to get away with underpaying employees who just don't speak up for themselves, you don't want your employees thinking a small raise is due to poor performance—or worse, malicious intent—if instead it's due to one of the legitimate reasons above. That kind of unvoiced resentment is deleterious to workplace culture.

#8 AVOID DOING ANNUAL PERFORMANCE REVIEWS NEAR WORK ANNIVERSARIES

Much like it's better to determine pay raises some other time than near each individual employee's work anniversary, it's also better to do performance reviews at some other time. While some performance review systems are better than others, many employees experience negative emotions at review time no matter what you do, and that's not what you want an employee to associate with their work anniversary (and by association the employee's decision to work at the organization).

However, reviewing everyone at the same time is time-consuming, so the everybody-at-once idea recommended for pay increases doesn't work as well here. Some organizations do pull off doing them all at once, but it's a big strain on managers and virtually ensures that employees will get less attention.

An option that often works better is to have an employee's first performance review six months after their hire date—and then every twelve months after that. You could also adopt a system of providing performance feedback much more frequently than annually.

Yet another option is to move away from the concept of backward-looking annual performance reviews altogether and toward the concept of future-focused career coaching. If you do opt for that approach, it's fine to do the career coaching around the same time as an employee's work anniversary: employees find the experience to be positive rather than negative. This is because the process becomes about an abundance-mindset-oriented curiosity regarding the future rather than a scarcity-mindset-oriented judgment about the past.

More details are again in the **Communicate performance review and pay raise timing** section starting on page 97.

#7 HOLD REGULAR ALL-HANDS MEETINGS

A sense of belonging is a powerful force that helps groups of people accomplish more together. But for there to be a sense of belonging, there needs to be something to belong to, and a way to belong to it. Getting together in an all-hands meeting is one way to express group identity. While the explicit purpose is to share knowledge, the existence of the meeting and mass attendance implicitly signals that the group has a meaningful identity and that everyone is on the same team.

One way to think of it is that the highest level of an organization that an employee can personally feel a connection with is the highest level that has all-hands meetings. If you want more interdepartmental cooperation and everyone working together toward common organization-wide goals, then have well-run all-hands meetings.

And as a side benefit, you can acknowledge work anniversaries at your all-hands meetings.

For more on announcing work anniversaries at all-hands meetings, see the **Do shout-outs at big meetings** subsection on page 56. For more on belonging, see the **Belonging** section on page 19.

#6 HOLD REGULAR ALL-MANAGER GET-TOGETHERS

In addition to getting everyone together, it's also valuable to specifically get together the people in your organization who are responsible for managing others.

Being a manager is hard. And it can be lonely. It's tough being caught between the interests of those below and those above. Sometimes it feels impossible to keep both groups happy. Pioneering research by Barry Oshry pointed to the importance of managers bonding with one another,[1, 2] and the first step to bonding is to get together.

A common approach is to have quarterly long lunches, though monthly is even better. But if you can only pull off something annually, that's still way better than not doing anything.

Top leaders can give presentations about the organization's direction or culture. Lower-level managers from the group can be asked to present about areas in which they excel that would be useful for the rest of the group.

All sorts of tips and best practices can be shared in these get-togethers, including ways to improve how managers can acknowledge work anniversaries.

For ideas on what managers can do on work anniversaries, which could be passed along in these meetings, see the **Ideas for managers and supervisors** chapter on page 107.

#5 INVEST IN EQUIPMENT TO ENABLE EMPLOYEES TO DO THEIR JOBS WELL

If an employee doesn't have the basics they need to do their job well, then any efforts to celebrate their work anniversary will come across somewhere between misguided and disingenuous. No employee wants a nice work anniversary gift when their potential is being hampered every day by not having the equipment, supplies, or environment to work as efficiently or effectively as they otherwise could.

Ask your employees what they need in order to do their jobs well and deliver that to them.

While you should never wait to get an employee what they need, a great way to be proactive about it is to check in on their work anniversaries. For more on this approach, see the **Ideas for IT support** chapter on page 139.

#4 FOCUS ON EMPLOYEE CAREER GROWTH (NOT ON AVOIDING ATTRITION)

The power of having an abundance mindset rather than a scarcity mindset has been well documented for everything from personal happiness to business performance. An abundance mindset makes you a better leader, improves collaboration, and even makes you smarter.[3, 4] In contrast, a scarcity mindset leads to many workplace culture eroding problems: increased stress; short-term thinking; reduced empathy; loosened moral standards; antisocial behavior; and self-centeredness.[5, 6]

Clearly, it's better to have an abundance mindset. Yet many workplace culture vendors will play up attrition anxiety as a reason to buy their product or service. "Attrition is expensive!" they exclaim, and go on to explain how preventing even a couple of employees from leaving will mean their product pays for itself—though they typically provide no evidence that their product has any impact whatsoever on retaining employees.

Organizations with great workplace cultures don't worry about attrition—they celebrate it! In a great workplace culture, employee growth is important. Managers know what their employees want from their careers and actively support them in getting there, so that when an employee has an opportunity to leave for a better position and chooses to take it, the organization is genuinely pleased. They view it as a win for the organization's career development program.

They're excited that another ambassador is going out into the world. They're also eager for the new perspectives they'll soon be welcoming into the organization with the new hire.

And what about the supposed costliness of losing employees? For organizations like these, the costs of attrition are low enough that the benefits far outweigh the expense. Because they have a good reputation, it's easier to find new hires, find them more quickly, and find them through lower-cost channels like referrals. Also, with all the focus on career development, for any non-entry-level position, there are likely already people in the organization ready to grow into the openings.

How does this relate to work anniversaries? In organizations that focus on encouraging career growth rather than discouraging attrition, work anniversaries become much more meaningful. They're no longer celebrations of the employees who simply never had the initiative to find a better job; rather, they're celebrations of the fact that the employees and the organization are an uncommonly good fit that continues to result in a relationship that's fulfilling and beneficial for them both.

#3 EMPOWER EMPLOYEES

Great cultures empower their employees. Trusting your employees to make good decisions without constant oversight not only makes working for the organization more rewarding for them, but also has the added benefit of making your organization nimbler.

It's also just more fun to be a trusted, empowered employee, and it's more fun to work with trusted, empowered colleagues.

Empowered employees will relish their work anniversaries more because they'll feel a deeper connection with the work that they helped shape. Empowering employees of course goes way beyond work anniversaries, but it's included in the discussion of job crafting in the **Set up a special career-focused one-on-one** subsection on page 119. It's also included in the **Ideas for IT support** chapter on page 139, which also includes references to the science backing up the value of empowering employees.

Are you concerned about your employees' abilities to make good decisions? Then you're probably not providing them with enough big-picture clarity on what's important—and your senior leadership team quite likely has the same problem. The next two tips will help.

#2 HAVE A CLEAR, WELL-COMMUNICATED, AND INSPIRING PURPOSE

Throughout the book, it is suggested that work anniversaries not be viewed as acknowledgments of time passing but rather as celebrations of the moment an individual and the organization joined together to work toward a common purpose.

For that to work, an organization needs to be unified by an inspiring purpose, which is then clearly and frequently communicated to employees.

Why does your organization do what it does? How does it make the world a better place? What's more important than just making more money for the owners?

Then, can every employee explain how their work contributes to the purpose?

Without answers to those questions, employees will view working at your organization as a simple financial exchange of time for money. That collective mindset will undermine any work to improve workplace culture.

For more on purpose, see the **Purpose** section on page 13.

#1 BE THE BEST IN THE WORLD

Even the clearest, most inspiring, best-communicated purpose ever put into words isn't enough on its own. If you want to avoid a workplace culture of cynicism and disappointment, your organization also needs to be good at actually *working toward that purpose*.

Better yet, your organization needs to be the best in the world at the purpose, or at least some aspect of it.

Being the best in the world might sound intimidating or impossible, but it doesn't have to be. "Best" can mean all kinds of things, depending on the context, and "in the world" can mean whatever geography constrains your customers. For example, you could sell the largest and cheapest slices of pizza within walking distance of a college campus and be "best in the world" at feeding hungry, budget-conscious students who like pizza and who live on that campus.

Another way to think about this is as your brand promise. Why do customers choose you? Who do you serve and what do you offer them that makes you the only real choice?

The important—and challenging—thing is making the hard decisions necessary to commit to a focus. Avoiding the pull of trying to be everything to everyone can be hard. Saying no to revenue that takes you away from your core strengths is counterintuitive. It requires a lot of discipline to resolve senior leadership disagreements by picking a side and embracing it wholeheartedly—rather than just doing some lukewarm, halfway compromise that diffuses resources across initiatives. At best that confuses your brand promise, and at worst actively works against it.

Employees care a lot about this, though they may come at it from different angles. Some employees have a strong drive to be personally competent; for others, the drive is to not disappoint other people. Some may be motivated by the desire to show off how impressive their organization is, while others are strongly driven by competition and want to be part of a winning team. But while the underlying drives are different, the end effect is the same: everyone wants to work for an organization that's the best in the world at something.

This isn't what most people expect when asking for recommendations to strengthen their workplace culture, but it's very deliberately #1. If I could only recommend one thing, it would be to make courageous decisions to limit what your organization does and who it does it for—so your organization can be the best in the world.

That's the kind of organization where celebrating work anniversaries will not only be quite likely to be done well, but also where work anniversaries represent something deeply meaningful to employees.

THREE LISTS OF THREE

This book is a combination of tactical ideas and conceptual frameworks. The previous appendices were all about bringing attention to key tactical ideas. This appendix is a summary of the three most important conceptual frameworks:

- **The three drivers of work anniversary value** – These are what you're trying to improve by celebrating work anniversaries

- **The three forces of work anniversary mediocrity** – These are the headwinds that every work anniversary program faces, which you need to be aware of to successfully sidestep them

- **The three components of work anniversary programs** – This is a simple framework you can use when designing or improving a work anniversary program

THE THREE DRIVERS OF WORK ANNIVERSARY VALUE

Work anniversaries can be strong contributors to three elements of culture that have been repeatedly and scientifically shown to improve organizational performance:

- **Purpose** – Instead of celebrating time passing, celebrate the moment when each employee became a part of something much bigger than themself *(page 13)*

- **Belonging** – Use work anniversaries to strengthen your organization's identity as a special group to belong to and signal to employees that they are valued members of this group *(page 19)*

- **Perceived organizational support** – Use work anniversaries to reinforce a reciprocal relationship of trusting support rather than a cold economic relationship where each side is trying to get by with minimal contribution *(page 25)*

By intentionally keeping these three elements in mind as your objectives, you can unlock the full potential of a well-run work anniversary program. This will lead to a positive return on investment for your efforts rather than the often net-negative impact of the uninspired, rudderless "at least we did something" approach.

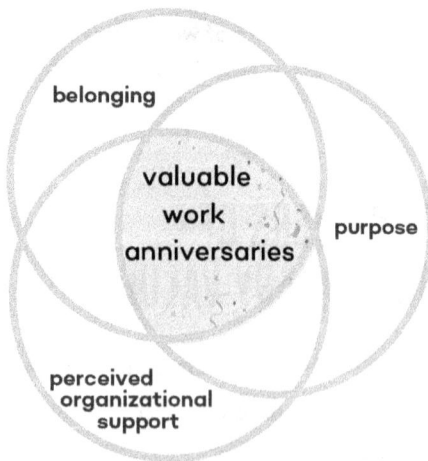

belonging

valuable
work
anniversaries

purpose

perceived
organizational
support

THE THREE FORCES OF WORK ANNIVERSARY MEDIOCRITY

Creating a sustainably great work anniversary program is hard because the three forces of work anniversary mediocrity are working against you:

- **Avoiding favoritism** – You can't treat some employees better than others *(page 32)*

- **Limiting spending** – You can't spend more than you can sustain through tough times or more than you're willing to spend on your least valuable employee *(page 34)*

- **Limiting effort** – You can't put more effort into work anniversaries than you can consistently sustain *(page 37)*

But now that you know about these three forces, you can decisively overcome them by intentionally aiming for the three drivers of work anniversary value on the previous page and implementing some of the many tactical ideas in this book.

the forces	the outcomes	the combined outcome
avoiding favoritism	generic	
limiting spending	low cost	mediocrity
limiting effort	low effort	

THE THREE COMPONENTS OF WORK ANNIVERSARY PROGRAMS

As you consider improving your work anniversary program, approach it as being made up of these three components:

- **Acknowledging** – The more that people acknowledge a work anniversary the better. Enroll and remind as many people as you can *(page 298)*

- **Giving** – Don't give something employees could get at any organization *(page 299)*

- **Strengthening culture** – Tying the organization's purpose to work anniversaries is the most important thing, but there's also much more you can do *(page 300)*

To create a new work anniversary program or improve an existing one, simply decide what you want to do in each of those three areas.

And remember that none of those three components stands alone. For a truly standout program, consider the intersections among them *(page 301)*.

acknowledge
employees

give
gifts

great work
anniversary
programs

strengthen
culture

HOW TO WRITE A GREAT CELEBRATORY WORK ANNIVERSARY SPEECH

Writing and giving a speech can be intimidating, especially if that's not a typical part of your job, but by following this step-by-step guide, you'll be able to craft a memorable speech you can give with confidence.

YOUR SPEECH'S OBJECTIVES

Every great speech has clear objectives, and a celebratory work anniversary speech has these two objectives:

- Making the long-serving employee feel special and appreciated
- Helping those listening to the speech feel a deeper connection with the long-serving employee

Keep the goal of maximizing these objectives in mind as you choose what to include in the speech and what to leave out.

PREPARATION

Your knowledge and view of the long-serving employee is just one perspective. You can add to the richness and depth of your speech by reaching out to others who know the employee and can provide additional perspectives. Try to get to as many of the employee's past managers and *their* managers as you can, and get in touch with colleagues the employee is close to. If people from the employee's personal life will be there for the speech, reach out to them too.

Here are five great questions to ask about the employee, some of which will obviously be more relevant to some of the people you talk to than others:

- What would you consider their biggest accomplishments since they joined?

- What's your favorite memory of working with them?

- What do you appreciate most about them?

- Do you have any photos of them or their accomplishments? *(If you're talking to their friends or family, ask for personal pictures of them, maybe with pets or engaged in their hobbies, or even embarrassing photos from their youth)*

- Who else would be good to reach out to with these questions?

The answers to these questions will help you gather raw material for your speech.

YOUR SPEECH'S STRUCTURE

The person organizing the event should be able to give you an idea of how long the speech should be, but remember that shorter is generally better. Leaving people wanting more is preferable to overstaying your welcome. Don't be afraid to cut good material to bring more attention to the great material. The times in parentheses are just guidelines, assuming a five- to ten-minute speech.

Here's a recommended structure:

1. **Start by thanking your audience** – Thank them for joining you to honor and celebrate the past however many years the honoree has been with the organization—if the organization has a clear and well-communicated mission or purpose, be sure to mention that it's about more than just time spent; it's also about contributing to the mission or purpose (*15–30 seconds*)

2. **Show the photos from their personal life** (if you have them) – Your primary goal in this part of the speech is to help the audience get to know the employee better—if something from their personal life can in some way be connected to their accomplishments at work, mentioning that is fine, but it's not necessary (*0–2 minutes*)

3. **Mention their start date and year** – Share a photo depicting them when they started or a photo representing the organization, such as the original building, product packaging, or company logo from the year they started, or if you can't find those, share images from pop culture that year, like movies or songs (*15–30 seconds*)

4. **Tell the story of how you met them** – Share an old picture of the two of you, share a first impression that foreshadows their future contributions, and/or joke about how you doubt either of you were expecting or thinking about this moment back then, which can be a fun lead-in to mentioning how honored you are to be the one chosen to give the speech *(1-2 minutes)*

5. **For the bulk of the speech, share the best of the accomplishments, memories, and what colleagues appreciate most that you captured in the preparation** – Showing any related pictures adds to the interest level *(3-6 minutes)*

6. **End with heartfelt gratitude** – Once again, thank the employee for their contributions to the organization and for enriching the lives of so many people, and close by asking for a round of applause *(30 seconds)*

WHAT NOT TO DO

For those of you who find comfort in cautionary advice, here are the three things to avoid:

▸ **Don't make divisive or insensitive comments** – Unless you've run it by and got the okay from at least two folks who are more easily offended than you—avoid politics, race, religion, gender, and sex

▸ **Don't make anyone feel bad** – For example, don't dwell on big mistakes that the employee cleaned up or mention who the employee beat out for a promotion

- **Don't end by mentioning your desire for the employee to stay for a long time** – No one knows what will happen in the future, and the employee may well be thinking of moving on— the speech is meant to be a celebration of the past, not an attempt to influence the future

PRACTICING

Amazing speeches happen not because the speaker was especially talented at giving speeches but because they *practiced*, probably a lot. Celebratory work anniversary speeches may not be high stakes, but you'll honor the long-serving employee more—and look better yourself—if you practice.

Here are a few things to keep in mind when practicing:

- **Slow down.** Most people speak too fast when speaking publicly, which makes their words hard to understand and their thoughts hard to follow. Your speech is important. You want people to be able to *relish* it. Don't rush, be sure to enunciate clearly, and pause after particularly powerful statements.

- **Time your speech.** It's probably longer than you think, especially if you succeed at slowing down your speaking. Remember, shorter is better.

- **Ask whoever is listening for ideas for improvement more than once.** The first time, most people will say something encouraging but unhelpful like "It was great!" Let them know you're genuinely interested in making it better and would appreciate their honest thoughts on what to improve.

It's highly recommended that you practice a couple of times on your own and then practice a couple of times in front of at least one other person. Think the speech is too long for that? Then maybe make the speech shorter.

YOU'RE GOING TO DO GREAT!

Public speaking can be nerve-racking for people who don't do it often, but remember that everyone is rooting for you to succeed. *The audience is on your side.*

I've spoken to hundreds of people about their best and worst work anniversaries. Having heard many, many heartwarming stories, I can confidently say:

> You very well might create one of the most memorable highlights of someone's career

Have fun, and good luck!

YOU CAN DOWNLOAD THIS GUIDE

If you're organizing an event and have multiple speakers and you want to share this work anniversary speech-giving guide with them, download an editable version and customize it with any details specific to your situation:

WWW.WORKIVERSARY.COM/SPEECH-GIVING-GUIDE

APPENDIX VI

TAXES

UNSCRUPULOUS COMPANIES around the world have tried to avoid paying taxes on annual bonuses by giving work anniversary gifts instead. Since most governments *really* want to tax employee pay in all its many and varied forms, the rules around taxation and work anniversaries can get complicated.

This is the obligatory paragraph where I make clear that I'm not a tax lawyer or an expert in employment law, and I don't live in most of the countries listed below. Local taxing jurisdictions add another layer of complication. Further, laws can change and this book could easily be out of date by the time you read it. Plus, typos can happen. For all these reasons and more:

> You should consult with an accountant
> or attorney and not rely on this
> book for legal or tax advice

To get hyper-legalese about it, the publisher and I make no representations or warranties with respect to the accuracy or completeness of the contents of this book and specifically disclaim any implied warranties of merchantability or fitness for a particular purpose. No warranty may be created or extended by sales representatives or written sales materials. Neither the publisher nor I shall be liable for any loss of profit or any other commercial damages, including but not limited to special, incidental, consequential, personal, or other damages.

Phew. Now that we've got that out of the way, I do think this appendix can be helpful. It gives you a high-level understanding that allows you to draft your program in an at least reasonably informed way so you can save time (and thus money) when you talk to your lawyer and/or accountant before actually implementing it.

Since this book is in English, it will cover the countries with larger English-speaking populations. Here are the work-anniversary-related exemptions from taxes by country:

- **Australia** – The exemption limit formula is set as follows: $1,000 + ($100 × (RLS – 15)). RLS is the number of whole years of service, so essentially the exemption is $1,000 for the first fifteen whole years of service plus $100 for each additional whole year of service after that.

- **Canada** – $500 is exempt every five years for a non-cash award that is also not a gift card.

- **India** – No special rules for work anniversaries. Gifts in cash or convertible into money (like gift cards) are fully taxable. Gifts in kind for any reason, including work anniversaries, up to Rs 5,000 in aggregate per year are exempt, beyond which they are taxable.

- **New Zealand** – No special rules for work anniversaries. You can provide an employee with up to $300 worth of gifts, prizes, or subsidized or discounted goods and services each quarter and not pay FBT. As soon as you go over this limit, the full value of the benefit is subject to FBT. Employers who file annual or income-year returns have a yearly exemption of $1,200 for each employee. The maximum total exemption an employer can claim is $22,500 each year. If you pay FBT quarterly and the value of the benefits you provide exceeds $22,500 in total for the current and last three quarters, you must pay FBT on the full value of the benefits for the current quarter.

- **Nigeria** – The Personal Income Tax Act doesn't make any special allowances for long-service awards. Work anniversary gifts are taxable to the extent that they are "any salary, wage, fee, allowance or other gain or profit from employment including compensations, bonuses, premiums, benefits or other perquisites allowed, given or granted by any person to any temporary or permanent employee."

- **Philippines** – Awards for length of service, which must be in the form of tangible personal property other than cash or gift certificates, with an annual monetary value not exceeding P10,000 received by the employee under an established written plan that does not discriminate in favor of highly paid employees, are exempt.

- **Singapore** – Cash awards are taxable. Non-cash work anniversary awards are not taxable if they don't exceed $200. If the award exceeds the exemption threshold, the whole value is taxable.

- **United Kingdom** – You don't have to report or pay on a non-cash award to an employee if all of the following apply: they've worked for you for at least twenty years; the award is worth less than £50 per year of service; and you haven't given them a long-service award in the past ten years. For example, you can give a non-cash award with a value of up to £1,000 for twenty years' service.

- **United States** – Gifts must be "tangible personal property"—that is, not cash or cash equivalents. The value of the gift is limited to $400. The gift must be given as part of a "meaningful presentation," cannot be given to employees until their fifth anniversary, and can only be given every fifth anniversary after that. "De minimis" gifts are allowed. Although *de minimis* isn't well defined, case law has established the single data point that $100 is not de minimis.

For more up-to-date information on taxes and information from other countries, check out the tax guide at:

WWW.WORKIVERSARY.COM/TAX-GUIDE

ACKNOWLEDGMENTS

THERE'S ONLY ONE person's name on the cover, but don't be deceived:

Hundreds of people contributed
to the writing of this book

"Hundreds?" you ask, skeptical eyebrow raised.

Yep, hundreds. And they're listed on the following pages. How will I organize hundreds of names? First by category, and then either chronologically or by reverse alphabetical order.*

---

* Why reverse alphabetical order rather than regular alphabetical order? Google the phrase "alphabetical discrimination" and all will be clear. Admittedly, this book isn't going to do much for social justice, but I tried to do what I could. In addition to fighting alphabetical discrimination, this book takes the position that gender-neutral language is better—there is no gendered language in this book. The book also tries to bring a tiny bit of attention to the wrongfully marginalized story of Elinor Smith (pages 219 and 366–367). More directly related to work anniversaries, the book encourages a barrier-breaking focus on belonging (pages 19–25), regular pay equity audits (pages 51 and 324), religious sensitivity (pages 81-82 and 241), and a fairer way of giving employees access to senior leaders (pages 130–135, 154–155, 172–177, 289, and 317–318). If you spot any ways this book could have been more inclusive, please let me know. That will help me make the next edition better.

And hundreds is actually a gross underestimate. The true number is in the millions. To understand what I mean, reread the introduction or google "I, Pencil," by Leonard Read. And consider this paragraph my humble thanks to all the many millions of people not listed who contributed to this book in the "I, Pencil" sense.

FAMILY

Writing a book is a big commitment, so thanks go first to my parents for being there and for always encouraging me to believe in myself, which came in especially handy for the endeavor of writing a book. Thanks to my immediate family for their support throughout the process, including through a few deadline-driven nail-biting weekends. And thanks to my extended family both for their direct support of me and for their support of those who supported me.

Mom, Dad,
Wyatt Joi, Piper "Quinn" Joi, Jack Joi, Donna Joi,
Wayne Lloyd, Wanda Lloyd,
Mike Crawford, and Jodi Crawford

ESPECIALLY INFLUENTIAL TEACHERS AND MENTORS

I wouldn't have written this book without the help of a lifetime's worth of teachers and mentors who had an outsize influence on my career, leading me to the moment where I decided to write this book. Listed in chronological order.

Lois Marie Harrod, John Sakalarides, Donna Joi,
John Sternberg, James Frayman, Doug Claffey,
and Bruce Ernst

RECURRING-MEETING FRIENDS

Writing a book takes a lot of time and can be lonely. Thanks to my many "recurring-meeting friends"* for being there throughout the process.

Lacey Williams, Kinsey Smith, Ethan Salk,
Pat Ruddy, Eric Rubino, Jill Ramondo,
John Quillen, Clara Pitts, Victoria Peltonen,
Anth Moquin, Weld McIlvain, Moe Lynch,
Zach Leaman, Dan Kessler, Arianne Gasser,
Chirayu Desai, Christian Delcid, Josh Cole,
Doug Claffey, Lisa Burke, Lisa Black,
and Stephen Bernal

---

* One of the silver linings of the COVID-19 pandemic has been the impact of video calls on friendships. Whenever someone says, "Let's keep in touch," I ask, "When do you want to get together next?" Then, if at that meet-up we agree to keep meeting, I say, "Let's set up a recurring meeting!" We then set up a recurring (weekly, biweekly, monthly, quarterly, annual) calendar invite (thirty minutes, sixty minutes, breakfast), and we stay in touch more regularly than before. COVID-19 made high-quality videoconferencing and working from home commonplace, which has made staying meaningfully connected to the people we care about easier than it's ever been. These changes are also useful for book authors who want to acknowledge their friends but find that knowing where to draw the friend line is complicated and who don't want anyone to get hurt by being left out. Want to be on this list for the next edition of this book? Let's set up a recurring meeting!

EARLY DRAFT READERS

The early drafts of this book weren't very good, but these wonderful people were generous with their time and read them anyway. I am deeply grateful for how substantially they improved the book—each in their own unique way—with their extensive feedback.

Erika Westbay, Dan Suwyn, Kinsey Smith,
Kourtney Schmiedeke, Denise Schatz, Ethan Salk,
Eric Rubino, Debbie Rosen, Yvette Delemos Robinson,
Laura Riordan, John Quillen, Cliff Piontek,
Kaye Peloquin, Anthony Moquin, Weld McIllvain,
Wayne Lloyd, Zach Leaman, Brad Kielinski,
Dan Kessler, Piper "Quinn" Joi, Amber Harley,
Arianne Gasser, Kathleen Gallon,
Lori Donofrio-Galley, Christian Delcid, Doug Claffey,
Lisa Burke, Alicia Bressler, Lisa Black,
and Stephen Bernal

THE PUBLICATION TEAM

Producing a book isn't easy. Thanks to all these wonderful professionals who helped make it a fun and educational journey. Listed in chronological order.

Jane Ryder – book shepherd and line editor
Peter Gelfan – developmental editor
Doug Wagner – copy editor and proofreader
Caerus Kourt – book designer
Leigh Westerfield – proofreader
Heike Martin – back cover photographer

WORK ANNIVERSARY EXPERIENCE CONTRIBUTORS

Writing a valuable book requires a deep understanding informed by lots of viewpoints beyond the author's original perspective. Thanks to the hundreds of people who shared their personal work anniversary experiences with me.

Jim Zhai, Pablo Zamorano, Anna Yudina,
Jasmine Young, Jamie Young, Ryan Yoshua,
Devyn Woodfield, Lacey Williams, Krista Welz,
Nelly Watetu, Keisha Washington, Chris Ward,
Jasmine Wang, Jan Waldeck, Jacob Van Rooyen,
Chinedu Umebolu, Gökhan Uluöz,
Tonia Eirini Tsoumali, Sarah Tahiri,
John Syracopoulos, Gaurav Suryawanshi,
Manu Sud, Balaji Srinivas, Lisa Sordilla,
Daphne Soh, Kinsey Smith, Megan Skalka,
Marianna Shlak, Zane Sheldrake, Jagriti Sharma,
Farhan Shaikh, Farjad Shah, Denise Schatz,
Tuğba Sarıkaya, Ethan Salk, Silita Sadhu,
Alex Rusthoven, Garrett Russell, Pat Ruddy,
Eric Rubino, Chelsea Roughton, Debbie Rosen,
Yvette Delemos Robinson, Luiz Felipe Ribeiro,
Ife Ramsey, Jose Luis Ramos, Sariksha Ramlall,
Elizabeth Rabago, Geet Ponkshe, António Pólvora,
Clara Pitts, Juan Lee Pinzón, Gianni Piccininni,
Julia Peterdozzi, Ola Perenc, Victoria Peltonen,
Beatriz Paiva, Mark Osborne, Michael O'Donnell,
Maggie O'Connor, Nurhadi, John Nunn,
Akhona Nqiwa, Matt Nicoletti, David Ngunjiri,
Denzel Ndegwa, Twice Nathan, Thato Myeza,

Yvonne Muthoni, Kelsey Moss, Anth Moquin,
Tshepo Mokgata, Delina Mok, Sharon Miller,
Yiselle Mejias, Jacqueline Medenblik,
Florencia Meaño, Craig McLain, Rich McKee,
Weld McIlvain, Mosala Masoetsa, Michael Martin,
Rick Marshall, Martim Margarido,
Chuck Marcelin, Andrew Marceau, Pat Malone,
Emeldah Makwana, Erin Mahlstedt,
Sandeep Mahajan, Rita Maciel, Dingiwe Mabuya,
Danny Ma, Moe Lynch, Avery Ly, Dharmita Lutz,
Shayna Love, Sharanabasappa Vithalrao Lokhande,
Wayne Lloyd, Doug Lloyd, Tanya Letson,
Covadonga Salvador León, Maranda Lender,
Zach Leaman, Young Kwon, Vishal Kumar,
Pappu Kumar, Niranjan Kumar, Gaurav Kumar,
Raph Kosmicki, Dimitar Kirchev, Felix Kigongo,
Rajendra Khalbadaniya, Dan Kessler, Hannah Keogh,
Mark Katz, Anderson Karrim, Shiru Karim,
Mukund Kadkol, Fiona Joyce, Kerstin Jost,
Monte Jones, Piper "Quinn" Joi, Donna Joi,
Sue Johnson, Melissa Johnson, Catherine Jobe,
Viola Jefimova, Kathleen Ioannou, Andreea Ioanna,
Tania Huiny, Amy Hudson, John Hockley II,
Allison Gail Hermoso, Ankur Hazarika,
Mikal Harden, Lee Hansrod, Dillon Green,
Tara Gordon, Candace Goodwin,
Caroline Gateri, Arianne Gasser, Janean Ganser,
Rich Gallagher, Tanner Frost, David Frerking,
Noel France, Tim FitzPatrick, Angus Finnigan,
Inês Carolina Ferreira, Anna Faddeeva,
Janelle Ellis, Warren Detres, Chirayu Desai,
Christian Delcid, Elizabeth Delaney, Jabez Deger,
Rogério Gomes da Silva, Jens Currlin,
Francisco Cristancho, Jodi Crawford,
Ashleigh Coward, Kira Cooksley, Josue Colon,
Josh Cole, Matt Colby, Doug Claffey,

Darren Chung, Ncomeka Chikovha, Lily Chiang,
Yan Chen, Daniel Charlong, Lokesh Chandawar,
Feargal Cassidy, Rodolfo Carvalho,
Cherilyn Carlsen, Stefanie Calello, Kamen C,
Robin Burtner, Lisa Burke, Amanda Brown,
Alex Brennessel, Fria Bola, Matt Blose,
Kirsten Blose, Lisa Black, Philip Bieg, Phil Bieg,
Stephen Bernal, Jamel Beckford,
Giuliano Battista, Carlos Bastos, Greg Barnett,
Naomi Badger, Pranav Arora,
Paulina Pérez Aparicio, Dave Anand,
Solange Alvito, Catarina Costa Alves,
Suha Alhabaj, Aaron Adeniran, Lynn Adams,
and Alexa Adams

Thanks also to the many other unnamed work anniversary experience contributors who must have thought, *That fellow sure makes weird small talk.*

THE CITED RESEARCHERS

The research cited throughout the book is listed in the endnotes in a fairly obtuse format and in a smaller font. I worry that the formatting of endnotes obscures that there are living, breathing humans behind that research who have dedicated their lives to helping us all understand how humanity might work together better. So here they are,* with a hearty thanks for helping advance the science.

---

* There are, of course, many more researchers working in this field who weren't cited. If you're one of them and are doing research that you think contributes to furthering the understanding of work anniversaries, please reach out. I'd love to be informed by your work and include you here in the next edition of this book!

Ben Zweig, Jiaying Zhao,
Rosamund Stone Zander, Benjamin Zander,
Tom Yates, Longqi Yang, Dimitris Xygalatas,
Kaitlin Woolley, Manda Winlaw, Jeffrey Weston,
Christopher M. Wegemer, Philippe N. Tobler,
Jaime Teevan, Desney Tan, Wendy Suzuki,
Siddharth Suri, Sabrina Strang,
Jeanine Stefanucci, Maclen Stanley, Shilpi Sinha,
Michiko Shinohara, Kevin Sherman, Neha Shah,
Eldar Shafir, Bill Schaninger, Alexi Robichaux,
Andrew Reece, Eric Raufaste, Dennis Proffitt,
Elder H. Burke Peterson, Nicolas Pellerin,
Eiluned Pearce, Randy Pausch, Annie Murphy Paul,
Soyoung Q. Park, Yang-Yen Ou, Barry Oshry,
Ngozi Angela Ogwo, Roger Norham,
Sendhil Mullainathan, Marino Mugayar-Baldocchi,
Jing Meng, Peter Marsh, Anandi Mani,
Thomas Malnight, Gary Markle, Carole Love,
Wanchen Li, Jacques Launay, Chun-Chia Kung,
Craig Knight, Anthony Klotz, Carlina Kim,
Gabriella Rosen Kellerman, Thorsten Kahnt,
Connor Joyce, HanShin Jo, Sonia Jaffe,
Steven Huang, Joan Hope, David Holtz,
Brent Hecht, Alexander Haslam, Robert Hannah,
the Google People Analytics Team,
W. Tecumseh Fitch, Ayelet Fishbach, Ernst Fehr,
Naomi Eisenberger, Charlotte Edwardson,
Amy Edmondson, Connie Eble, Robin I. M. Dunbar,
Bonnie Dowling, Azade Dogan, Charles Dhanaraj,
Andrea Derler, Aaron De Smet, Melanie Davies,
Fang Cui, Chaitanya Charan Das, Michael Dambrun,
Steve Cole, Evan Carr, Donald T. Campbell,
Ivy Buche, Tracy Brower, Simon Bradley,
India Bohanna, Jon Bischke, Rikia Birindelli-Fayne,
Stuart Biddle, Julia Basso, Varshini Balaji,
and Patrick Alexander

ENDNOTES

INTRODUCTION

1   **"SHRM Survey Findings: Employee Recognition Programs 2015"**
SHRM, the Society for Human Resource Management
https://www.shrm.org/hr-today/trends-and-forecasting/research-and-surveys/Documents/SHRM-Globoforce-Employee-Recognition-2015.pdf
(accessed May 1, 2023)

2   **"SHRM Survey Findings: Employee Recognition Programs 2015"**
SHRM, the Society for Human Resource Management
https://www.shrm.org/hr-today/trends-and-forecasting/research-and-surveys/Documents/SHRM-Globoforce-Employee-Recognition-2015.pdf
(accessed May 1, 2023)

3   **"SHRM Survey Findings: Employee Recognition Programs 2015"**
SHRM, the Society for Human Resource Management
https://www.shrm.org/hr-today/trends-and-forecasting/research-and-surveys/Documents/SHRM-Globoforce-Employee-Recognition-2015.pdf
(accessed May 1, 2023)

4   **"Employee Tenure in 2022"**
Bureau of Labor Statistics – U.S. Department of Labor
https://www.bls.gov/news.release/pdf/tenure.pdf (accessed May 1, 2023)

5 **"Entelo Study Shows When Employees Are Likely to Leave Their Jobs"**
Jon Bischke, founder and CEO – Entelo
https://blog.entelo.com/new-entelo-study-shows-when-employees-are-likely-to-leave-their-jobs (accessed May 1, 2023)

6 **"For Employee Retention, 'Workiversaries' Are Key"**
Timothy Roeper, economist – Revelio Labs
https://www.reveliolabs.com/news/macro/for-employee-retention-workiversaries-are-key/ (accessed May 1, 2023)

7 **"The Promise and Risk of Boomerang Employees"**
Anthony C. Klotz, Andrea Derler, Carlina Kim, Manda Winlaw
Harvard Business Review
https://hbr.org/2023/03/the-promise-and-risk-of-boomerang-employees (accessed May 1, 2023)

8 **"Entelo Study Shows When Employees Are Likely to Leave Their Jobs"**
Jon Bischke, founder and CEO – Entelo
https://blog.entelo.com/new-entelo-study-shows-when-employees-are-likely-to-leave-their-jobs (accessed May 1, 2023)

9 **"For Employee Retention, 'Workiversaries' Are Key"**
Timothy Roeper, economist – Revelio Labs
https://www.reveliolabs.com/news/macro/for-employee-retention-workiversaries-are-key/ (accessed May 1, 2023)

10 **"The Promise and Risk of Boomerang Employees"**
Anthony C. Klotz, Andrea Derler, Carlina Kim, Manda Winlaw
Harvard Business Review
https://hbr.org/2023/03/the-promise-and-risk-of-boomerang-employees (accessed May 1, 2023)

CHAPTER 1: WHY WORK ANNIVERSARIES ARE SO VALUABLE

1 **"3 Crucial Discoveries about Purpose in Life"**
Maclen Stanley
Psychology Today
https://www.psychologytoday.com/us/blog/making-sense-chaos/202109/3-crucial-discoveries-about-purpose-in-life (accessed May 1, 2023)

2 "The Power of Purpose and Why It Matters Now"
Tracy Brower
Forbes
https://www.forbes.com/sites/tracybrower/2021/08/22/the-power-of-purpose-and-why-it-matters-now/?sh=7b57cdfa163a (accessed May 1, 2023)

3 "Put Purpose at the Core of Your Strategy"
Thomas W. Malnight, Ivy Buche, Charles Dhanaraj
Harvard Business Review
https://hbr.org/2019/09/put-purpose-at-the-core-of-your-strategy (accessed May 1, 2023)

4 "Guide: Understand Team Effectiveness"
The People Analytics Team – re:Work – Google
https://rework.withgoogle.com/print/guides/5721312655835136/ (accessed May 1, 2023)

5 "Belonging"
Peter Marsh, Simon Bradley, Carole Love, Patrick Alexander, Roger Norham – SIRC, Social Issues Research Centre
http://www.sirc.org/publik/belonging.pdf (accessed May 1, 2023)

6 "Social Neuroscience and Health: Neurophysiological Mechanisms Linking Social Ties with Physical Health"
Eisenberger NI, Cole SW
Nature Neuroscience, 2012 Apr 15;15(5): 669-74. doi: 10.1038/nn.3086. PMID: 22504347

7 "Why Does Belonging Matter at Work?"
Steven Huang – SHRM, the Society for Human Resource Management
https://blog.shrm.org/blog/why-does-belonging-matter-at-work (accessed May 1, 2023)

8 "The Value of Belonging at Work"
Evan W. Carr, Andrew Reece, Gabriella Rosen Kellerman, Alexi Robichaux
Harvard Business Review
https://hbr.org/2019/12/the-value-of-belonging-at-work (accessed May 1, 2023)

9   "'Great Attrition' or 'Great Attraction'? The Choice is Yours"
    Aaron De Smet, Bonnie Dowling, Marino Mugayar-Baldocchi, Bill
    Schaninger – McKinsey & Company
    https://www.mckinsey.com/capabilities/people-and-organizational-
    performance/our-insights/great-attrition-or-great-attraction-the-choice-is-
    yours (accessed May 1, 2023)

10 "The Neuroscience of Belonging"
    India Bohanna – BrainBlogger
    https://brainblogger.com/2012/09/17/the-neuroscience-of-belonging/
    (accessed May 1, 2023)

11 *The 4 Stages of Psychological Safety: Defining the Path to
    Inclusion and Innovation*
    Timothy R. Clark
    (Oakland, CA: Berrett-Koehler Publishers, 2020)

12 "Psychological Safety: Underpinning Innovation"
    Ngozi Angela Ogwo, Michiko Shinohara, Rikia Birindelli-Fayne, Robert
    Hannah
    https://www.grantthornton.global/en/insights/articles/Inclusively-
    leading-through-change/psychological-safety-underpinning-innovation/
    (accessed May 22, 2023)

13 "Perceived Organizational Support"
    Robert Eisenberger, Robin Huntington, Steven Hutchison, Debora Sowa
    Journal of Applied Psychology, 71(3): 500-507 (1986)

14 "Perceived Organizational Support: A Literature Review"
    Li Sun
    International Journal of Human Resources Studies, 9(3) (2019)

CHAPTER 3: IDEAS FOR HUMAN RESOURCES

While there aren't any specific citations, and our views diverge when it comes to timing, the thinking on performance reviews, career coaching, and pay raises in this chapter was heavily influenced by the highly recommend book *Catalytic Coaching: The End of the Performance Review*, by Gary Markle. Also, Gary is an amazing speaker—I highly recommend you see him speak if you get a chance.

CHAPTER 4: IDEAS FOR MANAGERS AND SUPERVISORS

1   "A Recipe for Friendship: Similar Food Consumption
    Promotes Trust and Cooperation"
    Kaitlin Woolley, Ayelet Fishbach
    Journal of Consumer Psychology, January 2017

2   "Entelo Study Shows When Employees Are Likely to Leave
    Their Jobs"
    Jon Bischke, founder and CEO – Entelo
    https://blog.entelo.com/new-entelo-study-shows-when-employees-are-
    likely-to-leave-their-jobs (accessed May 1, 2023)

3   "For Employee Retention, 'Workiversaries' Are Key"
    Timothy Roeper, economist – Revelio Labs
    https://www.reveliolabs.com/news/macro/for-employee-retention-
    workiversaries-are-key/ (accessed May 1, 2023)

4   "The Promise and Risk of Boomerang Employees"
    Anthony C. Klotz, Andrea Derler, Carlina Kim, Manda Winlaw
    Harvard Business Review
    https://hbr.org/2023/03/the-promise-and-risk-of-boomerang-employees
    (accessed May 1, 2023)

5   "Belonging"
    Peter Marsh, Simon Bradley, Carole Love, Patrick Alexander, Roger
    Norham – SIRC, Social Issues Research Centre
    http://www.sirc.org/publik/Belonging.pdf (accessed May 1, 2023)

6   "Why Does Belonging Matter at Work?"
    Steven Huang – SHRM, the Society for Human Resource Management
    https://blog.shrm.org/blog/why-does-belonging-matter-at-work (accessed
    May 1, 2023)

7   "The Value of Belonging at Work"
    Evan W. Carr, Andrew Reece, Gabriella Rosen Kellerman, Alexi Robichaux
    Harvard Business Review
    https://hbr.org/2019/12/the-value-of-belonging-at-work
    (accessed May 1, 2023)

8 "'Great Attrition' or 'Great Attraction'? The Choice is Yours"
Aaron De Smet, Bonnie Dowling, Marino Mugayar-Baldocchi, Bill Schaninger – McKinsey & Company
https://www.mckinsey.com/capabilities/people-and-organizational-performance/our-insights/great-attrition-or-great-attraction-the-choice-is-yours (accessed May 1, 2023)

9 "The Neuroscience of Belonging"
India Bohanna – BrainBlogger
https://brainblogger.com/2012/09/17/the-neuroscience-of-belonging/ (accessed May 1, 2023)

10 The 4 Stages of Psychological Safety: Defining the Path to Inclusion and Innovation
Timothy R. Clark
(Oakland, CA: Berrett-Koehler Publishers, 2020)

11 "Guide: Understand Team Effectiveness"
The People Analytics Team – re:Work – Google
https://rework.withgoogle.com/print/guides/5721312655835136/ (accessed May 1, 2023)

12 "Perceived Organizational Support"
Robert Eisenberger, Robin Huntington, Steven Hutchison, Debora Sowa
Journal of Applied Psychology, no. 71(3): 500-507 (1986)

13 "Perceived Organizational Support: A Literature Review"
Li Sun
International Journal of Human Resources Studies, 9(3) (2019)

CHAPTER 5: IDEAS FOR IT SUPPORT

Much of the research cited in this chapter was originally collected in the highly recommended book *The Extended Mind: The Power of Thinking Outside the Brain*, by Annie Murphy Paul.

1 "The Infocockpit: Providing Location and Place to Aid Human Memory"
Desney S. Tan, Jeanine K. Stefanucci, Dennis R. Proffitt, Randy Pausch
https://www.researchgate.net/publication/2494537_The_Infocockpit_Providing_Location_and_Place_to_Aid_Human_Memory (accessed May 1, 2023)

2 **"The Infocockpit: Providing Location and Place to Aid Human Memory"**
Desney S. Tan, Jeanine K. Stefanucci, Dennis R. Proffitt, Randy Pausch
https://www.researchgate.net/publication/2494537_The_Infocockpit_Providing_Location_and_Place_to_Aid_Human_Memory (accessed May 1, 2023)

3 **"The Effects of Acute Exercise on Mood, Cognition, Neurophysiology and Neurochemical Pathways: A Review"**
Julia Basso, Wendy Suzuki
Brain Plasticity, 2(2):1-26 (2017)

4 **"Effectiveness of the Stand More AT (SMArT) Work Intervention"**
Charlotte L Edwardson, Tom Yates, Stuart J.H. Biddle, Melanie J. Davies
BMJ Clinical Research, 2018;363:k3870

5 **"The Relative Merits of Lean, Enriched, and Empowered Offices: An Experimental Examination of the Impact of Workspace Management Strategies on Well-Being and Productivity"**
Craig Knight, S. Alexander Haslam
Journal of Experimental Psychology Applied, 16(2):158-72 (2010)

CHAPTER 6: IDEAS FOR CEOS (AND OTHER TOP LEADERS)

1 **"Entelo Study Shows When Employees Are Likely to Leave Their Jobs"**
Jon Bischke, founder and CEO – Entelo
https://blog.entelo.com/new-entelo-study-shows-when-employees-are-likely-to-leave-their-jobs (accessed May 1, 2023)

2 **"For Employee Retention, 'Workiversaries' Are Key"**
Timothy Roeper, economist – Revelio Labs
https://www.reveliolabs.com/news/macro/for-employee-retention-workiversaries-are-key/ (accessed May 1, 2023)

3   **"The Promise and Risk of Boomerang Employees"**
Anthony C. Klotz, Andrea Derler, Carlina Kim, Manda Winlaw
Harvard Business Review
https://hbr.org/2023/03/the-promise-and-risk-of-boomerang-employees
(accessed May 1, 2023)

4   *The Advantage: Why Organizational Health Trumps Everything Else In Business*
Patrick Lencioni
(San Francisco: Jossey-Base – Wiley, 2012)

CHAPTER 8: IDEAS FOR GRAPHIC DESIGNERS

1   **"Entelo Study Shows When Employees Are Likely to Leave Their Jobs"**
Jon Bischke, founder and CEO – Entelo
https://blog.entelo.com/new-entelo-study-shows-when-employees-are-likely-to-leave-their-jobs (accessed May 1, 2023)

2   **"For Employee Retention, 'Workiversaries' Are Key"**
Timothy Roeper, economist – Revelio Labs
https://www.reveliolabs.com/news/macro/for-employee-retention-workiversaries-are-key/ (accessed May 1, 2023)

3   **"The Promise and Risk of Boomerang Employees"**
Anthony C. Klotz, Andrea Derler, Carlina Kim, Manda Winlaw
Harvard Business Review
https://hbr.org/2023/03/the-promise-and-risk-of-boomerang-employees
(accessed May 1, 2023)

CHAPTER 11: IDEAS FOR FRONTLINE EMPLOYEES

1   *Aviatrix*
Elinor Smith
(New York: Harcourt Brace Jovanovich, 1981)

The Elinor Smith quote at the beginning of chapter 11 is broadly misattributed to Leonardo DaVinci across the internet, which tragically misappropriates attention from a truly inspirational pioneer.

Who was Elinor Smith?

In 1927, as a sixteen-year-old, Elinor Smith became the youngest licensed pilot in the world. While Amelia Earhart is now better known, pilots of their day considered Smith a better flier, voting Smith female pilot of the year in 1930. Smith set many solo endurance, speed, and altitude records and was the first woman featured on a Wheaties cereal box. While technology has moved on and most of Smith's records have since been broken, Smith is still the only person to ever have flown a landplane *under* (?!) all four of New York City's East River bridges. The chapter 11 quote is in reference to Smith's thinking ahead of that flight. Full of chutzpah to the end, in the year 2000 at age eighty-eight, Smith was invited to NASA's Ames Research Center and became the oldest pilot to complete a simulated space shuttle landing.[1, 2, 3, 4]

2   *The Art of Possibility: Transforming Professional and Personal Life*
Rosamund Stone Zander, Benjamin Zander
(New York: Penguin Books, 2002)

3   "A Neural Link Between Generosity and Happiness"
Soyoung Q. Park, Thorsten Kahnt, Azade Dogan, Sabrina Strang, Ernst Fehr, Philippe N. Tobler
Nature Communications 8, 15964 (2017)

4   "The Neural Substrate of Self- and Other-Concerned Wellbeing: An fMRI Study"
HanShin Jo, Yang-Yen Ou, Chun-Chia Kung
PLOS ONE, 14(10), Article e0203974 (2019)

5   "Selflessness and Happiness in Everyday Life: An Experience Sampling Method Based Study"
Nicolas Pellerin, Eric Raufaste, Michael Dambrun
Journal of Individual Differences, 42(3), 107–115 (2021)

6   "Self-Centeredness and Selflessness: Happiness Correlates and Mediating Psychological Processes"
Michael Dambrun
PeerJ. 2017 May 11;5:e3306. doi: 10.7717/peerj.3306. PMID: 28507820; PMCID: PMC5429736 🐛

7   "Selflessness, Depression, and Neuroticism: An Interactionist Perspective on the Effects of Self-Transcendence, Perspective-Taking, and Materialism"
Christopher M. Wegemer
Frontiers in Psychology, 23 September 2020, 10.3389/fpsyg.2020.523950

8   "Selflessness: A Pattern for Happiness"
Elder H. Burke Peterson – The Church of Jesus Christ of Latter-Day Saints
https://www.churchofjesuschrist.org/study/general-conference/1985/04/selflessness-a-pattern-for-happiness (accessed May 22, 2023)

9   "The Starting Point of Happiness Is Selflessness"
Chaitanya Charan Das – The Church of Jesus Christ of Latter-Day Saints
https://gitadaily.com/the-starting-point-of-happiness-is-selflessness/ (accessed May 22, 2023)

CHAPTER 12: WHY WORK ANNIVERSARIES ARE BETTER THAN BIRTHDAYS

1   "Why Don't Jehovah's Witnesses Celebrate Birthdays?"
JW.ORG – Jehovah's Witnesses
https://www.jw.org/en/jehovahs-witnesses/faq/birthdays/ (accessed May 1, 2023)

2   "Questions from Readers"
Watchtower Online Library - *The Watchtower Announcing Jehovah's Kingdom*, 1998
https://wol.jw.org/en/wol/d/r1/lp-e/1998766 (accessed May 1, 2023)

CHAPTER 14: WORK ANNIVERSARIES AND THE POWER OF CULTURAL UNIQUENESS

1   *Slang and Sociability: In-Group Language among College Students*
Connie Eble
(Chapel Hill: University of North Carolina Press, xi +228, 1996)

2   *Ritual, How Seemingly Senseless Acts Make Life Worth Living*
Dimitris Xygalatas
(New York: Little, Brown Spark, 2022)

3   **"The Ice-Breaker Effect: Singing Mediates Fast Social Bonding"**
Eiluned Pearce, Jacques Launay, Robin I. M. Dunbar
Royal Society Open Science, 2150221150221 (2015)

4   **The Evolution of Language**
W. Tecumseh Fitch
(Cambridge: Cambridge University Press, 2010)

CHAPTER 15: USING WORK ANNIVERSARY METRICS TO MEASURE WORKPLACE CULTURE

1   **"Campbell's Law"**
Wikipedia
https://en.wikipedia.org/wiki/Campbell%27s_law (accessed May 22, 2023)

2   **"Assessing the Impact of Planned Social Change"**
Donald T. Campbell
Evaluation and Program Planning, Volume 2, Issue 1, 1979, Pages 67-90, ISSN 0149-7189

APPENDIX II: TOP TEN IDEAS ESPECIALLY FOR REMOTE EMPLOYEES

1   **"The Effects of Remote Work on Collaboration Among Information Workers"**
Longqi Yang, David Holtz, Sonia Jaffe, Siddharth Suri, Shilpi Sinha, Jeffrey Weston, Connor Joyce, Neha Shah, Kevin Sherman, Brent Hecht, Jaime Teevan
Nature Human Behavior 6, 43–54 (2022)

APPENDIX III: TOP TEN WORKPLACE CULTURE RECOMMENDATIONS

1   *Leading Systems: Lessons from the Power Lab*
    Barry Oshry
    (San Francisco: Berrett-Koehler Publishers, 1999)

2   *Seeing Systems: Unlocking the Mysteries of Organizational Life*
    Barry Oshry
    (San Francisco: Berrett-Koehler Publishers, 2007)

3   **"Adopt an Abundance Mindset to Boost Your Leadership Potential"**
    Joan Hope
    Recruiting & Retaining Adult Learners 24:5, 9-9 (2022)

4   **"5 Reasons Why an Abundance Mindset Will Make your Organizational Culture More Collaborative"**
    Varshini Balaji – Mindhatch
    https://www.mindhatchllc.com/5-reasons-abundance-mindset-collaboration/ (accessed May 1, 2023)

5   **"Poverty Impedes Cognitive Function"**
    Anandi Mani, Sendhil Mullainathan, Eldar Shafir, Jiaying Zhao
    Science 341, 976-980 (2013)

6   **"Scarcity Mindset Reduces Empathic Responses to Others' Pain: The Behavioral and Neural Evidence"**
    Wanchen Li, Jing Meng, Fang Cui
    Social Cognitive and Affective Neuroscience 18:1 (2023)

ENDNOTES

Yes, these are the endnotes listing the research that was cited *in the endnotes*. One of my editors thought having endnotes within endnotes was, well, unconventional—and suggested I remove them. I have left them in anyway as a tiny (and arguably unworthy) way of honoring Elinor Smith's unconventional life.

1   *Aviatrix*
    Elinor Smith
    (New York: Harcourt Brace Jovanovich, 1981)

2   "Elinor Smith"
    Wikipedia
    https://en.wikipedia.org/wiki/Elinor_Smith (accessed May 1, 2023)

3   "Elinor Smith"
    Cradle of Aviation Museum and Education Center
    https://www.cradleofaviation.org/history/history/women-in-aviation/elinor_smith.html (accessed May 1, 2023)

4   "Elinor Smith: Born to Fly"
    Denise Lineberry – The Researcher News – NASA Langley Research Center – NASA
    https://www.nasa.gov/topics/people/features/elinor-smith.html (accessed May 1, 2023)

INDEX

LOOKING FOR MORE?

The Workiversary Group's purpose is to dramatically improve work anniversaries for the billions of workers around the world. This book by our founder, Rick Joi, is just one of the many initiatives we are supporting to achieve that purpose.

Through our website, workiversary.com, we offer lots of resources for continuing your work anniversary journey, and most of them are free:

- **Blog**. The workiversary.com blog provides bite-size insights into the many quirks and mysteries of work anniversaries and how you can improve them at your organization

- **Vendor guide**. The workiversary.com vendor guide shares our top picks for vendors that help organizations deliver great work anniversaries

- **Tax guide**. The workiversary.com tax guide provides quick overviews of how work anniversary gifts are taxed in various English-speaking countries

- **Printable certificate templates**. These printable work anniversary certificate templates are classic, simple, and low cost yet still meaningful—select from a variety of Word and Google Docs templates you can customize and print

▸ **Onboarding preferences template**. This printable questionnaire makes it easier to get started capturing employee preferences as part of the onboarding process, which makes it easier for managers to give thoughtful work anniversary gifts

▸ **Speaking**. Book a speaker who can talk about a universal topic affecting every workplace for your human resources networking group, management event, or podcast

▸ **Consulting**. Talk to an expert about how you can have a world-class work anniversary program while saving time and money

▸ **Innovation**. If you're a fan, supporter, enthusiast, or believer in great work anniversaries, be a part of our effort to create a software product that's low cost, low effort, and free of favoritism while simultaneously being priceless, deeply meaningful, and uniquely personalized

Contact us at hello@workiversary.com or through our website:

WWW.WORKIVERSARY.COM

OH, AND ONE LAST THING

There are seven unicorns hidden somewhere in this book.

Did you find them all?

Want hints? Email us at

HELLO@WORKIVERSARY.COM